Young
at Heart

Chicken Soup for the Soul: Young at Heart
101 Tales of Dynamic Aging
Amy Newmark

Published by Chicken Soup for the Soul, LLC www.chickensoup.com
Copyright ©2024 by Chicken Soup for the Soul, LLC. All Rights Reserved.

The publisher gratefully acknowledges the many publishers and individuals who granted Chicken Soup for the Soul permission to reprint the cited material.

Front cover illustration of car courtesy of iStockphoto.com (©lemono), illustration of road and sky courtesy of iStockphoto.com (©unizyne)
Back cover and interior photo of man with child courtesy of iStockphoto.com (©triloks), interior photo of woman playing pickleball courtesy of iStockphoto.com (©adamkaz), interior photo of women drinking wine courtesy of iStockphoto.com (©wundervisuals)
Photo of Amy Newmark courtesy of Susan Morrow at SwickPix

Cover and Interior by Daniel Zaccari

Publisher's Cataloging-in-Publication data

Names: Newmark, Amy, editor.
Title: Chicken soup for the soul : young at heart / Amy Newmark.
Description: Cos Cob, CT: Chicken Soup for the Soul, LLC, 2024.
Identifiers: LCCN: 2024932475 | ISBN: 978-1-61159-115-6 (paperback) | 978-1-61159-350-1 (ebook)
Subjects: LCSH Aging--Literary collections. | Aging--Anecdotes. | Older people--Literary collections. | Older people--Anecdotes. | BISAC SELF-HELP / Motivational & Inspirational | SELF-HELP / Personal Growth / Happiness | SELF-HELP / Aging
Classification: LCC HQ1061 .C447 2024 | DDC 305.26--dc23

Library of Congress Control Number: 2024932475

PRINTED IN THE UNITED STATES OF AMERICA
on acid∞free paper

30 29 28 27 26 25 24   01 02 03 04 05 06 07 08 09

Young at Heart

101 Tales of Dynamic Aging

Amy Newmark

Chicken Soup for the Soul, LLC
Cos Cob, CT

Changing your life one story at a time®
www.chickensoup.com

Table of Contents

❶

~Embrace Your Years~

❷

~Get Physical~

❸
~Try Something New~

❹
~Happily Ever Laughter~

❺
~Love and Love Again~

❻

~New Adventures~

❼

~Second Wind~

8

~So Much to Give~

9

~The New Normal~

10

~Who Are You Calling Old?~

Chapter
1

Embrace
Your Years

My Reflection in the Mirror

*In your own life it's important to know
how spectacular you are.*
~Steve Maraboli

I stared at my reflection in the full-length mirror for what seemed an eternity. Next to me were the dozens of dresses I'd already tossed into the "reject" pile.

Dress shopping for my thirty-year high school reunion had become very frustrating. I'd gained weight slowly over the years and wasn't used to my new large bosom and tummy pouch.

How could I possibly find a dress that looked good on me and how could I attend the reunion looking like this? I hadn't seen most of my classmates since high school graduation. Surely, everyone would notice I had gained weight. I felt embarrassed and ashamed. I finally settled on a simple black dress, one size too big, so it would be loose and cover my curves.

That evening I tried on the dress again at home. Who was I kidding? The dress looked horrible! Just then, as if on cue, my husband and young son walked in.

"Mom, what are you wearing?" My son giggled. "That dress is too big!"

My husband agreed. I looked at my reflection once more; I looked like I was wearing a sack. I don't know what came over me, but I started to laugh until happy tears fell. It felt so good to laugh! It must have been contagious, because we all stood there roaring with laughter.

I returned the dress the next day and in its place I bought a bright red, formfitting dress! This time when I stood in front of the mirror, I couldn't believe it — I loved what I saw.

"Wow, you're beautiful!" my husband said, when I twirled around to show him.

On the day of the reunion I was nervous. I timidly walked into the venue.

"Honey, there's no way you can't be seen with that beautiful red dress," my husband said. "Flaunt it!"

He knew just what to say to make me feel better, and he was right. Just then, one of my friends ran over to hug me.

"You look amazing," she said, excited. "I couldn't miss you walking in with that cute dress!"

That evening I reminisced, laughed and danced the night away.

That was nine years ago. Since then, I have learned to love my body and embrace my new curves instead of hiding them.

That moment I stood in front of the mirror was a turning point for me. I realized later that those dresses I tried on didn't look bad on my body; it was my insecurities that made them look bad.

My reflection in the mirror was the reflection of my lack of confidence. But nowadays, I love what I see!

— Dorann Weber —

Hair Today, Gone Tomorrow

Anyone can be confident with a full head of hair.
But a confident bald man — there's
your diamond in the rough.
~Larry David

I giggled along with my husband, Gerry, as we looked through the before-and-after pictures in the colourful brochure he had received from the hair club. It was hilariously difficult for us to imagine him having hair again after being pretty much bald for the past twenty-some years. Now in his early fifties, he longed to fulfill his dream of once again having a full head of hair.

After much research, he settled on a provider that was seven hours away and would require crossing the border from Canada into the U.S. He was not discouraged by the fact that he would need to go for "maintenance" appointments every four weeks.

This non-invasive procedure was one whereby a custom hairpiece would be created for him out of human hair, coloured to match the little hair he had left, and then fused to his head via a special taping process. When he shared the details of this with me, we both cracked up, unable to quell the notion that this was nothing more than a glorified toupee!

Gerry, though, was still determined to go through with it, and I wanted to be encouraging. After all, I reminded myself, he wasn't out buying an expensive sports car or strutting around in skinny jeans and cowboy boots! If wanting hair would be the full extent of what I humorously referred to as his mid-life crisis, then I would gladly climb aboard for the ride.

Deciding that we would make these monthly trips a little getaway for both of us, I had Gerry drop me at the mall while he went to have his first hairpiece applied. As I hurried back to where he was to pick me up, I felt the laughter begin to bubble up inside me as I tried to imagine what he would look like. Not wanting to offend him, I struggled for control as I pushed open the door and walked outside. I caught sight of him through the car window as he sat waiting for me. As our tear-filled eyes met, I could tell that he was already laughing hysterically, having anticipated my response. Now I was doubled over in mirth as I awkwardly made my way to the passenger side of the car.

It wasn't that the hairpiece looked bad; it didn't. In fact, they had done a marvelous job. It was more the shock of seeing my husband with hair for the first time in many years that had us both consumed in fits of laughter.

Overcoming this initial transformation, we settled into the four-week routine of traveling to the hair club for washing, maintenance and sometimes a replacement of the hairpiece, while stocking up on the many "needed" hair products.

Joking that Gerry was now more the diva in our relationship than I was found me labouring to reapply the mandatory tape to his head in an effort to keep the hairpiece in place.

Upon entering the fourth year of hair maintenance, we now had the wonderful addition of grandkids, which found us lagging a few weeks behind the compulsory appointment dates. We had also run out of the special tape, which meant that Gerry's hairpiece was becoming extremely loose as well as a little ratty looking. Desperate to keep the hairpiece in place, we experimented with various kinds of adhesive and eventually ended up using Krazy Glue. Although the product immediately bonded to the skin, it would only work for a short time, which had Gerry wearing a ball cap over the hair during the day to keep it in place and removing it at night when he slept. After one such night, our little grandson — who had slept over and was eager to wake

Grandpa in the morning — saw Gerry for the first time without hair. He exclaimed, "Grandpa! You have bald hair!" Of course. we laughed our selves silly over this, and had to admit at the same time that this whole procedure was getting ridiculous.

Later that same morning, as we were heading into the city to do some shopping, Gerry was again wearing his baseball cap over the hairpiece, which I laughingly pointed out was enormously counter-productive. Yet still holding onto the dream, he simply grinned and gave the brim of his hat a firm tug.

The mall had been well attended that day, and as we exited through the side door, we were forced to follow behind a large line of people who were also making their way to the parking lot. All of a sudden, a strong wind blew up, causing Gerry's hat to fly off his head. I watched in awe as, with lightning speed, he grabbed the hat, but not before his hairpiece took flight! It soared through the air, eventually hitting the ground and rolling like a tumbleweed through the parking lot. Shocked, we stood there motionless at first, along with a growing crowd, staring in disbelief at this bizarre scene.

"Just leave it," I managed to whisper under my breath while trying not to laugh. "Let it go." Abruptly, I began walking and then running toward our truck. Thinking Gerry had heeded my advice and was following behind me, I was stunned to see that he instead was running after his hair! Uncontrollably laughing now and on the verge of peeing my pants, I stared in disbelief as a very large man viciously stomped down on the runaway hair. Picking it up, he handed it to my embarrassed husband and casually remarked, "@#$% happens." Then he turned and walked away. With the cap back on his head, Gerry quickly shoved the hairpiece in his jacket and sheepishly returned to the truck. Seeing the condition I was in sent us both again into uncontrollable gales of laughter. With tears streaming down our faces and our stomachs aching, we got in the truck and headed for the nearest gas-station restroom.

True to form, the humour of this experience far outweighed the embarrassment, so when Gerry finally regained his composure, he said, "I think it's time to let this hair go."

"Set it free!" I chimed in heartily.

As we turned onto the highway, Gerry reached into his jacket, extracted the matted and dusty hairpiece, and threw it out the window. I watched through the side mirror as it settled on the shoulder, much more resembling a dead animal than something one would actually wear on one's head.

Though my husband did grieve his hair loss for a second time, he eventually came to embrace his baldness, happy to be finally free of his need for hair and equally as happy to have such a great story to tell.

Laughter has always been an essential part of our lives, especially with Gerry at the helm, and this outrageous event continues to be one of the best "ha ha moments" we have ever had!

—Jan Kendall St.Cyr—

Grandma's the Name

Grandmas are moms with lots of frosting.
~Author Unknown

I am a fourth-generation writer and a first-generation "Grandma." My own grandmother was called "Honie" by all of us, and that started because she called us "honey," and we returned the favor. Or so I thought. What actually is true is that Honie felt too young to be called Grandma and so encouraged something less age-related. Since her name was Helen, she contracted it to Honie.

That tradition continued with my own mother when I had my children. Having a career in the glamorous field of writing and possessing a special talent, she considered these names: "Glamour" and "Talent." I believe we all discouraged that, but there was a name waiting for her.

In addition to possessing talent, my mother also possessed a pet Capuchin monkey named "Bomba." My children were quick to realize that she was, in fact, Bomba's Momma, and that got shortened to "Bomma." And she has been Bomma to all of her grandchildren since.

Just as her own mother did, my mother felt too young to be labeled with a name that implied generation seniority.

I forgive them both. It's not their fault that they lived through a time when a woman's age was never a thing to discuss or disclose. Thank goodness times have changed!

They didn't have the good fortune to live (or work) where aging and aging well are badges of honor.

How lucky I am to be working in a retirement home and seeing first-hand every day that age is irrelevant, and it's not how long one lives that matters, but how well one lives.

And that's why, when my darling first grandchild, Audrey Caroline, was born on November 5, I claimed the name of "Grandma" with as much pride as the men who planted the American flag on the moon.

I'm Grandma! I am Grand MA! And I have to say, it's the best title I've ever held... well, next to MOM, that is.

— Linda Williams Aber —

The Zezimas' Christmas Letter

There is nothing in the world so irresistibly contagious
as laughter and good humor.
~Charles Dickens

Since I am in the holiday spirit (and, having just consumed a mug of hot toddy, a glass of eggnog and a nip of cheer, the holiday spirits are in me), I have decided to follow in that great tradition of boring everyone silly by writing a Christmas letter.

That is why I am pleased as punch (which I also drank) to present the following chronicle of the Zezima family, which includes Jerry, the patriarch; Sue, the matriarch; Katie and Lauren, the daughtersiarch; Dave and Guillaume, the sons-in-lawiarch; and Chloe, Lilly and Xavier, the grandchildreniarch.

Dear friends:
    It sure has been an exciting year for the Zezimas!
    Things got off to a rocky start when Jerry had a kidney stone. He is sorry to have to number them like the Super Bowl, but it was Kidney Stone VI. Mercifully, this, too, did pass.
    Also on the medical front, Jerry took a CPR class in which the instructor used him as a dummy. The other class members couldn't tell the difference.

To keep in good physical condition, Jerry won a one-day gym membership. He didn't exercise very strenuously, proving to be the biggest dumbbell there, but afterward he went to an adjacent bar and did 12-ounce curls.

Continuing to show his commitment to a healthy lifestyle, Jerry attended a Wine Stomp Party at a vineyard and, re-creating a famous I Love Lucy episode, climbed into a vat of grapes and stomped them with his bare feet. To ensure the health of the vineyard's customers, the grapes were thrown away.

Jerry may not have made his own wine, but he and Chloe did make their own ice cream. They went to a shop where the owner, impressed by Chloe's natural ability to pour in the ingredients but not by Jerry's pathetic incompetence at measuring them, allowed the dynamic duo to make a batch of honey-cinnamon. It was delicious, prompting the owner to tell Chloe, "Now you can say you taught your grandfather how to make ice cream."

Jerry, Sue and Lauren took Chloe and Lilly on their first visit to the zoo, where humans were the wildest creatures, and Jerry, an acknowledged oldster, was carded by a flirtatious young woman while buying beer for the adults in the group. He roared louder than the lions.

One of the proudest moments of the year occurred when Chloe graduated, magna cum little, from preschool. She had a prominent role in the ceremony, which was attended by Jerry, Sue, Lauren, Guillaume and Lilly, and was tops in her class. Afterward, everyone had milk and cookies. Yale or Harvard couldn't have done better.

A milestone was reached when Lilly celebrated her first birthday. Big sister Chloe, who's 4, helped her blow out the candle on her cupcake and, as their little friends applauded, helped her eat the cupcake, too. Talk about sisterly love!

And there was an addition to the family: Xavier, Katie and Dave's beautiful boy, made his grand entrance into the world. Sue and Jerry, aka Nini and Poppie, went on a road trip to meet him, and Jerry quickly learned that changing diapers on a boy is a lot different from changing them on a girl. That's because boys have an apparatus that is not unlike a water cannon or, considering the oscillation, an in-ground sprinkler system. It was a geyser on a geezer.

But Jerry didn't mind because he got to do some male bonding. On a subsequent visit, Jerry introduced Xavier to the Three Stooges, making him giggle uncontrollably by doing Shemp imitations. The women, naturally, were thrilled.

Xavier met cousins Chloe and Lilly on a visit to Nini and Poppie's house. The three adorable children had a ball, laughing, playing and, not surprisingly, proving to be more mature than Poppie.

We hope your year has been fun-filled, too.

Merry Christmas with love and laughter from the Zezimas.

— Jerry Zezima —

Deconstructing My Birthday

Plant flowers in others' gardens and your life becomes a bouquet!
~Author Unknown

"**W**hat do you want to do for your birthday?" my husband asked in an exasperated voice.

"I... I want... I don't know," I stuttered. "Something special."

"You want to go to that new restaurant?"

"No."

"Go out with friends?"

"No."

"What?"

"Something special, so I don't just feel old." Maybe I just needed to bite the bullet and get some hair dye or some new skin cream.

"Hmm." He disappeared into the garage. I've always thought garages were built just so men had a place to escape.

With no party in sight, I decided to use my positive thinking. How to celebrate? I couldn't think of any event that would improve my attitude toward my birthday. I had no idea what I truly wanted or needed.

Christmas time had always been my favorite celebration. I loved to give gifts to family and friends. And that's when I realized it. If I loved giving gifts, then I could do that for my birthday! Why not?

This is how I came up with my annual Birthday Person.

In the months before my birthday, I think of all the people who have blessed me. I search for a small token — a gift. Then I plan what I want to say. After writing my first rough draft, I get a clean sheet of paper that doesn't have tearstains on it. And then I create the finished product and mail it with my gift. There have been many tears involved in writing notes to my Birthday Person, tears of joy, tears of healing — tears shared on the giving and the receiving end.

I chose my mom the first year. I was her eighth child. She gave me life and added a great deal of fun and love along the way. Next was my sister, Ouida. We shared everything. Best of all, she shared her faith with me and many others. She died a few years after I made her my Birthday Person.

I've chosen a Birthday Person or Persons each year: my sisters, brothers, daughters, youth directors, pastors, grandchildren, family and friends — all people who have changed my life in amazing ways. Some years it has been more difficult to choose a Birthday Person and several times I've selected a whole group — my Sunday school, Facebook friends and more. It has blessed me beyond any gift I could have received.

By changing my thinking from getting older to focusing on others, I have eliminated the fear of more wrinkles and gray hair. I'm amazed when glancing back over the copies of these letters to see many people on my list have now passed away — my mom, sisters, brothers and friends who changed my life. These were people who gave me so much, people who I could never thank enough — but at least I was able to thank them on my birthday.

Now I look forward to my birthday every year. Taking the time to say thank you not only makes me happy, it has changed my life.

My "Birthday Person" tradition has spread to many of my friends. The power of turning a potential negative into a positive, of saying thank you before it's too late, is more rejuvenating than any box of hair color or skin cream could ever be.

— Peggy Purser Freeman —

Kindergarten Grandma

It takes a very long time to become young.
~Pablo Picasso

elen entered my life after a parent approached me and asked if I would consider hosting a foster grandparent volunteer in my kindergarten class. My answer was an immediate yes.

As a teacher, I strove to make the classroom feel like a family. Many children did not have grandparents or had ones who lived far away, so I thought this was a wonderful opportunity for children to be nurtured by an older adult. I introduced her to the class by the name Grandma Helen.

I was not quite certain what to expect when Helen first came to us. I had envisioned a little old lady, possibly frail, who would read and spend time with the children. Little did I know that Helen would walk into the classroom with a spring in her step and a twinkle in her eye. She said she was available up to three days a week for about four hours. She was anxious to help in any way she could.

Helen's enthusiasm was contagious. Her energy level was so high I would joke that if we ran a race, she would win. She was agile getting up and down from those little kindergarten chairs even though "grown up" chairs were available.

The students gravitated to her right away. It turned out that she did not want to read to groups of students, but really enjoyed sitting at learning stations while students were working. There they would talk and she would make note of their questions and concerns. Not all students were able to focus and finish their work on time, so she helped the ones who needed a little extra guidance. She had endless patience helping a child learn to cut with scissors or tie shoelaces.

Wintertime always brought the battle of the coats and boots. The children had about twenty to thirty minutes of outside recess. Grandma Helen helped zip thousands of jackets. When the students came inside there were always a few stuck in their coats when the lining of their jackets got caught in their zippers. She would patiently lift the offending coats over their heads and work to loosen the zippers. This even happened to me, and I was grateful that I didn't have to wear my jacket until lunchtime!

Helen was only scheduled to work a few days a week, but that soon turned into every day. I looked forward to her cheerful presence and extra help. The students eagerly waved to her from their tables when she walked through the door. If she didn't arrive by snack time the students wanted to know where she was.

Her volunteer hours stretched into longer periods of time where I would find her standing at the sink washing paintbrushes, putting materials together or cutting the miles of laminated paper materials. Pitching in and doing these activities saved me so much time. Her work allowed me to leave school by 5:00 so I could spend more time with my family.

Grandma Helen loved coming to school. She was always disappointed when I called her on extremely cold and icy mornings and told her not to come. This lovely seventy-eight-year-old woman drove to our school from a town that was thirty minutes away. The school parking lot was situated a distance from the front doors and I was worried she would slip on the ice.

It was very exciting when the Department of Aging honored her and three other foster grandparents at a recognition dinner. Their families, teachers and principals were invited to join them. Grandma Helen remarked that she didn't understand why so many of her friends were content to stay home and be lonely instead of having meaningful activities to look forward to during the day.

She enjoyed attending class parties and delighted in the children's excited reactions when she gave them candy on Valentine's Day and books at the winter holiday party. She felt wonderful when she helped a child complete a craft. We were all grateful for the many times she cleaned up paint spills and kept papers from sticking together after an enthusiastic student used too much glue.

Grandma Helen became a special friend to me. I looked forward to her calming presence. I was filled with curiosity to see what she might pull out of her canvas bag on arrival: would it be hats and mittens, extra socks, maybe a snack for the class or even a teacher supply I needed?

She was supportive of me as a teacher and became a compassionate confidante. We shared stories and events about our lives and families as we became close over the years. We even met occasionally over the summer months.

Grandma Helen spent years in my classroom. Amazingly, I retired before she did. She graduated to second grade and continued to spread her kindness and generosity.

—Jean Ferratier—

All Things New

They must often change, who would be constant
in happiness or wisdom.
~Confucius

"**M**om, you don't need to call all the time to check on me," our twenty-year-old son, Joe, said. "I've got to go. And Mom, you need to get a life."

Before I could say goodbye, he hung up. His words echoed in my head. "Get a life." I felt like I'd arrived to work at the best job in the world and been handed a pink slip. Being a mom meant everything to me.

It seemed one day our house bustled with activity, and then the next day it was quiet. There were no teenagers bursting through the front door asking, "What's for dinner?" There were no more late-night chats about school, crushes, or jobs.

In an effort to lift our spirits, one weekend my husband Loren said, "Let's go for a drive." We caught the ferry and drove up Whidbey Island. Standing on the bluff at Fort Casey, Loren and I watched tugboats drag barges through the Straits of Juan de Fuca. We'd visited the favorite Washington state park dozens of times with our kids.

Tears dripped down my cheeks as a chilly March wind whipped off the water. "It feels strange to be here without them. I can hear their laughter in the air and see Ben chasing Joe down the beach, whacking him with kelp."

"I know." Loren pulled me close under his arm while we strolled to our car. "I wonder what they're doing today."

Scenes from their childhood played in our minds as we drove from the park. The emptiness we felt with half our family missing ruined our outing. A few miles from the ferry I interrupted the silence. "Well, we can't just mope around the rest of our lives. I think we need to go to new places, places we never took the kids, places not already filled with memories. We need to build new memories of our own."

"Hmm… " Loren nodded. "You might be right."

While my idea simmered, Loren and I talked of dreams long left dormant. We considered changes we needed to make to move forward. Plans took shape as we envisioned our future together.

In May we traded our family car for a sporty SUV. In June Loren took a two-week vacation. We packed our clothes, loaded an ice chest filled with fruit and sandwiches into our new car, and hit the road. Instead of heading north or east like we'd always done as a family, we drove south.

Traveling down Highway 101, we explored the Oregon and Northern California coastlines. Whenever we needed a rest, we pulled off the highway at the nearest beach. Seated on the tailgate of our vehicle, we ate meals from the ice chest. We held hands, strode miles of oceanfront beaches, and sat on driftwood logs to watch the sunset.

We booked a room at a B&B, something we'd never done. The innkeeper operated a side business making fused glass and offered classes to guests. We marveled over glass vases and platters, swirled with color, displayed in the dining room. "Do you want to sign up for a class?" I said to Loren.

He gave me a skeptical grin. "I don't know. We've never done anything like that before."

Smiling, I shrugged my shoulders. "That's the point. Come on, it'll be fun."

We paid our forty dollars and signed up for an afternoon class. Huddled over a workbench in the innkeeper's studio, we spent several hours learning the process of fused glass. I watched Loren select colored glass chips from numerous supply bins and arrange them in unique patterns. We each made two coasters, had hours of fun, shared a new experience, and learned a new craft.

We had so much fun on our trip we started a list of other places we wanted to visit.

However, when we returned home once again, we faced a quiet empty house. After twenty-two years of raising kids, we felt lost until we realized we finally had time to focus on our own interests. We cleared out the kids' bedrooms and turned one into a study. Loren registered for college and earned a degree. We repainted our daughter's old room and transformed it into an art studio. Loren built me a painting table and I signed up for watercolor classes with a local artist.

We skated along fine until that first holiday season approached. Without the flurry and excitement of our kids it was miserable. Alone, we slogged through the field of the Christmas tree farm our family visited each year. From a dark corner of our closet Loren retrieved cardboard boxes labeled "Christmas." I loved the sights, sounds, and smells of the season, but when we unwrapped the first decorations, I held up a calico cat fashioned from wallpaper with buttons sewn on to attach the legs. "Bethany made this," I sniffed. "And here's the rabbit Joe made, but he's not here to hang it on the tree."

Loren wrapped his arms around me and pulled me onto the couch. "Hey, I've got an idea. Why don't we buy new ornaments?"

His suggestion seemed a wild extravagance. I gazed into the box of homemade decorations. Each one came with years of memories. "Okay." I jumped up from the couch. We rewrapped the ornaments in tissue. Loren carried the boxes back to the closet.

On Saturday we went to the store. "I feel like newlyweds on our first Christmas together," I said.

Loren laughed. "We're a long way from those days." Eyes wide with delight we strolled each aisle. A string of twinkly lights for the tree and several packages of shiny ornaments lifted our spirits and helped us glide through the season.

One evening early in the new year Loren said, "Hey, let's catch a movie."

"What, right now?" I glanced at my watch. "It's nine o'clock."

After a moment's thought I raced to grab my coat. "You're on."

Near midnight, stars twinkled in the sky as we strolled from the theater. "I don't remember the last time we went to the late show."

Loren gave my hand a gentle squeeze. "Not since we were dating."

When we arrived home we spotted the answering machine blinking. Loren pressed the button and we heard Joe's voice, "Hello... Hello... Pick up the phone... Hey, it's ten o'clock. Where are you guys?"

I laughed as Loren and I snuggled into bed. "He told me to get a life."

— Kathleen Kohler —

The Beauty of Age Spots

*Years may wrinkle the skin, but to give up
enthusiasm wrinkles the soul.*
~Samuel Ullman

"Don't worry, those are just age spots," the esthetician said in a reassuring tone, as she handed me a small tube of beauty cream.

"Are you absolutely certain that these are age spots?" I questioned, pointing to the dark spots on my hands.

Angie, the esthetician, smiled warmly and pronounced, "I'm 100% positive."

I let out a squeal of delight and hugged her tightly — letting the tube of beauty cream fall to the floor.

"You have no idea how long I've waited for these to appear," I confessed.

Angie looked slightly bewildered, and I realized there was no possible way I could explain my excitement. I was just a little disappointed that she hadn't mentioned the wrinkles around my eyes and the sprouting gray hairs near my temples. I was so proud of them! In fact, the whole visit was a huge letdown, but since I was using a gift certificate — given to me by a friend — I didn't want to seem ungrateful.

What Angie didn't know was that I wasn't supposed to live to see age spots, wrinkles or gray hair! At age forty, I wondered if I would live long enough to see any signs of aging. I was in the battle of my life — fighting breast cancer — and all I really wanted to see was my boys, ages nine and fourteen, through safe passage into adulthood. (And maybe a grandchild or two!)

After the five-year mark of being cancer free, I started to have hope. I saw the actual beginnings of wrinkles. I called them laugh lines because I couldn't stop giggling at the squiggles on my face; I was actually getting older! In fact, I attended my older son's high school graduation wearing no make-up, just so everyone could see my new wrinkles.

When I got my first gray hair, I quickly pointed it out to my husband. "Look, honey, a gray hair," I announced, fluffing it up so he could see it better. Mark, my husband of thirty years, always seemed a little disinterested in hair issues, but I think it had something to do with the fact that he was bald by the age of thirty.

On our thirty-fifth wedding anniversary, while I danced at our younger son's wedding, I was giddy with excitement because I had sprouted two new gray hairs and lip lines. There was no way the make-up artist was going to cover up those beauties; I simply wouldn't let her!

There was so much to look forward to because age spots hadn't made their appearance yet... (or so I thought) and I was approaching my sixtieth birthday and our fortieth wedding anniversary.

While I was taking a trip down memory lane, Angie interrupted my thoughts. "Here's another sample of fade cream that you can put on your hands twice a week before going to bed. During the day, use liberal amounts of sunscreen," she warned. And then I gasped when Angie mentioned the second option. "Of course, you can always have your age spots removed with lasers," she said matter-of-factly.

"Remove them?" I protested. "Why would anyone want to do that?"

Angie stared at me — not understanding — while I explained; "I'd very much like to keep them — all of them — if you don't mind."

She shook her head as she handed me the spot-fading cream and asked if I would like a follow-up appointment.

"No thanks!" I said with a grin. "I won't need the anti-spot cream or a follow-up appointment."

As I walked out the door of the spa, I was beaming with gratitude to have such a wonderful "diagnosis" of age spots! Absolutely nothing could have prepared me for that.

Later that year, I celebrated two milestones — my sixtieth birthday and twenty years of being cancer free. I'm absolutely thrilled to be growing older with gray hair, wrinkles, and now — age spots. I'm not sure why anyone would want to take them away or make them disappear because they are — after all — long-awaited gifts.

And I can see the beauty in all of them!

— Connie K. Pombo —

The Bon Jovi Challenge

*It's a great thing when you realize you still have the
ability to surprise yourself. Makes you wonder what
else you can do that you've forgotten about.*
~Alan Ball

ot long after I turned forty, my husband surprised me with tickets for the local leg of Bon Jovi's Have a Nice Day Tour. The band had been a favorite of mine since the 1980s, when I couldn't get enough of "You Give Love a Bad Name," "Wanted Dead or Alive," and "Livin' on a Prayer." I was excited to see the Jersey boys again and enjoy a blast from my past, and possibly hear a hit or two from their more recent musical endeavors.

I headed off to the show ready to revisit those bygone glory days. At the time, I wasn't depressed about hitting middle age, but I had come to believe that all the "big moments" of my life were behind me. I had married a wonderful man, had three beautiful children, written several reference books, published articles in national magazines, and worked on a number of television productions. I viewed my remaining years as a time of a quiet complacency, devoid of any fresh conquests. Sure, there would still be things to look forward to — my children's graduations, their weddings, becoming a grandmother one day — but those would all be milestones "once removed," where I would be a spectator watching from the sidelines rather than an active participant on the field.

The concert opened with "Last Man Standing," a song from Bon Jovi's most recent album. Its lyrics promised "there's magic in the night" to fans attending the show, and that's exactly what the band delivered. From that first song, I was struck by the complexity of this new music, and it dawned on me that Jon and his fellow performers were approximately the same age as I was. But they were continuing to grow and expand and develop creatively, whereas I had taken myself out of the game. As the concert went on, I began thinking that I should challenge myself to venture off in new, untried directions. If they could do it, why couldn't I?

The following day, I purchased the *Have a Nice Day* CD and played it all the way through, at least once a day, over the next few weeks. I found the song "Welcome to Wherever You Are" especially inspiring since it seemed to speak directly to my situation. The words warned against giving in to doubt and encouraged belief in the power of untapped potential. As I listened, I resolved to stretch my own horizons and push myself toward goals never before imagined.

For me, that meant taking a stab at writing fiction. As a journalist, my background was in newswriting and editorial research, and I didn't consider myself capable of producing creative works. After all, I had always told myself I was a word technician, not an artist, but now the time had come for me to step beyond that self-imposed boundary.

Within four months — aided by Jon's dulcet tones — I had written and sold my first short story, a piece about a grieving father who copes with loss by helping the homeless. Another sale soon followed, and then a poem I penned about summer giving way to fall garnered a national award. By the end of that year, I had a half-dozen published fiction credits to add to my résumé.

Buoyed by that success, I decided to try something I never thought I could do: write a children's book. It took two years and eight drafts, but I did find a publisher for my tale, and the work remains in print to this day. And it all began at that Bon Jovi concert, when what I thought was a destination turned out to be a crossroad. Taking the unfamiliar path has led to incredible places that I would not have even believed existed before that night, and there is still much uncharted territory awaiting me.

So, thank you, Bon Jovi, for showing me that creativity doesn't come with an expiration date, and that the only limits constraining us are the ones we put on ourselves. The road ahead is as wondrous and rewarding as we choose to make it, and I can't wait for whatever lies beyond the next curve!

— Miriam Van Scott —

An Introvert on the TODAY Show

Say yes and you'll figure it out afterwards.
~Tina Fey

So, what was a mild-mannered, middle-aged librarian doing on the TODAY show? I'd written an essay, "At Ease with a Body Fighting Gravity," about the fact that I'm more comfortable in a bathing suit at age fifty-eight than I was in my youth, when I actually had the body to rock a Speedo. This, apparently, was so unusual that after it was published in *The New York Times*, a TODAY show producer invited me onto the show to talk about it.

"I'd love to," I replied, "but not in a bathing suit."

I had my doubts about whether a librarian gabbing about an essay would make for riveting TV. While I can be funny on paper, I'm no dazzling wit. You'd never use the words "life of the party" to describe me. Plus, the prospect of being on national television was, to put it mildly, terrifying. At work, I'm always ready to entertain a crowd of toddlers with "The Wheels on the Bus" or "The Itsy Bitsy Spider." But entertaining millions of people on live TV? That sounded more like an Itsy Bitsy Heart Attack.

My library colleagues assured me that I could do it. "If you can handle Tiny Tot Story Time," they told me, "you can handle anything."

So, what's it actually like to be on the TODAY show?

It wasn't my usual day.

A limo turned up at 5:00 a.m. to take my sister Diane and me from my suburban Philadelphia home to 30 Rockefeller Plaza. (Trust me, this isn't how we librarians usually roll.)

After arriving, we were shown to the Green Room (which wasn't green; it was actually orange and purple). There was yummy-looking brunch chow I was too nervous to eat, and wall-mounted flat screens playing the show I was about to be on.

"Toto," I said to my sister, "we're not in Kansas anymore."

For the next ninety minutes, I was efficiently passed from one earbud-wearing, clipboard-wielding young staffer to another, each of whom filled me in on what was happening and what to expect next.

"Roz Warren? You'll be here for twenty minutes, and then we'll take you to Hair and Make-up."

Hair and Make-up, it turns out, is just a beauty salon, but at warp speed. Fifteen minutes after I hit the salon chair, my straight blond hair had been transformed into something with shape and body. My face was spackled with glamorous gunk, including burgundy lipstick and heavy mascara — a look my sister pronounced "garish" when I rejoined her.

"But I'm sure it'll look great on screen," she said. (It did.)

We waited in a new lounge with a random assortment of other garishly made-up strangers, again watching the TODAY show. A woman who'd been with us in the Green Room earlier was now onscreen promoting a parenting book.

I was, I realized, on a TV-guest conveyor belt, swiftly carrying me toward my three minutes of fame.

"Your segment is scheduled for 8:35," a staffer told me. "It's a beautiful day, so you'll be out in the plaza instead of in the studio."

At 8:15, I was taken to a "dressing room" to change into the Eileen Fisher garb I'd brought with me. To my surprise, it wasn't a room at all, just a curtained-off corner of Hair and Make-up. I ducked behind the curtain, stripped down to my undies and suited up.

Once in Eileen Fisher, I felt more confident. I might soar on my segment or fall flat on my face, but at least I'd be well dressed. (And my local EF store had given me a whopping "She's wearing this on the *TODAY* show" discount!)

My producer turned up to wish me well. My segment, she said, would start with an upbeat clip of AARP-aged women talking about feeling beautiful. Not only that, but staffers had offered any woman in the crowd watching the show who was over sixty the chance to "background" my segment if she'd stand behind me holding a brightly colored placard proclaiming her age.

Sure enough, when I took my place on a chair out on the plaza, I was cheered by a happy group of middle-aged women (my peeps!). They had no idea who I was, of course. All they knew was that, thanks to me, instead of being stuck at the back of the crowd, they were also about to be on national television.

Two minutes before airtime, Savannah Guthrie, a slim woman in a stunning turquoise cocktail dress, took the chair opposite mine and shook my hand. (Folks have since asked if she looks as good in person as she does on TV. You'd better believe it.)

"I'm Savannah," she said. "I liked your article!"

A writer I know who is often on television had advised me to look as upbeat and animated as possible. "You may feel as if you're grinning like a crazy person," she said. "But it'll come off great on camera."

I wasn't finding it difficult to grin. This was pretty amazing.

Somebody was counting down. Five… four… three… two…

We were on the air.

Savannah Guthrie is, without question, worth every penny they pay her. I am now her biggest fan. Guthrie made sure I didn't make a fool of myself on national television. Every question was calibrated to make me sound well informed and entertaining. And when it became clear that I'd never finish my final anecdote in time, she zipped in, nailed the punch line, and ended the segment on a laugh from the crowd.

Okay, so maybe I'm biased, but I think it was terrific television.

The cameras stopped. Guthrie moved on. "Great job!" said my producer.

Twenty minutes later, my sister and I were back in the limo, headed home. (And by five that night, I was back at the circulation desk, checking in books.)

It was an amazing, incredible, once-in-a-lifetime adventure.

And I'm really glad it's over.

If you ever get invited on to *TODAY*, here's my advice: Get plenty of sleep the night before. Bring your sister. Wear Eileen Fisher. Don't expect the Green Room to actually be green. Smile like a crazy person. Enjoy yourself.

And give Savannah my best.

— Roz Warren —

Editor's note: If you look up "Roz Warren *TODAY* show" on the Internet you'll find a video of Roz's appearance. It's fun to watch.

Get Physical

Silver and Gold

To dance is to be out of yourself. Larger,
more beautiful, more powerful.
~Agnes de Mille

When I discovered my passion for Irish Dance in my mid-forties I learned everything I could about it. This was despite the disparaging comments of some of my friends. They tried to talk me out of my dream, saying I was too old to master this art form.

I didn't listen to them. I took classes, practiced every day, paid for private lessons, went to workshops, and constantly listened to music for competitions and shows. Frankly, I never liked being in the competitions. But, they forced me to practice and improve my technical merit. Over the years, I accumulated a few silver and bronze medals.

And then, at age fifty, I won a gold medal for performing the hornpipe, a difficult solo step, at an Irish Step Dance competition in Estes Park, Colorado. This was the reward for all my hard work and the validation of my dream. I had done it despite the naysayers.

At the end of the competition, while I stood in the dancer tent admiring my medal, a pair of Irish dance shoes went flying past my head. The shoes were not intentionally aimed in my direction. But the words of an angry fellow competitor were: "You have no right to that medal, Padgett. You are way too old to be dancing, competing or even thinking about performing an art this demanding and athletic. Even if you were of an appropriate age to enter this level of competition, I should have won. I am so much better at technique, timing, and all around dancing than you will ever be."

I didn't know what to say. I felt like I was reliving all the negative words I had heard over the years, from all the people who said I couldn't do it. I stood there, hurt, trying to regain my emotional balance. Then I felt a hand rest gently on my shoulder. An unfamiliar voice asked, "Do you believe her?"

I turned to face the judge who moments ago had awarded me the gold.

"Yes ma'am. She has better technique and sense of musical timing. She is just all around better than me," I admitted.

"No, she isn't," the adjudicator told me. "Do you know the difference between the silver and gold? Do you know why you were awarded this medal today?' she asked.

I dropped my gaze from hers and shook my head.

She lifted my chin, looked into my teary eyes and said, "You reflected hours of practice and honing of your craft, just like many others. You managed to keep the beat and execute a difficult step, like many others. Your posture was straight, and you demonstrated ability to remember the intricacies required. You were up against some tough competition out there today, and you gave a flawless performance. From a judge's point of view, it can be difficult to select one dancer over another when awarding medals.

"But, if mechanics and technical merit are equal, the decision will fall to the one who dances with her heart. Some *do* the dance; others *are* the dance. Today, you were the dance. And that, my friend, is gold."

That was my last Irish Dance competition, not because I feared decapitation as the result of airborne footwear. It was because the calendar does not lie. My years of hard, competitive Irish dancing were over. I entered the contest knowing it would be my last.

I am not prone to melancholy over things out of my control — like the passage of time. And I honestly cannot say I spend a lot of time looking at the dance medals I accumulated over the years.

Nonetheless, the medals do come in handy once in a while. For example when someone tells me they cannot realize a dream because of age, perceived inabilities or opinions of critics, I extend this invitation, "Would you come to my house for tea, please? I want to show you something."

—Laura L. Padgett—

A Weighty Revelation

To feel "fit as a fiddle," you must
tone down your middle.
~Author Unknown

When Bob and I got married 39 years ago, he weighed a good 50 pounds more than I did. I'd been self-conscious for years, being one of the tallest in my class at 5'9"... taller than many of the boys in my high school. That was a hard insecurity to shake. To realize that Bob was "bigger" than I was weight-wise was a welcome boost for my self-esteem.

I enthusiastically welcomed my added pounds and beach-ball contours when I became pregnant with our children, Jennifer and Wade, but managed to stay active enough afterwards to drop those extra pounds and reclaim my original shape. Now that decades have passed, my metabolism has crashed, and our kids have grown and left us with an empty nest; my waistline and the numbers on our scales seem to be growing uncontrollably.

I used to try dieting, but Jen and Wade told me to eat because I was too grouchy. I've half-heartedly tried to eat more healthily, yet realize eating healthy meals isn't enough. I still find myself sneaking the sweets I crave — and I know my body deserves better. Those calories are not only fattening, they're dangerous to my health. My brain knows this, but my mouth and taste buds betray me when I least expect it... and I'm disappointed in my lack of self-discipline.

I used to run for exercise until my joints gave out. I powerwalk and work out at the gym now, but since my hips and waist stubbornly stay the same, perhaps that's not enough.

Some try to tell us not to worry about the actual size of clothes we wear... what matters is for our clothing to fit well. Reluctantly, I recently followed that advice and swallowed my pride as I purchased a size of jeans I swore I'd never buy. I needed some "well-fitting" jeans to take on a weekend trip with Bob. Yes, the size was hard to accept, but they were made with "stretch" denim, and the labels said they would make my tummy "seem slimmer." That dulled my ego's pain a little.

I hoped these were the right choice of jeans, because I wanted to look and feel my best on this romantic getaway to a picturesque southern New Mexico lodge Bob had heard about. The inn was lovely and the room we stayed in was quaint, albeit very tiny. That meant the little dresser only had a couple of small drawers and there was no closet.

Because of the lack of space, I just folded my new jeans and placed them on a shelf. I planned to wear them the next morning on a scenic drive and hike which Bob was anxious to share with me.

When I came out of the diminutive bathroom, drying off from my shower, I found Bob standing in front of the mirror with a puzzled look... staring at the pants he'd just zipped up. "What's wrong with these jeans? The pockets are in the wrong place and the legs don't feel right."

"No!" I gasped in horror. "I laid your jeans out on the chair. You're wearing mine!" Bob just laughed, but I was devastated. After 39 years of marriage, Bob put on the wrong pants and they fit him.

I tried to tell myself the reason they fit was because of the stretchy denim, but knew in my breaking heart that I could no longer deny it. I'm as big around the middle now as Bob is. I don't know how much Bob actually weighs, but even though he still weighs more than I do, I'm sad to admit that my body's shape has morphed into his twin.

This wrong-pants revelation has given me a new determination and focus to get my act together.

I was blessed with good health and a slim body in my youth, and I became lazy. I'm grateful to be older now, but with that gift, I need to take more responsibility. I know I can do this. I deserve it.

I can no longer be lazy and just eat whatever... whenever, because I want to live a long, happy life with my husband and dear family. Sweets and fatty foods must be cut out, and as long as I'm physically able, I want to push myself harder at the gym and take more frequent walks. I have no desire to be the size I was at our wedding, but I do need to take better care of myself.

If I can firm up and slim down at least enough that Bob can never wear my jeans again, I'll be thrilled... yet I know that shouldn't be my only reason. They say what's really important is to be healthy, but my new determination to try harder makes me feel better about myself. That's important too. Bob has always loved and supported me, but even after being married 39 years, I realize some of my insecurities still linger. By no longer being lazy and taking better care of myself, I will grow as a person. That's much better than growing around my middle! Bob may have picked the wrong pants, but I know now more than ever that he picked the right woman.

— Lynne S. Albers —

13

Chased by Zombies

Run. Because zombies will eat
the untrained ones first!
~Heather Dakota,
Zombie Apocalypse Survival Guide

Three times a week, my husband forces me to meet him in town after work and pretend to be chased by zombies. Or maybe it was my idea. The details are fuzzy.

We are actually preparing for a community 5K held every year in our town to raise money for those battling cancer. As 45-year-olds who are overweight and incredibly out of shape, with me recovering from two major surgeries last year, I'm not really sure why we don't just write a check and help hand out water bottles or something. That seems like the practical, logical thing to do. But then I suppose we wouldn't get the T-shirt.

This all started when we flew to the West Coast and spent a week with our two-year-old grandson. When we returned, we realized that if we didn't do something soon, we would never be able to keep up with that child. There's a reason we had our children in our twenties, but we're still young enough that following a toddler around the playground should not be so exhausting. So we returned to the East Coast, took a nap, and started a 5K training program.

We are using an app for couch-to-5K training. The idea is that anyone can run if they work into it slowly. This particular app has a story line involving zombies to help make the training a bit more interesting. Because, let's face it, running is hard and boring. The really nice — or really horrible, depending on the day — thing about this app is that it incorporates additional exercises such as knee lifts or heel lifts to strengthen our legs. So not only can our muscles scream in pain from running, but they can be stretched out to feel pain in different ways!

Advil is now a staple on my grocery list. After the first week, my husband, suffering from horrible shin-splint pain, bought special "shin-splint socks." These are a real thing. He realized a week later that he should have read the instructions when he found out that he was wearing them backwards. When I pictured our empty-nest years, this was not quite what I had envisioned.

Then around week four, something amazing happened. I jogged five minutes straight without stopping. For most people, that won't sound like much. I'm not even comfortable calling it running at this point. But I was definitely jogging.

For me, it was a major accomplishment considering my past history. For the past few years, my iron was so low that I could barely walk across a room without being out of breath. Even after surgery to fix my iron issues, walking was still difficult. Then I tore the meniscus in my knee. The surgery to repair the tear was not, as I had hoped, an instantaneous fix. The recovery took months, not the three days I had allotted it on my calendar. I had thought the doctor was just being super cautious, but he actually meant it when he said it would take six months to a year to stop swelling and hurting so much. Mid-forties bodies, especially those not well taken care of, do not recover like 20-year-old bodies.

But, eight months after the first surgery and six months after the second, I'm jogging. Five minutes is not going to get me through a 5K, and I don't see how three more weeks will get me to a point of running for 40 minutes straight, but right now I'm just happy to jog five minutes straight. For a woman who could hardly walk across a room last year, that's a big step.

So, to recap, three times a week, a very overweight, out-of-shape, middle-aged couple meets in town to pretend to be chased by zombies along a historic canal path so they can pay $25 for a "free" T-shirt later this summer. And one of them has his socks on backwards.

— Heather Truckenmiller —

14

Chicken Soup for the Soul

Showing Up

I want to feel my life while I'm in it.
~Meryl Streep

I'm seventy-nine years old. Several years ago, I witnessed the sudden and unexpected death of my husband Don after thirty-two years of marriage. Eighteen months later, I met Jim, a gentleman who opened my heart to love again. Sadly, four months after we met, he passed unexpectedly due to a fall.

My grief therapist said one doesn't have to be a soldier to experience PTSD. I felt as if I'd been wounded in combat and wanted to remain hidden in a foxhole.

Now, almost three years later, I have emerged from the foxhole. I feel that life is good again, with no disrespect to loved ones who have passed.

As crazy as it may sound, I give the sport of pickleball a lot of the credit.

After my losses, I was fortunate to have tremendous support from family and friends, but pickleball provided an outlet with unexpected benefits. The obvious one was physical activity, but it delivered so much more.

My husband and I were introduced to the game in 2015 at our summer residence near Flagstaff, Arizona, where the pickleball courts were a two-minute walk from our door. We got hooked on the game but also enjoyed the friendships that quickly developed. Hey, when people see you a few minutes after you wake up with no make-up and accept you, there's an instant comradeship.

When Don passed in April, the first time I went to the pickleball court in May without him was hard. But, once again, fellow picklers pulled me through — and running around the court and working up a sweat surely released precious endorphins, not to mention the release of anger (that often accompanies grief) when you slam the ball as hard as you can.

When I returned to my winter residence in Phoenix, I discovered that the nearby senior center offered pickleball indoors and outdoors. They also had it at my local YMCA. I began to play at each place, and it was easier in some ways because many of these people never knew Don. It was a new circle of friends.

Now, in addition to the physical benefits, here's the *real* secret to the magic of pickleball. It's the social time on the bench or bleachers while you're waiting your turn for a court. You'll meet people from all walks of life with interesting past lives, all ages, and they come in all shapes and sizes. You don't have to be a super athlete to play. It's a short court and a short game; with only eleven points to win, it takes about fifteen minutes per game.

Many mornings, I awoke with a heavy heart after my losses. Some days, I just wanted to burrow back under the covers, but pickleball was an easy option to choose when I was trying to convince myself to go out. I didn't have to sign up ahead of time, and it gave me a reason to get dressed and show up — not just showing up for the game but for life itself. Having a place to go each morning and meeting new people who soon became friends was a great start to each day. It's a great pastime for couples to do together and for singles to meet other singles who have a similar interest.

This year, I've been invited to play in a ladies' pickleball league. We practice each week for our matches with other leagues in the area. Now, in addition to fun, there's a competitive edge and a beautiful comradeship that comes when you are part of a team.

I've played at many different locations and have found each one to be friendly and welcoming to newcomers. When I visited my children in Chicago at Christmas, I found an indoor court at a senior center near their home. Now it's "have paddle, will travel."

My life is so good now that sometimes I feel guilty enjoying myself so much when I've lost two dear people, but perhaps those losses make me appreciate life more. I never take one day for granted and I live life as fully as possible.

—Violetta Armour—

15

What Could Go Wrong?

Our grandchildren accept us for ourselves,
without rebuke or effort to change us,
as no one in our entire lives has ever done.
~Ruth Goode

t was Labor Day weekend, the last weekend in a summer full of outdoor adventures with my grandsons. Twelve-year-old Noah and I headed up north to go white-water rafting. It was my idea. I'd gone rafting dozens of times. Who cared that the last time was almost thirty years ago? What could go wrong?

We arrived at the meet-up spot near Pembine, Wisconsin. Our guide, Derek, fit us with life jackets and helmets. Along with the other six rafters, two women and four men, we boarded the bus with our driver, Bill, who took us to the launch spot on the Menominee River.

The first section of the trip was flat water, and Derek used the time to review the safety instructions and practice paddling in unison. We all listened carefully.

The next section was class 2 rapids, which I now know means "some rough water and rocks, some maneuvering." Only a basic skill level was required. Yahoo! We got wet. Everyone was laughing. We gave a high-five salute with our paddles.

The next section was class 4 rapids, which I now know are waves, rocks, sharp maneuvers, and a considerable drop. "Exceptional" skill level is required.

Off we went. Derek was calling out paddling instructions. However, the people paddling on the left were paddling way harder than the people on the right, so we smashed straight into a giant rock face. The force bounced us into a ricochet, which catapulted me into a backward somersault out of the raft.

My helmet popped off, and I was trapped underneath the raft. I was really, really scared. After a death-defying amount of time, the raft and I drifted apart. But now I was going down the "considerable drop" all by myself. Whitewater crashed over my face. I thought I was going to drown.

Noah was screaming, "Grandma! Grandma! Grandma!" That really drove home the point that I was out of my league. Derek was shouting at me, "Nose up, toes up!" He yelled at the rafters to paddle hard, and they finally got close to me. Derek reached over and grabbed the shoulders of my life jacket. "One, two, three," he said and hauled me into the back of the raft. The bottom of my suit fell down to my knees. I was facedown, bare keister up. As I wriggled around to pull up my suit and find a more comfortable position, Derek said, "Sorry, ma'am."

We got through the rest of the rapids and glided to the riverbank. No one was laughing. "Grandma, are you okay?" asked a wide-eyed Noah. My heart was pounding out of my chest, and my hands were shaking, but I did my best to keep my composure.

We hiked a little way to rendezvous with the bus driver. Bill said, "Wait until you see the video! Some of you are really going to want a copy."

I had forgotten about the video. Bill had been perched above the falls recording.

I rationalized it away. How close could he possibly have been? Plus, the mishap was in the back of the boat. Only Derek really saw it. I told Noah about it just in case and he thought it was funny, but he wasn't concerned. "They would probably fuzz it out anyway," he says.

Back at the meet-up spot, everyone gathered around a small, flat screen to view our exciting journey. Sure enough, there it was — my big, white derriere for the whole world to see. Noah shook his head and said, "Oh, Grandma."

The two other women in the group realized how awkward this was and yanked the men away. I threatened to stalk anyone who wanted to buy the video. Noah consoled me, "It's okay, Grandma. It's not that bad. Everyone has a butt."

I gave Noah a big hug. I'm so grateful that our memory of this trip will be a really funny, embarrassing thing that happened and not something horrible. He tells me that rafting was the most fun he had all summer.

—Elaine Maly—

16

You've Been Geezered

I have a plan...
To live forever...
So far... It's workin'.
~Steven Wright

'm Geezer Doug and my story begins in January 1997. As I read the sports section of *The Orange County Register*, I found a big picture of Baz Hawley, a design engineer from Australia whom I hired back in 1973. The picture showed Baz hugging a young lady just as she crossed the finish line at his trail race. It really was the Baz Hawley I knew. The article stated that Baz was the Race Director for something called the Winter Trail Run Series held in the mountains of the Cleveland National Forest.

I wondered what a trail race was. I couldn't imagine people running in the mountains. I had backpacked in the Sierra Nevadas on multiple weeklong trips and had even made it to the top of Mount Whitney in 1995. However, I never saw a single person running in the mountains. Could people actually run in that thin air?

Fortunately, the newspaper article had Baz's contact information. I called him and we ended up getting together several times. He always invited me to try his races and I always responded, "No way." I could never run up hills, let alone in thin air. I had the road runner's mentality that if I ever had to stop and walk, I wouldn't be a *real* runner. I also thought Baz was lying to me when he told me that many of the runners walked the steep sections. Besides, the last time I did a serious run was the Los Angeles Marathon in 1993, four years earlier. I remembered that my back bothered me the next morning.

It took a year of prodding, but Baz finally coerced me into attempting his 12K, the shortest race of his series. I had to get up pretty early to drive the long way out along the twisty Ortega Highway to get to the Cleveland National Forest and the Blue Jay Campground where his trail races were held. This was January 1998, and I was already 58 years old. I really thought I was too old; however, I soon found out a man older than me, Lee Francis, was running. He was 65.

Although I planned to run the entire course, I failed. I had to walk some of the steeper sections. I observed quite a few other racers walking them, too. Perhaps Baz wasn't lying to me after all.

The next morning, my back felt great — as if I had had a magical massage. A week later, I decided to sign up for Baz's 15K. Later, I joined the 18K and eventually his 21K (half marathon), which had 3,700 feet of climbing.

I started to love trail running, but it took a while for me to figure out why. Eventually, I realized that since the early 1980s, this new-to-California boy from flat and gray Chicago had loved backpacking in the Sierras. I had been taking annual, week-long hikes with my neighbor, retired U.S. Marine Major Bob Johnson, and that was with 45-pound packs. With these races, I got to run through that same gorgeous, remote, uncrowded scenery with less than a three-pound pack!

I also found that the up-and-down of the trails was surprisingly easier on my body than the hours on end I spent running on constant, near-level paved roads. Of course, I was initially concerned about all the rocks and roots one encounters on trails. I felt it would be almost insane to try to run through those sections. I did learn to slow down a bit and be careful. I am absolutely sure this has helped me keep my balance skills in good shape as I age.

My daughter, Michelle Barton, started joining me in my trail-running training about a year after my granddaughter Sierra was born in January 2000. Three years later, Michelle did her first trail race. Yes, it was a Baz Winter Trail Run Series race. Michelle has since evolved into a now-famous ultrarunner with numerous 50K and 50-mile course records to her credit, including some she set while beating all of the men. I am very proud of her. These adventures together in the scenic mountains evolved into a special, long-term bond.

In 2007, things changed for me once again because Michelle entered something new called TransRockies. It was the inaugural year for the race. TransRockies is held in Colorado in August and involves trail running above 8,000-feet elevation with the high point being Hope Pass at 12,600-feet elevation. It is 120 miles in total distance, but spread over six days. The new term I learned was "stage race." Back then, it was strictly teams of two racing together. Michelle and Adam Chase from Boulder, Colorado won the Mixed Team category that year.

After seeing all of her scenic pictures and asking her endless questions about this multi-day stage concept, I became convinced I could enjoy that race, too. Imagine all new mountain scenery in Colorado to toodle through and no 45-pound pack to carry! Just a three-pound hydration pack with a few lightweight emergency supplies. Aid stations, too.

I did my first TransRockies in August 2008. At age 68, I was the oldest runner. Steve Harvey and I were Team "California Old Goats." I have done it six times now and have *always* been the oldest runner. I am currently signed up to run it again in 2019 — at age 80. This will be my third time teamed with Gordy Ainsleigh (age 72). If we pass you on the trails there, we hope you enjoy receiving one of our "California Old Goats" semi-famous "U Bin GEEZERed" cards.

Trail running, even at my easy pace, has kept me healthy, especially for my age. No one likes the thought of getting old and useless, so why allow that to happen? I hope my story gives all "young" people under 60 an awareness that if they keep walking and running, they can continue to do the same. If Geezer Doug (me) can do it and still have fun at 80, so can everyone. I'm proof that there is no reason to retire from physical activities and the health they bring.

— Doug Malewicki —

Back in the Saddle Again

*The essential joy of being with horses is that it brings
us in contact with the rare elements of grace,
beauty, spirit, and fire.*
~Sharon Ralls Lemon

Was this what menopause was all about? I'd known there would likely be hot flashes. A thickening waistline. Mood swings. What I hadn't figured on was falling into an ever-deepening funk as I moved further and further into my fifties. I'd scold myself when I'd become weepy for no reason. I had nothing to be unhappy about. I had a wonderful husband, three happy kids who are on their own, a roof over my head, shoes on my feet and no worries about where my next meal was coming from.

It wasn't that I didn't have enough to keep me busy. I had a too-big house to clean and a too-big lawn to mow. A garden to tend. Meals to cook and dishes to wash. I volunteered at church and at a neighborhood elementary school. On top of all that, my husband and I lived on a small farm. Though the cattle, goats and chickens that we'd once cared for were gone, we still had horses, cats, and Sophie, our three-year-old Boxer mix who clearly relished being a farm dog.

But Sophie's waistline was thickening, too, and I knew it was my fault. Did I feed her too much? Yes. (Somehow it made it easier to justify my own overeating.) Did I exercise her enough? No. (Most days, I had no desire to walk through the woods behind our house or around the pond in our pasture. Surely, Sophie didn't either.)

We did, however, climb the steep stairs to the hayloft in the barn every morning. I'd cut the rough twine away from a couple of hay bales and toss them, flake by flake, down into the horses' manger. Then Sophie and I would descend the loft stairs and make our way back to the house. We were both out of breath by the time we got there.

Pathetic. It was clear that Sophie and I needed to find something to bring physical fitness — and, along with it, zest — back into our lives. But what?

On a sunny morning in early April, we headed to the barn as usual. And as usual, our three horses stood in the pasture and followed us with their gaze. But on this day, they didn't sprint to the barn. Instead, they dropped their heads and tore at the new-green grass that had, seemingly overnight, begun to poke through the pasture's brown stubble. When I got to the loft, I saw that the hay I'd tossed out yesterday still littered the barn floor.

I knelt down and threw my arms around Sophie's neck. "It's spring, girl," I told her. "No more hay chores!"

Sophie wagged all over.

"How about if we take a walk?"

More wagging.

As we began our first loop around the pond, I noticed that Sunny, our palomino gelding, was following us. I stopped to scratch between his ears and discovered that his mane and forelock were matted with cockleburs. "You poor thing," I told him, "let's take you to the barnyard and get you cleaned up."

Sunny stood patiently as I combed the burs out of his hair. He lifted his feet so I could use the hoof pick to clean out the dried mud and rocks. He practically grinned when I began rubbing the curry comb over his coat. As he grew cleaner and I grew dirtier, I noticed myself humming and wondering how long it had been since I'd groomed this horse. More than that, how long had it been since I'd ridden him? Or any other horse for that matter.

Two years at least. Not so long ago, I had ridden almost every day. But I'd fallen out of the habit. Allowed other things to get in the way. Let myself and my animals get fat and lazy. Perhaps the time had come to change that.

Except that you can't just jump on a horse and ride him as if he's a bicycle. It's important to make sure he's in decent aerobic shape. Free of leg and foot problems. And safe to ride. (A horse that's used to being a pasture ornament just might morph into a bucking bronco!) I needed to work Sunny on a lunge line for at least a couple of weeks to make sure he was sound. He seemed to have no objection. In fact, he seemed to enjoy our daily sessions. As did Sophie, who romped and played the whole time Sunny and I were working.

When it was clear that Sunny was ready to be ridden, I lugged his tack out of the barn. I draped the saddle blanket over a fence rail and beat the dust out of it with a broom. I cleaned the saddle and bridle and reins with saddle soap and rubbed them with Neatsfoot oil until they gleamed. I polished the bit until it shone like new. Then I got Sunny tacked up. He looked beautiful. And, as crazy as it might sound, happy.

The time had come to untie Sunny from the fence post and climb onto his back.

My fifty-five-year-old heart was beating hard. Was I too old for this? Were my muscles still strong and limber enough to mount a horse? Could I keep my balance once Sunny started to move? Did I remember how to use my hands and legs and voice to make him stop and go and change directions? There was only one way to find out.

I put my left foot in the stirrup, grabbed a clump of Sunny's perfectly coiffed mane with my left hand, and sprang off my right foot into the saddle. It felt good. No, not just good. Wonderful. I relaxed my grip on the reins and squeezed Sunny's sides with my legs.

"Giddy-up, fella," I said.

And with that, Sunny and I headed for the woods, with Sophie following close behind. We rode for more than an hour that day, taking in the sights and sounds and smells of spring and having a perfectly marvelous time. I collapsed into bed that night with every muscle in my body groaning. They were groaning even louder the next morning. But no matter. As soon as my housework was done, I headed straight for the barn.

I whistled once. Here came Sophie. I whistled again. Here came Sunny. Both of them ready—just like me—to put a little fun back into our lives.

—Jennie Ivey—

The Marathon Miracle

Miracles happen to those who believe in them.
~Bernard Berenson

t's 6:15 in the morning and the pavement is flying beneath me. With each stride through the dark, frosty morning, I'm gobbling up yards of San Vicente Boulevard as I head for the final stretch back to the office. Even though I'm cold and clammy, there's a certain exhilaration knowing that there aren't many others up at this hour, let alone preparing for an event like the marathon: 26.2 miles of grueling, energy-sapping punishment.

I had wanted to run a marathon for more than twenty years. But even during the fog of my alcohol and drug addiction, I somehow acknowledged that subjecting my body to the rigors of long-distance running would be a more expedient death than a bottle or another line of coke. But, when I finally got clean and sober on October 21, 1986, the world opened up to me. For the first time in my life, goals and aspirations seemed within reach without the artificial obstacles of youth, immaturity or my own physical and mental limitations. I could do anything I put my mind to.

Ironically, what complicated the issue was my college degree — in particular, my area of study. In 1983, I graduated from San Diego State University with a degree in Exercise Physiology and went to work for a cardiac rehabilitation clinic. My denial allowed me to drink to excess every night while I counseled patients on the value of taking care of one's health by day. For the next several years, every patient that I came in contact with naturally assumed that I was the picture of health and a marathoner. After all, haven't all exercise physiologists completed at least one? I struggled with my disease while in my own mind I felt invalidated as a fitness expert who was touting the benefits of a healthy lifestyle.

When I finally entered recovery, I had no excuses or limitations. I was determined to go for it. Over the next six months, I read every conceivable book on the subject of marathon training. I experimented with everything from diet, running shoes, shorts and fluid replacements — even underwear. Every Saturday morning was reserved for my long runs (between 15 and 25 miles) while the weekdays were peppered with shorter hill climbs and weight training. As the mileage and dirty laundry piled up, I became a fit and highly-tuned running machine.

With one week to go before the Los Angeles Marathon, short cruising runs were the order of the day; the concept being after months of preparation, it's time to cruise and relax. Just keep limber and get ready for the big race on Sunday.

As I approached the final stretch of my pre-dawn run, out of nowhere a pothole suddenly appeared, dropping me to the asphalt. On the way down, I heard an audible "pop" from my left knee. In one split second, six months of training evaporated in the wake of my dislocated knee. By the time I hobbled back to the office, it had swollen to the size of a cantaloupe.

While I wasn't immediately sure just how badly I was injured, I had taken enough anatomy classes to know that knees were not supposed make sounds and look like cantaloupes. But the thought of missing the marathon in five days concerned me far more than my physical infirmity. I had not just given the marathon a small place in my life; it had become my life. I had shared all of my competitive dreams of running my first marathon in my hometown with my friends and everyone else who was important in my life. Now my dream was gone.

I managed to see an orthopedic surgeon the next day, having already lost one valuable day of training. For the uninitiated, losing a single day of training when preparing for a marathon begins a downward spiral that can potentially erode the confidence necessary to complete a race that defies the limits of common sense. Lying on the exam table with a synovial fluid-filled syringe protruding from the side of my knee was not exactly instilling the type of pre-race confidence that I had hoped for.

The good news was that after a thorough examination, X-rays and an MRI, nothing appeared to be permanently damaged. When I stepped into the pre-dawn rut, I stretched every ligament, tendon and joint capsule to the extent of their unnatural limits; but nothing was broken. The first thing I asked the doctor was, "When will I be able to run again?" Remaining cautious, he explained that as soon as the swelling went down, I could do whatever I felt I could tolerate. The gauntlet was thrown down.

Later that afternoon, my self-confidence began to return to normal, even though my knee hadn't. The injury damaged my body, but not my spirit. The next day, I hobbled into a local running store and asked if there were any marathons later in the year. With all of the training that I had put in, I was certain that I'd be back on the streets within a couple of months.

"There aren't any more marathons until the last part of November," said the clerk. "Oh, wait. There is one smaller race next month: the Long Beach Marathon." A ray of hope emerged.

Even despite the rosy picture the orthopedic surgeon painted, I was convinced as I limped along on my gammy leg that there was no way I could pursue the Long Beach Marathon. It was only three and a half weeks away. Impossible. But, Aristotle once said, "Hope is a waking dream." My dream was only three weeks away.

Fortunately, due to my area of study, I knew more about physiology than the average weekend athlete. I knew that if I could sustain my fitness at its current level while my knee mended, there was a possibility that I could run the race and maybe even finish it.

The next morning, I embarked on a self-prescribed training regimen unlike any you'll read about in *Runner's World*; probably the first time anyone has ever prepared for a marathon without running. I was fortunate enough to be working in a hospital fitness center that had a wide variety of stationary bikes, treadmills and free weights. One of the bikes was a Schwinn Airdyne, arguably one of the finest pieces of fitness equipment ever invented. The Airdyne is an over-sized contraption that has not only pedals, but arm cranks that thrust up from the flywheel. With a large fan mounted in front of the rider, the faster that you pedal the greater the resistance. Hmmm… This could actually work.

I hooked myself up with a series of electrocardiograph leads designed to monitor the heart rate and rhythm of cardiac patients during exercise. Having already calculated my training heart rate range based on my previous program, I knew that I could theoretically maintain my fitness if I could persevere through 90 minutes a day at a minimum of 150-165 beats per minute. I dragged a barstool up next to the bike and propped my ice-packed knee on it and proceeded to pedal with my good leg and both arms until I reached 150 beats per minute.

Over the course of the next week, I downed prescription-strength anti-inflammatories like candy. The swelling in my knee went down as my fitness level climbed. I was actually becoming fitter without putting in so much as a mile of running. After about two and a half weeks, I solicited the doctor's approval to start running again. He gave it.

The first day back out on the street was torture. I was handicapped more by my mental fitness than physical. After a few easy miles, I returned to the office with renewed confidence that I just might be able to finish my first marathon.

Within a week, I was back up to 10 miles. The Long Beach Marathon was now only days away. At a time when I should have been tapering down, I was ramping up. Trainers advise anyone contemplating running a marathon to run at least one run of 20 miles or more before the event. Fortunately, I had already completed mine, so I just considered my injury a minor "interruption" in my training schedule.

By the time race day arrived, I was fit and motivated to run the race of a lifetime. I completed the race in just under four hours, running the first 18 miles faster than I had ever run before. As I crossed the finish line, the loudspeakers announced my name and hometown to the crowd of cheering spectators. I immediately broke down in tears as the preceding seven months of stress finally oozed out of every pore of my body. I could finally relax; I had completed the Long Beach Marathon.

Over the next few years, I completed three more marathons, but none of those victories was a sweet as the first. The power to overcome overwhelming odds to attain an impossible goal made it even better than if my training had gone exactly as planned.

—Allen R. Smith—

It Pays to Keep Walking

Afoot and light-hearted I take to the open road,
Healthy free, the world before me,
The long brown path before me
leading wherever I choose.
~Walt Whitman

My husband and I are both very creative. Dave is currently the househusband, but in his spare time he plays guitar and writes songs. I sew quilts and do freelance writing when I'm home from my full-time job. We are building our own house from the ground up. As a result of constantly being involved in our projects, we are not very sports-minded. The most activity I usually do outside is gardening, and Dave fixes our vehicles himself and runs most of the errands around town. We are involved in church activities and we play with our grandkids. But most of what we do is indoors, sitting down.

We've had quite a few medical problems and managed to rack up a lot of bills in the past for doctors and medical tests. Then in 2007 Dave had a heart attack and I was diagnosed with the muscle disorder fibromyalgia. We took a good look at making some lifestyle changes. Dave worked on the meal planning, which I benefited from as well. We both started losing weight. But we were also advised to get more exercise.

Walking. That's all we needed to do. Just walk every day. Somehow that just didn't fit in with our normal schedule, and we knew we were in for a challenge. We had already tried going to a gym, using a treadmill, etc. but nothing worked to keep us walking. Even just remembering to walk every day was a drawback for both of us.

Our latest medical issues provided new incentive to get more serious about this, so we made our usual resolution to walk more. Dave drove down to the small lake below us and walked around it nearly every day, a good half hour of exercise. He admired the scenery, took pictures of the ducks and geese, and seemed to be doing fine with this routine, for a while. But as the initial shock of having a heart attack began to wear off, daily distractions took over and Dave began to plan less time-consuming exercise. A brisk walk down to the "Y" in our dirt road and back up the other side took only 20 minutes and was up- and downhill. That seemed to work at first. But he gradually grew more forgetful and when the weather was bad, it was difficult to keep it up.

My daily walking needed to be mostly at work because by the time I got home, I was too tired to do anything. Sometimes I even had to take a nap because of my fibromyalgia. I resolved that I would get away from the desk at break times and walk for 10 minutes. Two breaks would be 20 minutes. Unfortunately, I tended to be less dedicated when it was too hot, or too cold, or raining, or snowing, or I was too achy, or I wanted or needed to do something else during my break! I knew if I walked more I would feel better and maybe not need so many naps, but I still struggled with walking every day. However, my real worry was Dave. He had a life-threatening possibility if he didn't keep up his walking. Something had to be done, so I prayed for a way to keep us both motivated to walk.

At last one day I had an idea. It seemed kind of silly at first, but I actually thought it might work so I told Dave about it. What if we paid ourselves to walk? My plan was this: we would each keep track of our walking time on the calendar, adding it up as "walking points." Whenever we reached 120 points, we would get $10 to spend or save for whatever we wanted. In addition to the money, I figured there would be a little competition, which might add to the motivation.

Since our money is always budgeted for bills and living expenses, or catching up on credit cards, we don't often have anything extra to buy things that are not necessary. Dave is always window-shopping in catalogs and online for electronic equipment to go with his music playing or song recording. Yet he almost never has the opportunity to buy any. I often want some clothes or certain books that are out of our price range.

Dave liked the idea, so we started applying it, and to our surprise, it worked! Dave soon began keeping up his 20 minutes a day. One of the first things Dave bought was a bass guitar. (Now that's incentive!) Another time he got an MP3 player. As I write this, he has saved up $155 for some unknown item he hasn't decided on yet.

The plan worked for me as well. I was now more inclined to walk at work during my break time. There was a certain pair of fancy shoes I wanted to buy, and a $50 sweater in a catalog. I found myself walking specifically to earn points to be able to get those items.

The competitive side of the plan worked as well. We found ourselves telling others that we had to go out for walks so we could earn our walking points. "Dave is way ahead of me this week," I would say. One time I kept forgetting something in the car at a large church gathering outdoors, and Dave teased me. "You're just walking back to the car so you can get more points!"

When I first thought of this idea, I also wondered how we could afford it. But as I told Dave at the time, if we kept walking we might save on medical bills. Didn't it make sense to stay healthier and not need a doctor? We had spent thousands of dollars on medical bills in the past. Why not spend it on ourselves to stay healthy?

For us, this plan has worked 18 months and counting. Sometimes I just want $10 for something special, and other times I save it up for something more expensive. And thank God, we have been healthier—what a bonus! Our doctor bills have been generally lower this past year. Could it be that the walking points plan not only kept us walking but also actually saved us money?

We may never know the answer to that, but one thing we can say for sure: it definitely pays to keep walking!

— Laurie Penner —

20

Splash of Fame

Don't think, just do.
~Horace

I n 1968, Andy Warhol said, "In the future, everyone will be world famous for fifteen minutes." In a short time, the phrase "fifteen minutes of fame" became a standard promise. Like most people, I never really expected to have even a few seconds of this assured and grand limelight. And then it happened.

We were aboard the *National Geographic Explorer* on a cruise to Antarctica. The ship carried 148 passengers and 100 crewmembers. Excitement filled the air as we witnessed sculptured ice formations twenty stories high, snow-covered mountain peaks and glaciers.

Motor-driven boats called Zodiacs ferried us across the frozen sea so we could climb snowy mountain ranges and mingle with penguins waddling around like little old men. Enormous seals dotted the shoreline. Heavy snowflakes covered our parkas, and frosty air bit into our skin.

Like all the other passengers, we relaxed in the tranquility of the excursion and relished the serenity of the White Continent. Then one morning we saw a sign announcing an open invitation to all passengers: Polar Plunge at 12:30.

My husband and I gaped at the sign. His face brightened, hinting he wanted to give this reckless feat a fling, but I had a churn of panic in my stomach. Hundreds of reasons for not doing such a ridiculous act clicked through my mind. "No way," I declared.

"For starters," I protested, "we are much too old. The water is freezing cold. Heights terrify me. I'm not much of a swimmer. In simple language, I'm a wimpy coward."

I could tell by my husband's expression my rebuttal didn't dent his building enthusiasm. "Not only that," I moaned, "but it means I'd have to wear a swimsuit in public with a boatload of people gawking at my fat, wrinkly body."

He gave me a quick hug along with his endearing smile. "We'll never have another chance," he insisted.

My resolve gradually weakened. My hearty "No way" gave way to a weak "Maybe." Finally, I heaved a big breath, mustered my courage and forced myself to say with fake enthusiasm, "Okay. Let's go for it."

Dressed in our swimsuits and shaking with trepidation, we gathered with the other participants in the lower part of the ship called the mud room. I eyed the group. A daring, testosterone-driven teen clamored to be first in line. A twenty-something woman in a bikini barely covering her slender body also stepped forward. Her partner wore Speedo trunks and swim goggles, indicating his aquatic expertise. The remaining few ranged in age from exuberant young people to middle-aged adults joking and laughing. We two eighty-year-olds were visibly the ancient, senior citizens of the group.

Our turn came all too soon. Shivering in the arctic air and trying to forget the perils of freezing water, we moved through the doorway and onto the Zodiac that would serve as the jump-off point. We stepped up to the edge of the bobbing Zodiac, and for a split-second gazed at the churning, glacial water below. My legs felt like wilted lettuce, but it was too late to turn back. We clutched our hands together, took a deep gulp of air, and took the polar plunge into the frigid ocean.

After what seemed an eternity, we bobbed to the surface and splashed our way to the safety platform. Wiping saltwater from our eyes, we staggered to the mud room. Thankfully, towels and bathrobes awaited our quivering Popsicle bodies. Through chattering teeth and hysterical laughter, I proclaimed triumphantly, "I can't believe I did that!"

On the deck above, passengers gathered to witness the episode and click photos of the crazy polar plungers. That afternoon, I claimed my fifteen minutes of fame from our cruise companions. We became the celebrities of the day. I must admit I reveled in their admiring comments: "You were the couple who held hands and jumped together? How romantic. Was it cold? Were you scared? Awesome! What will your kids say? Bravo... and at your age, incredible." Most notable of all, I heard, "You are so brave."

In my memory bank, I've stored my fifteen minutes of fame, and it will last the rest of my life. However, I have no inclination to skydive or bungee jump to experience distinction again. I still cling to my natural tendency toward self-preservation. My one-time, totally wild stunt is enough. Ah, but my splash of fame felt glorious.

— Barbara Brady —

Chapter
3

Try Something New

21

Texas To-Do List

The nice thing about teamwork is that
you always have others on your side.
~Margaret Carty

romptly at 6:00 a.m., I stepped out of my car and into one of the hottest July days ever recorded in Houston, Texas. My thick cotton T-shirt was soon drenched in sweat as I waited in the local church parking lot. Experienced runners surrounded me, all wearing appropriate attire for intense heat and humidity. At the age of fifty-three, I was about to train for my first half-marathon with the assistance of an organized program. This was my plan for building friendships in an unknown city!

Houston was quite a change from Southern California, where I grew up, went to college, married, and raised two daughters. It's home to the world's richest rodeo, glorious barbecue, and bedazzled wardrobes. I had bravely faced my husband's job transfer, at a time when many couples were contemplating retirement. However, the last checkmark on my Texas "to-do" list was daunting: "Find friends." My future no longer consisted of PTA meetings, team mom activities and my children's' high school social functions. What would each day look like? Would two aging Labrador Retrievers be my sole companions?

The answer arrived one week after a moving van spilled musty cardboard boxes throughout our new suburban house. Annie, the real estate agent, phoned. "Dana, would you be interested in joining the local chapter of USA Fit here in town?" Honestly, I had no idea what she was talking about. What I did know was that Annie was a runner. I had even heard her mention marathons. I felt anxious already.

"What does it involve? I mean, is this about running? Because that's just not my thing." I was hoping she would hear the disinterest in my voice. Not Annie! She didn't give up easily.

"Come on! You'll love it! It's a group of both runners and walkers who meet for six months, training for the Houston Marathon and Half-Marathon. I think you would meet some nice friends. I'll be there!"

Excuses filled my head. "Annie, I am a walker, but who in their right mind walks a marathon? I've never heard of such a thing." It didn't matter. I was about to get schooled in the brilliant ways of USA Fit!

That day in the church lot, the beauty of Annie's plan came to light. We were divided into groups according to marathon or half-marathon, and pace. I decided to stand amongst the "purple people." That's code-speak for half-marathon walkers. I had a group. I had friends!

From the first day, four women with experience took me on as their personal project. Diane, Karen, Jill, and Betsy walked every step with me that initial Saturday. When we returned from the steaming three-mile course, my face was an unusual shade of red. Diane noticed immediately. She sat with me in the shade and covered the basics of proper clothing and hydration. I marveled at her kindness as I sipped a thick, green sports drink.

For the next six months, those four women never left my side. When fall arrived, we rejoiced in the beauty of the changing leaves and inhaled the scent of crackling fires as families rose and prepared breakfast. By now, our Saturday morning chats had become more personal. Kids, jobs, houses, dogs — no subject was off limits as we raced past the tranquil lakes surrounding our town. The sun rose, great blue herons soared, and deer wandered on the edge of the woods. I came to believe I could actually walk the half-marathon at the rapid pace required by the sponsors. My confidence grew not only from strict preparation, but also from a collective courage.

The USA Fit training schedule was taped to my kitchen wall. Every day for six months was recorded, with the required activity listed. I diligently crossed off each square until only the final week remained.

With that realization, panic set in.

That was also when I understood just how supportive my purple friends were. On the Monday before the race, I saw Diane in the busy produce aisle of the grocery store. "I'm so happy to see you!" I gave her a massive hug and, without warning, the tears started. They came from a place deep inside, from insecurity and the realization that I might not be up to the challenge ahead.

Diane steered me toward the racks of bread. The air smelled delicious, and a soothing calm enveloped me. "You are going to be just fine. You're ready! I'll be waiting for you inside the convention center first thing that morning. I'll help you through the whole process." Another hug and I was on to cereal and canned goods.

Then came a piece of bad news. Karen was experiencing knee problems. On Wednesday, she made the tough decision. "I just can't walk the course. Look for me at mile seven. That's when you'll need a cheering section the most. I'll be there." I wasn't certain I could accomplish the enormous task ahead without the full team; each woman added a different component to the group's success. Karen was steadfast. "Do not let this take away any of your joy."

Race day was exciting. Spectators lined the streets with noisemakers, banners, and loudspeakers. I found my purple friends at the designated meeting place without any problem. A group photo was taken, and then we clung to each other as 24,000 racers made their way to the starting line. The four of us huddled in the early morning chill, pep talks were given all around, and then the gun sounded. Finally, I would face the challenge Annie had invited into my life.

Back in July, my target had simply been to finish the half-marathon. At some crazy point, I decided to complete the race in less than three hours. In order to meet that goal, Jill and I kept constant watch on the time. "Dana, I have a plan. We need to walk for five minutes, then jog for one. That should keep our finish time to three hours." We grinned at each other, knowing that this rather large detail should have been worked out in advance!

The last mile was nearly intolerable. Our pace had been much quicker than during training. Luckily, the final stretch was bursting with enthusiasm from the crowded sidewalks. I sped along to cheers from Elvis impersonators, sumo wrestlers and a youth group dressed as chickens. Diane yelled from far ahead, "It doesn't get any better than this!"

Six months of preparation finished with one step over a thin black line. An aquamarine spiral of balloons reached into the cloudless sky. Confetti blanketed the road. On the other side of the line, my friends waited, patient as always. Enthusiastic volunteers, who had been so generous with their time, placed heavily inscribed medals around our necks. I fingered the shiny, grosgrain ribbon with an overwhelming sense of accomplishment. At that moment, I realized I had become part of my new community. A town where strength is a team effort and a dear friend will dry your tears in the grocery store.

— Dana Sexton —

Riding the Road to Friendship

When I see an adult on a bicycle, I do not despair
for the future of the human race.
~H.G. Wells

I was a Northern newcomer to a Southern adult community. I knew no one and was feeling very out of place and lonesome. I wanted desperately to make new friends.

Day after day, I saw groups of cyclers riding throughout the community and beyond the gates. Dressed in black Spandex riding shorts, brightly colored biking shirts, gloves and helmets, they appeared to be having a great time together. I looked longingly at them as they rode in pace lines of eight to twelve riders.

I knew how to ride a bike, but couldn't imagine myself ever accomplishing the level of riding I saw. I read an article in the community newspaper inviting those interested in biking to join a beginner's cycling group. It is not like me to join something where I know no one, but I pushed myself to attend an organizational meeting. I immediately began chatting with two women and we committed to our first group ride taking place later in the week.

Twelve men and women ventured out on our first eight-mile ride. We slowly pedaled in a long line through the quiet streets of our community. We began to meet three times a week, and steadily increased our distance and speed. Stopping for refreshments became the norm and we soon adopted our mantra, "We bike for food." As we sat chatting over coffee, strong friendships began to form. Many of us found we had other interests in common and began exploring them together.

Now, comfortable with several members of the cycling club, I decided to attend a few of their social events, a luncheon, a fifties party, and a holiday gathering. There, I met more folks. Men from the cycling group brought their wives to the social events and wives brought their non-cycling partners. Out of these gatherings grew a small dinner group and again my circle expanded. More opportunities for new friendships opened up when our club members planned a few overnight cycling trips in conjunction with other clubs from various parts of the state.

All of these new friendships were made possible by taking that first step outside my comfort zone. I now ride fifty to 100 miles a week, have improved my health, and have more friends than I ever imagined. Taking that first step and trying something new opened up a whole new world of fun and friendships for me.

— Mary Grant Dempsey —

23

Annual Reboot

A person needs at intervals to separate from family
and companions and go to new places.
One must go without familiars in order
to be open to influences, to change.
~Katharine Butler Hathaway

"Who's going with you to Sedona?" Mama asked. I hesitated, thinking of how to frame my answer. "I'll be with my co-workers at the Phoenix meeting, but then they're flying back to North Carolina. I have to go to a conference in San Francisco right after that."

"I don't like it," Mama said, her blue eyes looking straight into mine. "It's not safe for a woman to travel alone."

"Mama, if I can go through cancer treatment, I'm certainly not afraid to get in a rental car and drive across the state of Arizona."

"I still don't like it, you going by yourself."

I hoped my tone had not hurt her. She'd been through enough. She was just a mother looking out for her young, even if her young was forty-five years old. It was time to pull out my trump card. "I won't be alone. God will be with me," I said.

She took in the words of her determined, "headstrong" middle daughter. "Well, you'll be in the best of hands, but be careful."

And that's how my first solo journey started—a serendipitous trip to Sedona that was wedged between business in Phoenix and

San Francisco. Before that I'd been settled into my middle-aged life, working as a research nurse, married to a busy psychologist, raising two teenage sons. Life seemed like a predictable chain of events. The one creative outlet I had was writing, which had taken the form of a first novel about women who were also in midlife. My characters were in group therapy trying to become what they'd once dreamed of before they were weighed down by routines and responsibilities.

When I was diagnosed with breast cancer, my predictable chain of events suddenly became a scary journey into the unknown of surgeries, chemotherapy and radiation. I took each step with the help of my faith, family and friends. Over time, I learned that I could survive, and even thrive, when I faced my fear and kept going, choosing to live instead of cower.

Finally, I finished my treatment and was allowed to travel. I felt myself coming to life as I made plans for the trip. There were moments of fear when I wondered what I was getting myself into and how I would handle it if my rental car broke down or I suddenly became ill. I trusted that along my path there would be people to help me, just as there had been through my cancer journey.

Traveling alone gave me the freedom to interact with strangers, instead of limiting my conversations to companions, whether family or friends. On this trek, I enjoyed chatting with a shop owner (a fellow North Carolinian) and with a couple hiking in Oak Creek Canyon. In the past when I talked with strangers during a family vacation, my older son, embarrassed by my spontaneity, would remark, "Mom acts like she's just run into her best friend."

Unencumbered, I could be in the moment. I lingered at the sight of wildflowers next to the red rocks and watched the drama of nightfall with strangers, sitting atop our cars, not worrying I'd be late for any obligation.

I left Sedona renewed.

Back at home, I resumed my pre-cancer pace with work and family responsibilities — something I said I'd never do. Over the next few years, I piled on layers of stress. My life was out of balance. Then, with my fiftieth birthday approaching, I decided to give myself the gift I really wanted, another trip alone.

I chose Jekyll Island, Georgia, where I'd previously been on a family vacation, a place with natural beauty that pulled me like the tide. Each morning I laid out my goal for the day: to move as the spirit led me, freely living in the moment. I read Psalm 103:5 that spoke about youth being "renewed like the eagle's," which seemed appropriate with me turning fifty and needing to unplug from a busy life. I rode my bike on the half-mile loop through the marsh, stopping to watch morning unfold, freely breaking into song without any other person in earshot.

I rode to the historic village, shaded by huge, moss-draped oaks that reminded me of the trees I played under as a girl. Sitting in the grass, I felt as if it were a childhood summer day when I spent hours with pretend friends. At night I swam in the old-fashioned hotel pool with lights that added to its turquoise allure. Moving freely about the island, I discovered I'd been drawn to a place that took me back to my childhood — a time when I was free and lived in the moment.

When I crossed over the Palmetto-lined causeway, heading home from Jekyll, I felt as rested and renewed as I had when I left Sedona. I decided I would go on a trip alone every year from then on.

Over the years, I've kept that promise. I've traveled to Martha's Vineyard, where I had delicious conversations while staying in my first hostel. I've ridden my bike at sunset at Assateague Island. I've watched hydroplanes land on Mann's Harbor in the San Juan Islands of Washington State. I've ridden a horse through a Teton meadow.

It was something that started by chance and now happens by choice. I've opted to live my life fully.

— Connie Rosser Riddle —

24

Trying Something Different

I would rather have a mind opened by
wonder than one closed by belief.
~Gerry Spence

June 2016. I am driving on Highway 75 west of Atlanta. My wife Carolyn and I (both sixty-eight) are on our way to check out Tellico Village, a retirement community south of Knoxville. I am worried. I'm fine with our plans to move from our home in Florida. That's not the problem. The problem is that we booked two nights in a private home through one of those Internet home-sharing services.

"Why not stay at a motel like we usually do?" I had asked Carolyn when she first brought up the idea a month ago.

"This place is located right in Tellico Village," she said. "We'll be staying with someone who lives there and can give us an insider's view."

"A stranger. What if we don't get along with her?"

"We will. Her name is Jo Ann, and she's got great reviews."

"Wouldn't a motel be cheaper?"

"No. This place costs less, and we have kitchen privileges, so we'll save on meals too. Besides wouldn't it be nice to try something different for a change?"

I diplomatically chose not to answer her question. If I did, the answer would have been *No. I value my privacy and the idea of staying in a stranger's home does not appeal to me at all.* But I knew I had already lost the argument.

Our GPS leads us more efficiently than I would have liked to the front door of our host's home. If I could drag my feet outside the car to slow us down, I would. But here we are in a neighborhood of beautiful homes. Jo Ann has a lovely single-story house, well landscaped and with two large white rockers waiting on a porch festooned with flowers. The house is dark inside. It is 4:00 p.m., the exact time we said we would arrive.

"So where is she?" I ask. I have a hint of "I told you so" in my voice. "Didn't she confirm our arrival time?"

"Yes," says Carolyn. She rings the doorbell. No answer.

As I dial Jo Ann's number I think: This wouldn't have happened if we had booked a motel like we usually do. Jo Ann answers. She apologizes for not being here to greet us. She says she has been trying to reach us to let us know she is attending a church activity this evening. She tells me to look under the cushion of one of the porch rockers for the house key and garage door opener.

"Just park your car in the garage and make yourselves at home," she says. "Your bedroom and bathroom are located behind the kitchen, but feel free to use the living room, television, and back porch." She tells me that she cleared a shelf in the refrigerator for us and that she will be coming home late.

I am relieved. For the next several hours, we have a home away from home. The house is gorgeous, modern, immaculate, and tastefully furnished. We unpack and go for a walk around the neighborhood. The neighbors we meet outside their homes greet us and are happy to tell us their experience living in the Village. One gentleman tells us how smart we are for staying at Jo Ann's house so we can experience the neighborhood firsthand.

After a home cooked dinner, we watch the news and go for a drive to the lake to explore. In the evening we relax on the screened-in back porch. At 10:00 p.m. I hear a key turn in the door. Jo Ann is back.

Jo Ann is a gracious and welcoming host. She apologizes again for not meeting us when we arrived. She pours herself a glass of wine and offers some to us. We have a forty-five minute conversation about how she came to the Village several years ago, the growing pains of the Village, and her experience selecting a lot and building her house. She offers to put us in touch with a neighbor who is a Realtor if we decide to build or rent a home. We learn things about the Village from her that we would never have learned had we stayed at a motel. When she says good night, she informs us that she will not be home the next day. She says she likes to give guests as much privacy as possible.

"Just put the keys and garage door opener under the rocker cushion when you leave," she says. "Come back for another stay any time."

What little anxiety I have left vanishes. I couldn't have imagined a better stay. We make ourselves at home for the rest of our time. I kick myself for being so reluctant to try this. I worried so needlessly.

That summer we book several more stays in people's homes in three states: Tennessee, Wisconsin, and New York. Every stay works out wonderfully. Now whenever we travel, this is one of the options we consider. But if I hadn't endured the anxiety of "trying something different for a change," we would still be staying at impersonal motels. And we may not have moved to Tellico Village, where we are now living, pleased with our decision.

— D.E. Brigham —

The Makeover

*We cannot become what we want
to be by remaining what we are.*
~Max De Pree

The first half of my life had been devoted to my mother, husband, and four sons, shaping my days around what they needed from me. But now I was on my own. The children were grown. I was single. And my mother had moved 1,200 miles away to start her own new life.

It's time, I decided. I was turning fifty, after all. *The second half of my life will belong to me.*

First up was changing my look. When I saw women in long skirts, I thought they looked great, but I needed to muster up the courage to change my look so dramatically. I checked out the shoes, jewelry, and blouses that went with the skirts. Even the haircuts looked different.

My birthday arrived and one day I adopted my new look. I slipped into my new long skirt with appropriate shirt, added big drop earrings, bangles on my wrist, and sandals. I was embarrassed as I walked from my gift shop in a small, historical town to the bank and post office.

I went to the post office first. No one said a word. Wow.

On to the bank. No one said a word about my new look. This was much easier than I thought it would be. I went shopping that night and bought several colorful long skirts. Then I piled up all my old conservative clothing to give away.

Over the weekend, I had a second pair of holes put in my ears to accommodate the diamond studs my last husband, who recently passed away, gave to me. That made room for the dangly ones in the lower holes. A feeling of joy washed over me. This was fun!

My girlfriend Anne took me to her favorite hair salon.

"Time to wash away the grey," she said.

As I sat patiently in the chair, the hairdresser turned it one way and another, looking closely at my skin color.

"Hmm," she said.

When I left the salon. I had red hair! It was a bit startling when I passed a window and caught a glimpse of myself. It didn't look like me... until I got used to it Then I couldn't remember what I looked like before!

Then I started traveling. I flew several times to Europe. spending the same amount of money that it would have cost me to travel sixty miles away to the Jersey shore. I traveled extensively in the United States.

The last major change I made was buying a different car. I turned in my dark four-door sedan and bought a red Camaro.

I couldn't believe the little box I used to live in. Now that my mind had been opened, it would never close again. My attitude was different. I was happy and filled with gratitude.

A friend asked if I was trying to be young again. I thought about it and realized, no, I could care less about being young again. I wouldn't want to go through that again.

That was over twenty years ago. That little change of clothing changed my whole life! I have since written a dozen books, and stood in front of groups of women, teaching them to tell their stories. I encourage them to take charge of their lives, open their minds, and go back to school regardless of their age. Life is good!

— Arlene S. Bice —

26

No More White Walls

Our home tells a story about us, so we may as well
take the opportunity to make it a stylish one.
~Deborah Needleman,
The Perfectly Imperfect Home

small bell chimed to announce my presence as I pushed open the shop door. There went my hope of entering unnoticed. A salesman hurried to meet me with a broad smile. "How can I help you today?"

I resisted the urge to make a hasty exit and forced myself to greet him instead. "I'd like to see some paint swatches."

Our home was more than ten years old and way overdue for a fresh coat of paint. The past ten years had been good to us, too, as we developed special friendships. It was because of those friends that I found myself in the paint store.

It started innocently enough with visits to each of their homes. Then I invited them to ours. Two friends, Jan and Linda, graciously admired our home, but were curious about one thing. I steeled myself for what I knew was coming. Jan was the first to ask. "Beautiful... but, um, can I ask why all the walls are white?"

It was a natural question. Their homes included color-coordinated rooms, accent walls, and color-themed bathrooms. Every room proclaimed their confident decorating abilities. On the other hand, every wall in our home was stark white. The label on the paint can may have had a fancy name such as "Pearl Onion" or "Ice Cube," but I had to face facts: It was still white.

How could I explain my reasons for all white walls? It's not because I don't enjoy color. I had admired their homes. I watched HGTV, and I'm a fan of home makeover shows. I read *Better Homes and Gardens*. I learned to differentiate between "warm" and "cool" colors. I even knew the difference between saturation and intensity. And still my walls were all… white. When it came to actually selecting colors, I became paralyzed with indecision.

I learned the colors of the rainbow in grade school by memorizing the acronym ROYGBIV. Red, orange, yellow, green, blue, indigo, violet — so pretty when they form a bow in the sky. Or adorn wildflower petals. Or when they paint the clouds in glorious sunsets. I've always enjoyed splashes of color… as long as they stayed outside.

When it comes to painting my walls, I panic. Too many choices. *What if it doesn't look good when I'm finished?* Of course, I know I can repaint, but I barely have enough time to paint it once, let alone redo it. So in looking back at more than thirty years of marriage and four different homes, every wall in every home has sported a boring shade of white.

Not anymore. I was ready for a change. I *needed* a change. So I smiled at the salesperson and followed him to the rack of paint chips.

"What colors did you have in mind?"

It was a simple enough question. With my friends' encouragement echoing in my thoughts, I said I was thinking about starting with blue for the dining room. And perhaps gold for an accent wall in the living room. He nodded approvingly and pointed to groups of cards. Perhaps this wouldn't be so hard after all.

"What shade of blue were you considering?"

It was then the colors betrayed me. The wall of paint chips induced a familiar feeling of panic. We had moved way beyond ROYGBIV. Later, I learned this one store offered 231 shades of green, 152 variations of red, 188 shades of blue, and 154 variations of yellow. Even my old friend, white, was disloyal — with 134 different shades. Honestly!

Blue? No such thing. Too easy. Instead I read names such as Adriatic Sea, Oceanside, and Poseidon. Next to them were Gulfstream, Côte d'Azur, and Amalfi. *Amalfi? Really?*

I didn't fare any better searching for the right shade of gold. Auric, Nugget, and Alchemy were nestled next to Overjoy, Midday, and Nankeen. *Seriously?*

Giving in to curiosity, I glanced through the reds. Habanero Chile, Fireworks, and Heartthrob joined Valentine and Heartfelt as options. The green family also sported its own creative labels, including Julep, Argyle, and Picnic. I shook my head when I noticed one paint chip labeled Gecko. I may live in Florida, but not in a million years would I put a lizard on my walls.

Still, I was determined to do this. So I grabbed a handful of blue and gold paint cards that seemed to be the right hues, thanked the salesperson, and left. Back home, we held the various chips against our walls, compared them to our furniture and window treatments, and tried to imagine how the rooms would appear. The graduated intensity of color on each card made it even more difficult to choose. On some cards, it was almost impossible to discern the difference between the shades.

We finally settled on two choices. I called them blue and gold, but their official names are Caspian Tide and Mushroom Bisque.

Once we chose the colors, the next step was the prep work. Covering the furniture, taping the edges of the walls, and laying a drop cloth took almost as much time as the actual painting. The job lasted four days from start to finish — one day to prep, one day to paint, and one day to remove miles of blue painter's tape from the walls and ceiling. The last day was reserved for scraping permanent paint flecks from our hair and skin. With every drop that had landed on me, I marveled at how the decorators on television makeover shows can finish an entire room in one afternoon and not get a speck of paint on themselves.

I do have to admit, the final product looked terrific. Color really does make a difference. It even made me feel different. And I was thrilled to invite those same friends back to see the result.

In fact, the dining room and living room look so good that I've been eyeing our bathrooms. There may be a place in our home for Habanero Chile after all.

— Ava Pennington —

27

Lord, Make Me a Babe

*An empty lantern provides no light. Self-care is the fuel
that allows your light to shine brightly.*
~Author Unknown

I recently found out that my soon-to-be-ex-husband is dating someone. He and I were sitting outside of our son's classroom door at the middle school, waiting for our parent–teacher conference. At school events where parents are present, it's easy to spot the divorced parents. They look kind of stiff and surly. Generally, they are not talking to each other. They can be spotted at soccer games, too. One doesn't need a graduate degree in psychotherapy, which I happen to have, to figure out which couples are together now only by the necessity of parenthood.

Down the school hallway, a lady I did not recognize flounced by. "Hii-yii," she sang out in a lilting, singsong voice. She was not talking to me. The soon-to-be-ex turned beet red. Like a character straight out of a time-machine movie, I instantly morphed into a high school junior.

Harry's teacher came to the door and invited us in. Thankfully, I morphed back into my middle-aged-parent self. The focus shifted to Harry, our adolescent, soon-to-be-from-a-broken-home son. I survived the conference and walked to my car alone afterward.

As soon as I got home, I picked up the phone and called the soon-to-be-ex. "Are you dating?" I asked.

"Howdja know?" He never did know when to lie.

I don't know why, but it hit me like a kick in the stomach. Truly, this was the end to an eighteen-year marriage, where no one on the face of the earth could have tried harder than I did to save it. Several years earlier, my girlfriends had an intervention with me. "Linda," they said at a lunch meeting, "you're in an emotionally abusive marriage."

"I know," I said, "but it's still better than the alternative." The alternative is what I am now facing: the Big D. I still can't bring myself to say it.

So, there is no use crying over spilt milk or going into the maudlin details. Like the flaming co-dependent that I am, I tried to move heaven and earth to save my marriage. In fact, to borrow a phrase from a twelve-step program, I used to refer to it as rearranging the chairs on the deck of the *Titanic*. With icebergs rearing their ugly heads in the distance, I did everything I could and more.

And now, I am facing the D-word. He filed. Not only that, but now the other D-word is being thrown out there. He is *dating* someone. After eighteen years, he is not dating me.

So, if I explain that I woke up one morning several days ago with butt-kicking depression, one would understand why. This depression was like moving slowly underwater with a boulder on my back. I wanted to break into tears at the drop of a hat. I rehearsed calling a psychiatrist friend and telling her that it was time to sign me up for antidepressants. Through some serious hard times, I have resisted that option.

Friday morning, I trudged off to work. Keeping cash flow was a necessity at my stage of life. I sat down in my office. My client came in. I noticed a change from her previous appearance. She looked terrific! Her hair was natural and pulled back, instead of heavy and long. Her eyes looked wide open. This woman really knew how to put on make-up. Instead of winter brown and black, she was wearing pink and white with matching pink socks. She was getting enough sleep, and it showed in her complexion.

I marveled at the difference in her, especially the make-up. Then it hit me like a voice from God, like a bolt of lightning, like a revelation from above in a low, thunderous voice: "Linda, you can do this, too."

"What, God?" I asked the voice in my head, meanwhile listening empathetically to my client. (Only really experienced psychotherapists can listen to God and their clients at the same time.)

"You can do this, too." It was God's voice again.

Finally, the revelation came through loud and clear: "You can become a babe."

"A babe," I gasped internally. "But, Lord, what about the flab under my arms and my thighs?" No use arguing with God. The revelation was unequivocal. The still, small voice had delivered the message loud and clear. My calling, at this juncture, was to become a babe — a fifty-six-year-old babe.

Who am I to argue with God? My course is set. Whatever it takes — a trainer-diet-make-up consultant. I know what I've got to do.

My final court date is several months away, and what sweeter justice than to show up in divorce court having morphed into a veritable babe. Not for him, but for me, and for my girlfriends who will be cheering me on every inch of the way.

So, I'm on my way to Babedom. And you know what else? My depression mysteriously evaporated. Poof. Like the parting of the Red Sea. I am a woman with a mission.

Whenever I begin to mourn the past or even ponder the thought of my soon-to-be-ex with someone else, I say this little prayer, "Lord, make me a babe."

It's working. I'm looking better already.

— Linda Hoff Irvin —

28

Goodbye TV

*If it weren't for the fact that the TV set and the
refrigerator are so far apart, some of us
wouldn't get any exercise at all.*
~Joey Adams

I am addicted to TV, mind-numbing, time-sucking, waste-of-a-good-day TV. I know some will say I should just be able to turn it off and ignore it, but it calls to me: Cindy… just come and spend a little time with me to wake up… watch the morning news… you have to know what's going on in the world. An hour later, when I should be doing dishes or laundry or a million other things, I am intrigued by the promos and I have to watch the next show. Just a little, I tell myself, and another hour goes by.

Finally, I make myself turn it off and get busy with the chores of life. I make lists and check off items as I get them done: make beds, clean bathrooms, unload/load dishwasher, file papers, pay bills, etc. I work for an hour or two, and lo and behold, it's time for lunch. Who wants to eat lunch alone? I turn on the TV for a little "company." I watch some reruns of one of my favorites and enjoy my hour-long lunch break with my "friends."

Then I decide to keep the TV on, "just for noise," while I continue with my list of chores. I bring in laundry to fold, but end up watching TV and folding laundry only during commercials. I bring things into the living room so I can "listen" while I work, but once again, TV is too enticing and work is relegated to the commercials.

Suddenly, it's time to make dinner. I still keep the TV on while I cook, because the five o'clock news has come on and I need to "stay informed." My husband and I eat dinner while watching TV, because he, too, wants to "stay informed." After a long day at work, he wants to watch a little TV and relax. Who am I to deny him this privilege? Naturally, I keep him company, because I haven't seen him all day. The evening disappears in a few sitcoms and a "made-for-TV" movie. I even force myself to stay up and watch the last show, although I am clearly tired from such a strenuous day of TV watching. Being enlightened is so much work!

I calculate that the TV is on in our house for about fifteen hours a day! That's 105 hours a week, 450 hours a month, 5,400 a year! Gone are the days of reading, sewing, painting, taking walks, or sitting on the swing in the garden talking to old friends on the phone. All are put off until the next commercial or the end of the show.

It's time to take my life back. I'm taking the plunge and disconnecting from TV. Fortunately, my husband has agreed to this drastic measure. I have unhooked the cables, packed the equipment in the box, including the three remotes, and taped it up ready for shipping. No going back now.

Goodbye TV, I will miss you and all the good times we had together. A little tear comes to my eye. There will certainly be a big void in my life now that you are gone. Whatever will I do to fill it?

I think about the friends I have ignored and the things I loved to do and "never seemed to have time...." Well, now I've got the time. Where to start? I think I'll dig out my scrapbooking materials, turn on the radio, and put my time to a little better use. Where's that book I've been meaning to read and when was the last time I spoke to my sister? Hmmm, so much to do, and so much time. I'd better get to it.

—Cindy O'Leary—

29

I Wanna Rock and Roll All Nite

Music is feeling. You can try to verbalize it.
It really just hits you or it doesn't.
~Gene Simmons

What was he thinking? My husband had just bought tickets to the KISS concert. Never mind that we're close to retirement age.

Maybe it was a nostalgia thing. We both graduated from high school in the 1970s. That's when the band KISS first burst onto the music scene. Not that they were my cup of tea, mind you. I was a classically trained pianist, and my taste in music ran from classical to soft rock. Beethoven to Barry Manilow. Not KISS. They were more heavy metal. That was more my little brother's style. In fact, the only time I ever listened to this kind of music was if it leaked under his closed bedroom door. I was Miss Goody-Two Shoes. I didn't listen to that kind of music — the kind of music KISS played. And I'd heard about some of the shenanigans that occurred during concerts. Like Gene Simmons spitting out blood. Yuck. Very disturbing.

Still, I must admit, there was something about the rock group that intrigued me. Their Kabuki make-up, Harlequin black-and-white costumes, and perilously high heels definitely captured my attention. KISS was so popular during the 70s that some students dressed like the band and performed at my school's annual talent show. They lip-synced to one of KISS's hit songs. With strobe lights pulsating and a very active imagination, you would almost swear you were watching KISS. Except for the very crude pyrotechnics, which consisted of a guy spitting lighter fluid out of his mouth and lighting it with a BIC Lighter. Impressive — until the stage curtain caught on fire. That's probably why they only came in third place.

So, some forty years later, I found myself going to my first KISS concert. Crazy. The closer it got to the date of the concert, the more anxious I felt. What on earth was I, a relatively conservative middle-aged woman, doing? Still, I decided to go with the best attitude I could muster, and set about picking out the coolest black-and-white outfit I could find in my closet.

It was the night of the concert, and I had no idea what to expect. Our seats were close. As I looked around the concert hall, I was pleasantly surprised to see a lot of people who appeared to be close to my age. It made me feel a little more comfortable about the whole experience. As the time for the concert neared, the room filled. To my right, there was a group of men, I'd say in their thirties, except for the guy one seat over from me. Trying to make small talk before the show began, I asked his name and age. Turned out, he was my son's age. This was his first KISS concert, too. At least we had something in common.

Just before KISS took the stage, a tiny woman appeared at the end of our aisle, weaving her way around people's knees toward the only seat left in the row. It happened to be the seat between me and the young man. Wearing a faded KISS T-shirt, jeans, and tennis shoes, this dear lady sat down. She seemed so out of place. I feared the young guys would poke fun at her. As soon as she sat down, however, one of the them yelled out, "Cool, we've got a Rockin' Grandma sitting next to us."

I had to find out what her story was. Turns out, she was seventy-six years old, close to my mom's age. And not only was she a Rockin' Grandma, but she was a Rockin' Great-Grandma. And, amazingly, she was a huge KISS fan. In fact, she'd been attending KISS concerts since the 1970s. She showed me a ticket stub to prove it. Sure enough, the ticket was for a KISS concert, and only cost $12. Wow, those were the days. This gal was not just a fan, but a mega-fan of the group. She attended all their concerts that came to town. Impressive. Plus, this Rockin' Grandma had come to the concert solo, since her husband was not so much of a fan. This lady was clearly comfortable in her skin and right at home in this environment.

Once the concert started, the crowd jumped to their feet, including Granny. In fact, she stood on her feet during the entire concert. Not only was she standing, but her tiny, wrinkled fist was pumping the air for the entire hour and a half. Tennis shoes were definitely the way to go. Of course, Granny knew that, being the experienced concertgoer that she was. Positively amazing. She put me to shame.

Before the concert, I'd done a little research on KISS, and the rock group's average age was sixty — an even more amazing fact after I saw the height of their heels, especially Gene Simmons', complete with shark-like teeth. They were at least six inches tall, maybe more. And Paul Stanley even looked good in a costume that showed off his belly. He's still got abs. Visible abs. I've never had abs — well, I'm sure they're in there somewhere, but they have yet to show themselves. I would certainly not wear a sparkly crop top showing off my belly.

For a little while, at least during the concert, I forgot all about the arthritis in my hips and knees, and stood up for most of the concert — partly because the guy seated directly in front of me could have played center for the NBA, but mainly because I was having such a great time. I couldn't wipe the smile off my face. It appeared at the start of the show and stayed through the entire concert, right up until the final song. And, speaking of the final song, of course, they saved the best for last. Rockin' Grandma had mentioned earlier that she had some leftover confetti in her bag. Suddenly, two towering platforms rose on the stage carrying a couple of band members up with them. Simultaneously, huge confetti machines began shooting tons of multi-colored paper strips into the air as KISS sang their iconic tune, "Rock and Roll All Nite."

After the concert, as I was picking confetti out of my hair, it hit me. I'd loved this concert. And I got why Rockin' Grandma was such a major KISS fan. The concert was an absolute blast. Now, I'm a big fan, too.

— Tamara Moran-Smith —

30

A Year of New Things

Happiness is achieved when you stop waiting
for your life to begin and start making
the most of the moment you are in.
~Germany Kent

The year I turned fifty, I resolved to do something new every day. When I tell people this, they always want to know what my favorite "new thing" was. They assume that I did something really different and amazing, like moving my family to an exotic place or learning to fly a helicopter. And they are inevitably disappointed when I say that my favorite thing was doing something new. Every. Single. Day. For a year.

Balancing 365 new things with work and family, while still managing to do the laundry and get dinner on the table every night, was not always easy. In the early weeks of the project, I often found myself at 11:45 p.m. wracking my brain for something new that I could actually accomplish in fifteen minutes. Thankfully, it turned out there were lots of things I had never done before that I could complete in a short period of time. I finished my first sudoku puzzle. I signed up for an online class to learn Italian. I smoked a cigar. I curled my eyelashes.

As time went by, I found it was easier to just keep my eyes open to the possibilities that surrounded me. It turns out there were new things everywhere, and all I had to do was make a little effort to enjoy them. And so, on a bitterly cold Saturday when I would normally have stayed home curled up with a book, I bundled up and set off to attend an Ice Festival. I got up crazy early one weekday morning to see a Blood Moon. I celebrated National Dog Day with my pup.

It wasn't long before my friends learned that I was open to almost anything I could consider a new thing, and the invitations began pouring in — not just from friends, but friends of friends. As a result, I went dog sledding, enjoyed stargazing on New York City's High Line, had lunch with Antonia Lofaso, who has appeared on *Top Chef*, attended a Fashion Week fashion show, and met Pulitzer Prize-winning author Gilbert King. I went to numerous lectures on all kinds of topics that I never would have previously considered useful or interesting and found something to appreciate in every single one.

Whenever I learned about something that seemed remarkable, I compelled myself to pursue it. Instead of "Why?" I began to ask "Why not?" I made my default response "Yes." When I learned about a local group trying to get into the *Guinness Book of World Records* by having the most people jumping on mini trampolines at once, I signed up immediately. The designated morning was cold and rainy. None of my friends or family members wanted to join me on my quest, but when I got to the field where the event was being held I found hundreds of like-minded folks. Together, we jumped for more than an hour, exhilarated by the exercise and the joy of accomplishing something slightly weird but totally wonderful.

A fair amount of my new things involved food. I tried wild boar. I ate nettles. I sampled gooseberries. I drank Limoncello. I made home-made pesto and hummus for the first time. I made pizza from scratch. I discovered that Thai eggplants don't look like any other eggplant I've ever seen; they are green and round, but the flesh cooks up soft like a regular oblong aubergine. I found out that I don't like radishes roasted any more than I like them raw, but that I love passionfruit in all forms.

As I look back on the year, it doesn't matter to me that many of my "new things" weren't exactly meaningful. What mattered is that I discovered there is an endless number of new things for me to try. It seemed to me an obvious sign that at fifty, my life was lush and full of promise. I could continue to grow, stretch my wings, and learn more every day for the rest of my life. I enjoyed the idea of changing my mindset, making a mental stretch, and getting out of my comfort zone. If nothing else, it gave me a reason to welcome each day as an opportunity to experience the world a little differently, to counteract all that's easy, predictable, or monotonous.

I can't fly a helicopter yet. But I *am* in a *Guinness World Records* book!

— Victoria Otto Franzese —

31

Mammie's Doll Babies

*Children are the most beautiful legacy that can be
passed down from generation to generation.*
~Author Unknown

uring a break at work last spring, I took a quick glance
at my Facebook account. I had several notifications, and
one of them was a friend request. I looked more closely at
the screen and saw my grandmother's picture next to the
request. "Barbara Haywood sent you a friend request," the notifica-
tion stated. Maybe it was a joke. I hated to think that someone could
have opened an account under my grandmother's name.

I called my mom at the end of the workday. "I have a friend request
from Mammie. Is it really from her?" I asked.

"It is," my mom confirmed. She explained that my uncle Buster
had bought her a Kindle Fire and my cousin Courtney had helped
her set up the account.

"That is so awesome," I said. "Now I better go accept her friend
request before she gets annoyed with me!"

I opened my app and wrote a welcome message on my grandmother's
page. I told her how excited I was to see her on Facebook, and added
that her request was the best one I had ever received.

Mammie learned about Facebook gradually. At first, she simply
"liked" pictures of the family. After a while, she figured out how to add
comments. But if we responded to her or asked questions, we didn't
always receive an answer right away. She was still figuring things out.

Her Facebook proficiency is not of great importance. It's the fact that she's on social media and has access to pictures of her family on a daily basis.

My grandmother has four children, ten grandchildren, and ten great-grandchildren. We all live fairly close to her, but we also lead very busy lives. Collectively, our children are involved with theater, dance, soccer, baseball, cheerleading, volleyball and gymnastics. And though we invite Mammie to many performances and games, her lack of mobility limits her attendance. Now that she has a Facebook account, she doesn't have to miss a thing.

Mammie can keep up with the latest trends, view vacation pictures, and look at photos of baseball games and dance recitals. She will be able to follow her granddaughters who are heading off to college this fall and still feel very much involved in their lives.

Sometimes, Mammie's presence on Facebook makes me chuckle. One day, I woke up to thirty-eight notifications from her. She was up at 3:00 in the morning, liking pictures from two years ago. I figured she must have had trouble sleeping, and she was looking at pictures to help pass the time.

Then there's her special way of commenting on posts. She calls us all her doll babies, even those of us who are approaching forty years old, and she always signs her comments, "Love, Mammie." After I posted a picture of my kids and me on a recent camping trip, she commented, "Here are three of Mammie's little doll babies. Looks like a fun and happy time. Love you, Mammie."

A friend asked me the other day if I was going to tell her that she didn't need to sign her name at the end of her comments.

"I sure am not," I told my friend. "She can use Facebook however she wants. I'm not criticizing a thing about what she does."

Mammie seems to be enjoying her new social-media presence, and the rest of us are benefiting as well. Just a little while ago, I checked my account, and I had a comment from Mammie.

"What are you celebrating now, Miss Thing?" she wrote at the bottom of a picture I posted.

"Life!" I responded.

And I really am. I am celebrating life, family, and the fact that my eighty-three-year-old grandmother is on Facebook. And that I am one of her doll babies.

— Melissa Face —

Chapter
4

Happily Ever Laughter

32

I Am a Pickleball Putz

I am just going to put an "out of order"
sticker on my head and call it a day.
~Author Unknown

am a proud pickleball dropout. After a brief attempt to learn the game from my husband Larry, I realized that being interested in something and having enough talent to play at the most basic level are two different things.

What? You haven't heard of pickleball? According to the 2022 Sports & Fitness Industry Association (SFIA), there are 4.8 million people who play the game in the United States alone. It is the fastest-growing sport in the country.

Until Larry and I retired, I had never heard about pickleball. Larry had been involved in sports his entire life — basketball, baseball, and track in his youth, and running and cycling as an adult. When he turned sixty-five, we both joined the local YMCA. While I took classes and swam laps in the Olympic-sized pool, Larry started playing the game with friends from Congregation Beth Shalom and other members of the Y.

Both competitive and athletic, Larry fell in love with the game immediately. When we moved to Florida, our criteria for where we would live included aerobic classes and a lap pool for me and pickleball courts for Larry. We both found what we were looking for in our 55+ active-adult community. Larry joined the Smashers and found players at his level. To make his life even better, Larry found the Summit

County Pickleball Club ("We play with altitude") near where we rent in Colorado every summer.

Pickleball not only provided Larry with a great form of exercise, but it also provided a social outlet. In Florida, the Smashers had dances and breakfasts; in Colorado, the players had picnics and cocktail parties.

As a matter of fact, it was the social aspect of "pb'ing" at 9,100 feet that got my interest. Larry was playing the game at least four mornings a week, and he was meeting lots of people. I, on the other hand, spent my mornings either hiking by myself or with my grand-dog or, occasionally, swimming lonely laps in a pool that accepted Silver Sneakers. Maybe learning the game would help me become part of a community.

So, one day, I asked Larry to take me onto the Colorado courts during a time set aside for beginners. After giving me some basic rules, Larry gently lobbed me a ball; I hit it. *Hey! This wasn't so bad! Slow lob, hit. Slow lob. I got this!* I thought.

When he started hitting the balls to me at the normal rate of speed, however, I could barely keep up. Only thirty minutes into my private lessons, a slim, athletic couple came onto the court.

"We'd love some lessons, too!" they said. Larry quickly repeated some of the basics, and the two of them took to it right away. At that point, they told us they had been playing tennis their whole lives, so this was an easy transition. Larry suggested the four of us play a game together.

Now, it was a completely different game. Fast lob, Marilyn miss. Fast lob, Marilyn miss. Soon, Larry was covering both sides of our court.

I wasn't even close to hitting the ball. My lifetime lack of hand-eye coordination, exacerbated by vision problems brought on by age, resulted in my swinging at lots of air. The ball was usually two feet above or two feet below my pathetic paddle.

So, I did what any normal mature adult would do in that situation: I told Larry I didn't want to play anymore, went back to our car, sat in the front seat, and cried.

"I can't do it," I told Larry after he finished his session with the two tennis pros. "I hate it! I can't see the ball. I can't hit the ball. I can't even move in time. I'm done."

I was. And I am. I am in the eighth decade of my life. Up until now, I had proven myself lousy at tennis, baseball, racquetball and squash. I have now proved myself to be lousy at pickleball. The benefits of being part of a large group—there are at least 1,000 members of Smashers—are totally outweighed by how much I hate trying to hit a stupid ball with a stupid paddle that may result in my breaking a stupid bone.

"You should try playing with us," some friends have told me. "None of us play that well, and we won't care if you're not great at it."

"No, thanks," I tell them. "I'd rather walk, swim, bike or do an exercise class."

And, after hearing about all my friends with pickleball-related injuries, I am happy to stick to what I am doing. None of them require hand-eye coordination. None of them are competitive, so I don't have to always lose. Better yet, I won't be the player who no one wants on their team. Yes, my short stint as a pickleball putz is over! From now on, my pickle of choice is a kosher one in a jar.

— Marilyn Cohen Shapiro —

Dancing in the Kitchen

To watch us dance is to hear our hearts speak.
~Hopi Indian Saying

love my husband. I also love dancing. Over the years we learned from experience, however, beginning with our wedding more than forty years ago, that the two were not compatible. We just didn't dance well together. We seemed to have an abundance of left feet.

So when our son announced that he was getting married, I knew something had to be done. I was not about to let us stumble our way through the official parents' dance. I did what I thought was the easiest and fastest way to come up to dancing speed — I signed us up for dancing classes.

My husband grumbled. He complained that it is impossible to count the beats, do the variations, and feel the music at the same time.

"That's multitasking," I told him.

Women are used to it. Folding the laundry and helping with homework. Cooking dinner and talking on the phone. It comes naturally.

"I'm a focused kind of guy," he said. "I do one thing at a time."

"Good," I said. "Do one thing. Dance."

He was reluctant but, with the wedding approaching in a matter of months, he agreed to go.

Our instructor taught us the basic steps but warned that if we didn't practice, we would forget them by the next class. We knew she was right because by the time we got home that first night we were already struggling to remember everything she showed us.

But where to practice? Our house didn't have an appropriate dance floor. The den was too small, the living room too crowded. We decided to practice in the kitchen. We moved the table and chairs to one side. The room really wasn't big enough for an elegant foxtrot, and it would put a crimp in an enthusiastic swing, but it would do.

It was difficult at first. Our instructor told us that the male and female each have specific parts: he leads, she does the flourishes. Yet between my jittery energy and his resistance, our individual styles, limited as they were, frequently clashed. I would resort to leading when I thought my husband wasn't assertive enough, which irritated us both. With practice, though, we began to sense each other's strengths and respond to each other's timing. Our posture became more confident. We stopped staring at our feet, willing them to go where they were supposed to instead of being surprised by where they ended up.

We noticed that our dancing improved the more we practiced, so we practiced more. We noticed something else, as well. Things seemed to be changing between us — in a good way. We were rediscovering each other. As we accepted our differing approaches to dance, we began to be less critical in other areas. If dinner was a little late, Benny Goodman helped us while away the time. When we held hands as we got ready to dance, the anticipation of our dating days returned. We laughed a lot more when we danced, no longer upset by our mistakes. We started with our instructor's steps and then began making up our own. We were having fun!

We danced at our son's wedding and to our mutual surprise we keep on dancing. Sometimes it is at a party, often just in our kitchen. I can tell when my husband wants to take a swing around the kitchen floor. His eyes light up. I love the grin on his face when we finish a pattern and come out on the right step. I am even more delighted at our laughter when we don't.

Dancing has drawn us closer, renewed our intimacy. There is a lot more hugging, more innuendo, more delight. Maybe it's just our endorphins running wild. Dancing is, after all, an aerobic exercise that releases those wonderful chemicals of euphoria.

The wedding was the excuse to dance but the result was more than a physical exercise. It helped us remember the excitement of who we are together. And as we continue dancing in the kitchen, wrapped in each other's arms and looking into our happy faces, we rekindle our love.

— Ferida Wolff —

57 Steps to Paradise

To be a queen of a household is a powerful thing.
~Jill Scott

My husband and I live in two separate condos, fifty-seven steps apart on the second floor of a two-story condo building. We're happy, practically still newlyweds, having said our "I do's" in June of 2012. I was sixty-six and Jack was seventy-five at the time of what we lovingly refer to as our "geezer wedding."

We had no attendants, no ushers, no rehearsal, no rehearsal dinner. Just the two of us walking down the aisle of our church hand in hand, married by my cousin Jerry—a monsignor in the Catholic church—with more than one hundred of our relatives and friends there for moral support.

After the church ceremony they all joined us at our condo clubhouse for the most fun wedding reception I've ever attended in my life. We had live music, an open bar and a spread of mid-afternoon finger food that could've fed an army. My kids, their spouses, grandkids, brother, sister, their spouses, and one niece surprised us with an elaborate flash mob dance to the song "Get Down Tonight." It was a magical day.

And so our marriage began and continues… in two separate condos. We sleep at his condo, where most of my clothes and jewelry live. Then we go to water aerobics across the street six days a week from 9 to 10 a.m., and go back to his condo where we have coffee (he), tea (me) and breakfast. He still eats Frosted Flakes. I make my own granola.

Right after breakfast, it's like I have a job. "Bye, honey, see you later," and I'm off to the outside walkway, past five other units to my condo just fifty-seven steps away. The place I call home. It's where I work as a writer and where I prepare my speeches for my other career as a professional speaker. It's where I fix a little snack in the mid-afternoon for myself. Jack, after all, has his own refrigerator and cupboards full of snack food, the kinds of things I don't eat like hot dogs, white bread and potato chips.

My condo is where I prepare our evening meal. And that's because I like my kitchen and my pots, pans, utensils and dishes better than his. I also like being in control of having at least one meal a day that's nutritious for both of us. My kitchen is a place filled with lovely spices, bottles of sweet red chili sauce and a great collection of various flavored olive oils and balsamic vinegars — condiments that my meat-and-potatoes man wouldn't think of putting on a salad or on fresh veggies.

My condo is where I play on my computer after my workday is done. It's where I read books, pay my bills, paint my toenails, organize my stuff, make photo albums, read my mail, paint jars and watch the TV shows that I enjoy. If there isn't a ballgame on TV after dinner, my husband will come into my lanai, where my only TV lives, and watch a show or two with me. But the minute a baseball, football, hockey or basketball game comes on, and he gets that look in his eye, I smile sincerely at my beloved husband and say, "Bye, honey… see you around 11. Or maybe I'll be over earlier and we can play cards while you watch the game."

I can almost see the relief in his eyes as he gets up from one of the two recliners in my lanai and practically trots out the front door, down those fifty-seven steps to one of his three TV sets where he can settle in and do what God put him on this earth to do… watch sports from a recliner. In fact, at Jack's retirement party years ago, before his beloved wife of forty-three years passed away, she regaled the audience by telling them that Jack was "a recliner that farts."

Jack and his first wife had a wonderful, happy marriage, and to be perfectly honest that is one reason I married the man. He's a good person who knows how to make a marriage happy and calm. When he agreed that we would live in both condos I knew he was a keeper.

At our ages, another thing I didn't feel like combining was our names. I just couldn't face the work of changing my name, again. Like many couples our age who had been married before, I wasn't about to change all my medical, financial, social security, business, social, church and passport records. Besides, as the author of thirteen books, my byline is pretty important to me and I'm keeping it forever, thank you.

When I moved to Florida in 2004, I left a six-bedroom home in Oak Creek, Wisconsin, the home where I lived for twenty-four years and where I raised my four children. After the kids were all out of the house, through college and on their own, I decided to sell the place and buy a two-bedroom condo in Florida. So I sold or gave away two-thirds of everything I owned. Thank goodness my children wanted some of my things, because now I can visit those treasures in California, Ohio and Wisconsin.

Because of all that purging, when I moved into my condo in Florida, I only brought the things I loved and wanted around me for the rest of my life, including some antiques and heirloom furniture that my parents had given me during my early married years. I wanted to display the hundreds of brightly colored painted jars I'd made over the years. I wanted my crock collection. Over a dozen crocks in sizes from one gallon up to twenty-five gallons. Three of those crocks, the twenty-five-, twenty- and twelve-gallon crocks, are used as end tables in my living room. My dad made round solid oak tops for them, and they are not only utilitarian because they store my out-of-season decorations, but they are also great conversation starters.

Jack, on the other hand, is a more modern-furniture kind of guy. He actually has good taste when it comes to decorating… it's just not my taste exactly. So why shouldn't he be in charge of decorating his condo and I be in charge of mine? It sure works for us.

Another reason we live in two condos is that after raising four children, mostly as a single parent, and spending most of my life running, running, running to various activities those four kids were involved in, I have come to discover that I love being alone. Alone in a quiet condo. No music, no TV, just me and whatever I want to do.

As a woman who can organize a dozen people to meet for lunch or dinner at various restaurants, yuck it up every day at water aerobics class and speak from the podium to 300 women and then chitchat with them later, I find it an enigma that I am basically a loner. But I honestly find my own company more comforting than mixing with others, even one man, 24/7. I love being alone in my own condo much of the day.

And I'm sure Jack would say the same thing about his alone time during the day. As president of our condo association, president of the small pool and clubhouse association and head usher at our church, he has plenty to keep him busy during the day in his own condo.

Don't get me wrong. I love my husband with all my heart and enjoy the time we spend together... always from 11 p.m. until 11 a.m., and often more than that. We're back and forth between the two condos three or four times a day. Jack often brings my mail over and stops for a chat in my writing room office. Or I stop by his place to put on my swimsuit so we can go for an afternoon swim together. Or we go the movies mid-afternoon.

But the fact remains that I love being head of my household. I like knowing that I can buy new bookshelves for my office or new expensive windows in the dining room and kitchen without even discussing the price with Jack. I pay for everything that involves my condo and he pays for everything in his.

It's just that when one or both of us has the need to be alone, we can do it without hurting the other's feelings. If I had to watch him watch sports on TV so many hours a day I'd scream and think he needed to get a life. But this way, we each have our own space that we're in charge of. And we can do exactly what we want in our own homes. And by late afternoon I always look forward to seeing my man come in the door to have dinner with me.

I think he's happy, too, to hear me come in his door at night, ready to relax, stretch out on our comfy king-size bed and do what we do every night of our married life... kiss goodnight and reach for each other's hand before falling asleep.

— Patricia Lorenz —

35

My Wife Tried to Kill Me

*I did a push-up today. Well actually I fell down, but I
had to use my arms to get back up, so close enough.*
~Author Unknown

Anyone who has been married or in a relationship for a
long time knows what "support" means. When your
spouse is trying something new, it's your duty to help in
any way possible. You may not agree with the decision or
even believe it will work, but if his or her mind is made up, you need
to support the effort one hundred percent.

In my marriage, these little plans usually come and go, like the
time my wife decided we were going to use scent-free laundry soap or
start a cardboard recycling program to help save the world. No harm,
no foul. But imagine my trepidation when she included me in "our"
New Year's resolution to improve our physical fitness.

It sounded simple enough at first. We were already eating fairly
well, so all I had to do was join her in doing something called "plank-
ing." Since it seemed to involve staying still I was all in.

For those who don't know, a plank is basically a pushup without
moving. After my wife explained it to me, I figured this had to be the
easiest exercise known to mankind. "You mean, I get in a pushup
position and then don't actually do any pushups?" I was incredulous.
The world record for holding a plank is five hours; she suggested we

start with thirty seconds. I scoffed.

While she set the timer, I confidently dropped to the floor with dreams of my new rock-hard abs dancing through my head. She said, "Okay, go!" I lifted myself up, making sure my back was straight, and waited, wondering why the world record was only five hours for this. After some time passed, I noticed that my stomach muscles were complaining a bit. Surprisingly, my arm shook a little. I refocused. Then it shook again, but more pronounced. My arms started to shake a lot. "How much time?" I asked, starting to doubt my original estimate of an hour's duration for my first-ever plank.

"Twenty seconds to go," she said.

Twenty seconds to go? Meaning only ten seconds of our easy thirty had elapsed?

My stomach muscles started to complain. I started to regret how easy I had made their life. I'd been nicer to them than I was to our kids.

My wife called out, "Ten seconds!" My discomfort turned to pain, and I noticed that my arms were no longer the only things shaking. My shoulders and legs also shook like the paint mixer at a hardware store, while my stomach started a full revolt, threatening to collapse and leave me in a heap on the floor.

"Keep your back straight. You're slouching. Five more seconds!" she barked.

She was no longer the sunshine of my life. At this point, I was convinced that she was pure evil, the root of everything that is pain in this world. I'm also pretty sure she was laughing at me.

As my wife and personal trainer counted down from five, I glanced down, half expecting to see a pool of blood on the floor. Actually, I would not have been surprised if I found myself face to face with a small alien head as it ripped itself out of my stomach like in the movie *Alien*.

"Four!" she called out as I envisioned the alien climbing free of my innards.

"As seen on TV!" crossed through my mind, and I started to giggle.

"Three!" The countdown continued, and the giggles increased. Apparently, the pain was making me delusional.

"Hi, little guy," I imagined I'd say to my new friend as he peered out of my intestines. I started laughing harder. This chuckling did not match up well with the shaking the rest of my body was doing. It occurred to me that this whole fitness thing was a terrible idea. I decided I would rather walk an actual plank at knifepoint than do these planks any longer.

"Two!"

She had to be lying about the time. She was evil incarnate.

I realized that I wasn't breathing. That was probably part of her plan.

"One!"

My face hit the ground first. As I lay in a sobbing laughing, sweating, heaving pool on the floor, I did an assessment to see if I had a bloody nose. Apparently, the human nose is not designed to stop the body from a free fall, which is pretty poor engineering. I didn't dare look to see if any fluids were leaking onto the carpet. It was her idea. She could do the cleanup after I expired.

An hour later, after the stomach pains had subsided and I regained the use of my arms, I stood in front of the mirror, saw absolutely zero improvement, and considered moving to Tibet until my wife's fitness craze passed. But I am not a quitter! (Or I am not allowed to quit, which is kinda the same thing, isn't it?) With the same resolve that allows a woman to have another child after enduring the pain of childbirth, I decided I could press on. I mean, I'm only four hours, fifty-nine minutes and thirty seconds away from the record, right?

— Marty Anderson —

36

A Soft Whisper in the Ear

With mirth and laughter let old wrinkles come.
~William Shakespeare, The Merchant of Venice

Premature gray hair runs in my family. My dad was completely white by the time he was in his thirties. I found my first gray when I was eighteen. I spent most of my twenties and thirties in heavy combat, attacking the dreaded skunk-stripe that seemed to arrive only a few weeks after my monthly attempt to cover up what my DNA decided was my natural hair color.

In my late forties, I gave up the chemicals and let my white hair shine. My husband James was a big supporter of my natural look. Other women stopped me in shopping malls and at the grocery store to tell me how much they liked my long, frosty-white hairstyle. All in all, I was exceedingly pleased with my decision to go au naturel.

I must admit, though, that I'm asked far too often for my liking if I'm over sixty-five when I'm at a checkout that offers senior discounts. Usually, the clerk is under thirty and can be forgiven for not being able to distinguish between the sagging skin of an eighty-five-year-old versus the droopy flesh of someone barely fifty. I get it. I didn't pay much attention to the over-thirty crowd when I was her age, either.

However, my husband finds this particularly hilarious because he knows it annoys me. I've even been known to stifle the question before it escapes the dewy-skinned clerk's mouth when I happen to be in a store on a seniors' day.

"Don't ask," I say preemptively. And, thankfully, they usually oblige.

However, there have been occasions when my white hair has been the source of a good laugh. My husband and I like to frequent thrift shops and antique stores. I'm a genealogist and collector of old photographs. I often find old carte de visite photographs or cabinet card images in these shops. One of my hobbies is reuniting old family photos with genealogists.

On one of our visits to a local thrift shop, my husband was in an exceedingly goofy mood. We had watched an old *Saturday Night Live* episode the evening before, and James was doing a poor imitation of Steve Martin's "wild and crazy guy" character, Georg Festrunk, as we entered the store. I went off to look at the knickknacks, hoping to find old photos, while he went into the housewares section of the store.

I didn't find any interesting pictures or tchotchkes, so I headed over to join my husband in the hunt for some nice kitchen gadgets. I noticed he had walked up behind an older woman. She was wearing the same color and style of coat as mine and had beautiful, flowing white hair. I headed over just in time to hear him whisper into her left ear, "See anything you like?" in his most salacious, "wild and crazy guy" voice.

The woman turned around. She was clearly well into her eighties and didn't seem to find his closeness particularly unsettling. She gave him a good look up and down. "Maybe," she said with a smile.

The surprised look on James's face was priceless. I couldn't help it. I laughed out loud. The elderly woman looked at me, and then at James. She figured out the mistake immediately.

"Nice jacket," she said to me.

"Thanks," I replied. "And you have the most gorgeous hair."

We all had a good chuckle. I think the woman was quite pleased to be mistaken for someone thirty years her junior. And you know what? I didn't mind, either.

— Carol L. MacKay —

37

The "Invisible Chair"

You can't deny laughter; when it comes, it plops down
in your favorite chair and stays as long as it wants.
~Stephen King

Every week after our writing group I stop at the Habitat for Humanity ReStore. It's on my way home, and I enjoy browsing their eclectic collection. I usually find something I like, whether it's for me, my kids, or a friend. The prices are reasonable, so whatever I purchase is a good buy.

On one visit, I spotted an attractive, old oak chair with a high, curved back. I didn't need another chair, but it looked so inviting that I had to try it out. It was the most comfortable chair I'd ever sat in. I was hoping it would have one short leg, a broken spindle, a nail sticking out through the seat, or something to deter me. It didn't. It was flawless and in topnotch condition.

I was already rearranging furniture in my mind, trying to find a suitable place for this chair. If I moved my bulky, stuffed chair to the sunroom, I could put this more compact piece in its place. Or, if nothing worked, I would give the chair to my daughter. In any event, the price was right, and I took it home.

I carried the chair into the house and brought out the furniture polish. After a vigorous workout, the chair looked shiny and brand-new. I shifted furniture, set down my bargain and enjoyed my new acquisition. It took up less space than the bulky chair and made the room look larger.

I knew my significant other would flip out when he saw another chair in the house. I decided not to tell him and wait to see if he was observant enough to notice it on his own.

Art walked past the chair many times and didn't say a word. *Is the chair invisible?* I wondered. *Is Art waiting for me to admit that I bought yet another piece of furniture, or is he waiting for my next move as I am his? If I can notice a crumb on the floor or a candy bowl that has been moved just one inch within seconds, why can't Art notice a brand-new chair? It's not the size of an ant.* Trying to make it more conspicuous, I placed a brightly colored pillow on the "invisible chair." He still didn't notice it.

A week later, I decided to sit on the chair wearing a bikini. When Art walked past, he remarked, "Nice bikini."

If Art hasn't seen the "invisible chair," I hope he doesn't see the "invisible player piano" I'm having delivered in two weeks!

— Irene Maran —

38

Man Shall Not Live on Bread Alone

The only time to eat diet food is while you're waiting for the steak to cook.
~Chef Julia Child

Last night, as I put the finishing touches on a batch of roasted pumpkin meatballs, I got a text from my husband. "Hey, are you cooking tonight?"

I wiped my hands on a kitchen towel and replied, "Yep. Found a new recipe online today. It's almost ready."

He responded, "Running late. Won't make it home for dinner. Sorry."

That's when I realized my husband was cheating. Rather than having dinner with his wife, I knew he was headed across town, where he couldn't wait to get his hands on that old hen he'd been sneaking around with. And I knew when he came home I'd be able to smell the perfume on him — eau de fried chicken from the grocery-store deli.

I should've seen it coming. He showed signs of food infidelity the first time I served a Pinterest meal and told him it was time for us to incorporate clean eating into our lives. He poked at the zucchini noodles on his plate and frowned at me. "But I like it dirty," he said. And by dirty, he meant battered, deep-fried and extra crispy.

My husband doesn't like change, especially when it comes to food. He's a Midwestern boy who's spent a lifetime gobbling dinners comprised of his three favorite food groups: meat, potatoes, and bread. So, when I started making changes to the way I shop and prepare meals, he was convinced that I was trying to starve him to death.

For the past two years, I've been trying to prove to him that removing gluten, sugar and processed foods from our diet is a part of living healthy, not a form of punishment. But he's still trying to figure out what he did wrong. He used to finish a meal by patting his belly and telling me it was delicious. Now he leaves the table and asks, "Are you mad at me for something?"

My kitchen cabinets were once filled with food magazines and cookbooks. These days, my smartphone is my cookbook; I find all my recipes on websites and social media. Oh, I know, just because some Paleo expert posts it on Facebook doesn't mean it'll taste good, but I like to think of my kitchen as a healthy test lab.

However, just as in the laboratory, there are a few dangerous concoctions that should be avoided. I realized this when I made cauliflower soup for dinner and served black-bean brownies for dessert. That night, as he slept, my husband serenaded me with gassy honks so noxious and loud that the dog got up and left the room. Those two food items, along with cabbage steak and herbed Brussels sprouts, have been taken off the menu. Forever.

Don't tell my husband this, but some of the dishes I've tried have been hard for even me to handle. A few weeks ago, I cooked up a pot of chickpea pasta. The texture and smell were reminiscent of something we once used to patch our driveway. And recently, I attempted roasted eggplant. Minutes into slicing the ingredients, I discovered I was allergic to the purple produce. Just the process of handling it prompted an itchy rash that quickly spread across the backs of my hands and up my arms. The eggplant took a trip down the garbage disposal, and dear hubby still believes we have poison ivy growing amidst the herbs in our back yard.

All those relationship books that encourage couples to experiment probably aren't referring to gluten-free, low-sodium meal prep. But healthy adventure cooking is about as exciting as things get around here. I just hope there'll come a day when my husband no longer feels the need to cheat on his diet. Until then, I'll remind him that quinoa isn't birdseed, and kale isn't a conspiracy against the potato industry. Until then, he'll probably continue to sneak around with the greasy broad he met downtown. After all, she does come complete with a side of biscuits.

— Ann Morrow —

The Challenge

When we say yes, we do more, create more, live more.
~Author Unknown

The challenge came from my empty nester's group — the Happy Empty Nesters (Hens). Now that our chicks had flown from the coop, it was time to focus on our roosters. We gave each other two assignments for the next month. First: Say nothing negative or critical to our husbands. Second: When our husbands initiated an activity, say "Yes!" This could be something simple like taking a walk around the block after dinner or something more involved, like taking a cruise around the world.

I approached the challenge with trepidation; it is scary to give up control. What if I was tired or bored or afraid? But I was resolved to do it; I'd have to report back to the Hens the next month. To the best of my ability, I would agree to my husband's requests.

My first opportunity occurred that evening as I was making dinner. My husband asked tentatively, "How about if we eat out on the deck?" I had to admit it was a lovely day — puffy white clouds with sunshine — but his suggestion added work to my already long day. We'd need to clean off the patio furniture and shuttle all the food and utensils out there. We might be plagued by any number of annoyances — insects, gusts of wind, sun in our eyes.

I didn't say any of that. In the spirit of the challenge, I said, "Sure." My husband's eyebrows went up in mild surprise, and he wasted no time pulling out a tray and loading it up.

The clouds shielded us from the glaring sun for most of our spring dinner out on the deck. I could feel the warmth on my face and smelled a faint hint of jasmine from the yard. We heard the honks of Canadian geese at the pond in the distance. As we discussed our day, a Nuthatch landed on the deck rail just feet from where we sat. We froze in place. The tiny bird was joined by another (a mate?), and then they frolicked off. My husband caught my eye and smiled. At that moment, the clouds parted to reveal the sun setting low in the sky in a riot of color. We had front row seats to the delights of nature and a spectacular view.

We made a romantic memory that evening, and I would have missed it had I not consented to join my husband on a new mini-adventure.

A couple days later, my husband came home from work and said, "The latest action-adventure movie got good reviews, and it starts in half an hour. Wanna go?" Though not my favorite genre, I could do this. I said "Yes" again. The movie wasn't bad, and my husband appreciated my willingness to join him. He mentioned it multiple times.

That Saturday, we had planned to jog together, but the weather turned threatening. This time, I took the lead and asked my husband if he would run with me anyway. He agreed. We reached our farthest point before turning back when the clouds opened up and swamped us in a deluge of water. We laughed so hard it was difficult to keep running, and we returned home soaking wet and utterly happy.

When the month was up, the Hens met again. The reports were generally positive. But for one woman, the challenge sparked a complete turnaround in her marriage. I suggested we continue the challenge indefinitely, and everyone clucked in approval.

Throughout the next few years, my husband and I sought out adventure with each other. We flew kites on the National Mall during the National Cherry Blossom Festival; we tramped through newly fallen snow to capture photos; we drove Jeeps on the beach in the Outer Banks; we smelled the fragrant flowers of Longwood Gardens; we flew in a hot air balloon at the Albuquerque International Balloon Fiesta; we hunted down all the Fabergé Imperial Eggs in the country; and we built our own spa in the sand at Hot Water Beach in New Zealand.

The challenge changed my mindset from doing what is easy to thinking of ways to say "Yes" to my husband, "Yes" to adventure, and "Yes" to life. Of course, it would be easier to say "No." But this is a better way. This is living life and feeling truly alive — not just marking time, but living life to the fullest. Did this ever make me feel uncomfortable? It certainly did. But it has also been one of the best things I've ever said "Yes" to.

— Monica Cardiff —

A Stone's Throw

*Use your precious moments to live life fully every
single second of every single day.*
~Marcia Wieder

e had hiked just over a mile and a half. Our Golden Retriever was dragging a little bit and needed a water break. My wife grabbed her daypack and found the water bottle. She poured some water into a beat-up bowl, and the dog lapped it up quickly.

We settled onto an old tree trunk and rested our middle-aged legs for a few minutes. The dog was tired but happy. She loves to hike with us, and today was no exception. My wife was content as well. She enjoys every opportunity to exercise, and hiking in the fall tops her list of favorite things to do.

I had to be coaxed into the hike. My wife reminded me of how we hiked when we first dated and said, "It can be like that!" I moaned and groaned about wanting to watch football, but as the sun glistened atop the colorful leaves on this Indian summer day, I was swayed to join her. I also felt a twinge of guilt for not doing more of the things we did when we were first dating.

As our hike progressed, I had to admit that the fresh fall air and unexpected warmth helped make our time in the woods rather enjoyable. I glanced over at some kids playing near a stream. Two boys and their older sister chased each other around, and one of them exclaimed that he had found some shells. This was a stream in Southeastern Ohio, not the ocean, so both my wife and I looked at each other as if to say, "That kid has a vivid imagination." Within a minute, his sister was also holding up a shell. Sure enough, some shells had made their way to the edge of a stream in the middle of the woods in Ohio.

My wife loves shells almost as much as she loves hiking, so she jumped up and walked over to where the kids were playing. She grabbed a shell and held it up like a prize. I grabbed the dog's leash, and we walked over to join her. The dog jumped up and down and seemed to be telling my wife that the shell looked great. They both examined the shell closely as if they had found a gold nugget. My wife smiled as she picked up more shells.

I began looking around and saw a perfectly flat stone on the ground. In an instant, I recalled skipping stones near the lake where my grandfather took me fishing as a kid. I loved skipping stones! Watching a flat stone skip across the top of the water seven or eight times was like watching some sort of magic trick. I told my wife she could keep her shells; I had found a skipping stone. She gave me a puzzled look and then asked, "What's a skipping stone?" I walked over and showed her the flat, thin rock.

I said, "Watch this!" I flung the stone in a perfect motion so that it would hit the water just right and then skip along the top several times. She looked on in amazement and asked how I did that. To my surprise, my wife had never skipped stones. I gave her a quick lesson, and then she tried it. After just a few attempts, she was able to skip a stone like a pro. As she became more and more successful at skipping stones, her smile got bigger and bigger.

The dog looked on and was ready to chase each and every rock. I held her tightly so that she did not take a plunge into the muddy stream. A wet, dirty dog would ruin my wife's joy. For a few minutes, my wife and I took turns holding the dog and skipping stones. We had so much fun that we didn't notice the sun fading behind the trees. It was time to head back. We stood near the stream as we prepared to make the trek back to the car. For a couple of perfect minutes, I stood behind my wife and wrapped my arms around her waist. I could tell she was content and proud of her new skill. I was simply glad that I was there to share in it.

As a boy, I thought skipping a stone was magical. Now, as a middle-aged man sharing a moment with the woman I have loved for over twenty years, it was beyond magical. That's the beauty of life. The simple and unexpected moments are almost always the best ones, like a moment when you go hiking on a fall day and share something new with your spouse. Her joy of learning how to skip stones for the first time made me feel great, and it made me love her even more. We held hands as we hiked back, just like we did when we first dated. The dog led the way, wagging her tail with each step. The next time my wife wants to go hiking in the fall, I definitely won't want to skip it!

— David Warren —

Love and Love Again

Making My
House His Home

A house is made of walls and beams;
a home is built with love and dreams.
~Author Unknown

Widowhood was lonely, especially on weekends when my friends were enjoying activities with their families. Since my children live far away from me, I sometimes took myself to a movie or fussed with my dog. And I was surrounded by familiar possessions, helping me remember the life I had once lived. I felt no need for a man in my life, as that would be too complicated.

However, I had joined a widowed people's group where I met an intriguing man. "How would you like to go to dinner with me?" he asked one day. Our friendship quickly became romantic, despite the fact that my dog barked each time he hugged me. We saw each other every day. Eventually, my dog even grew to love him, too, because we walked her together.

My married children thought I was being hasty by dating this man exclusively. "Mom, you need to slow down. Date some more," they cautioned. I ignored their advice.

They had returned to their lives after their father's funeral while I searched for a life of my own. I was in my seventies, as was my new love interest. We didn't want to waste time. You might say it was a whirlwind romance, and it was, because we were both sure. We knew we had fallen in love.

About a month and a half after we met, he knelt on one knee in my dining room and asked, "Will you marry me?" I grinned and said, "Yes." And then I asked if he needed help getting back up with his arthritic knee.

Where would we live? I owned the house that had been built for my maternal great-grandparents. He was renting, so it seemed logical that he would move into my house.

I already had a houseful of furniture, but he had an equal amount. We had to decide what we wanted to keep and what we no longer needed. It was a challenge to discard belongings that held meaning and family history for each of us.

One day, I went to his apartment and showed him the items I hoped we could keep. "I'd love to have this in our home." Then a friend who had remarried after her first husband died gave me some great advice: "Try to make your house his home, too. Don't let him feel like a guest in your house." After a minute, she added, "I made that mistake when I remarried. My second husband told me he felt like a visitor in my house. There was very little of him in any of the rooms. And he didn't know where he could put his things."

I recognized that my friend had given me advice I needed to take to heart. My husband-to-be is a pilot and owns various artifacts related to flying. We found a place for his airplane propeller in the office we would share. That was a good beginning.

He received a huge print of a biplane when he retired from IBM. I removed the painting I had hung over my fireplace and hung the biplane print there instead. On the mantel, we placed his big sculpture of a seagull, which represents the character from Richard Bach's book, *Jonathan Livingston Seagull*. On a wall that had no ornamentation, we hung his photos of Waterford, Ireland, from which his ancestors had come.

All my old television room furniture went in a garage sale, replaced by my fiancé's bookcases, television, television stand, and futon. We also hung photos of his parents on the wall. Sometimes, I would walk into a room and not recognize it as being in my home because of the "new" arrangement of furnishings and decorations.

After we married, I easily grew accustomed to my home, and my husband did, as well. Not long ago, he said to me, "I really feel as if this is my home."

I am so grateful to my friend who offered me such good advice from her personal experience. Just as she suggested, I have made my husband feel at home here and not like a visitor. The things we owned aren't as important as the love we share and the home we've made.

— Sandy McPherson Carrubba Geary —

Doing the Chicken Soup Dance

*An expert is a person who tells you a simple thing in a
confused way in such a fashion as to make you think
the confusion is your own fault.*
~William Castle

We met on Match.com on December 8, 2008. Harvey was in New York; I was in Florida. The odds of our getting together were almost unimaginable. Yet here we were, two eighty-two-year-olds who stumbled onto each other on the Internet and were instantly smitten. I tried to follow the rules of the dating service... no telephone numbers, no addresses, pure anonymity... at least until I was sure that I wasn't talking to an axe murderer, as my daughter suggested.

But Harvey was almost too good to be true. Handsome, witty, a former executive at CBS, a widower looking for love. Our e-mails via Match.com burned up the airwaves. We were writing day and night, and after a week, he was begging for my phone number and address.

"I need to hear your voice," he pleaded. And after a brief resistance, I gave him my phone number. He called immediately, and his voice was warm and reassuring. We talked for more than an hour... about our backgrounds, our families, our careers... then I took time out.

"I'll call you this afternoon," he said tenderly.

"I won't be home," I apologized. "I'm doing a book signing."

"What is that?" he asked.

"I have stories in two new *Chicken Soup for the Soul* books and I'll be signing them."

"You've written two books of chicken soup recipes? I'm impressed. You must be a great cook."

"I don't cook," I laughed, "and they aren't recipe books. They're part of a series called *Chicken Soup for the Soul*. One book is *Chicken Soup for the Soul: My Resolution* and the other is *Chicken Soup for the Soul: Tales of Golf and Sport*."

"Let me get this straight. You've written an entire book about your New Year's resolutions? I hope I figure in that. Have you resolved to keep writing me?"

"Well, yes, I have that, but this was written long before I met you. There are 101 stories for your mind, body and wallet."

"Hm, so my wallet figures in there," he said suspiciously. "I guess I'd better get a pre-nup!"

"Me, too. I have a daughter-in-law who's a lawyer."

"So you've made 101 resolutions?" he asked.

"Only two."

"What do you mean only two? What about the other ninety-nine?"

"Somebody else wrote them."

"You're signing a book that you only have two stories in? What do the other ninety-nine people have to say about that?"

"I assume they're just glad to have me selling their book."

"Okay. And what about the other book... the golf one. Do you only have two stories in that one?"

"One."

"You only have one story in the golf book, and you're signing it, too? Well never mind. I never figured you for a golfer, but I'm happy to hear that because I'm quite a golfer myself. Maybe we can play a game when I finally meet you."

"I'm not a golfer, and I did not write about golf," I sputtered. "I wrote about football."

"I see. So you play football. Now I'm really impressed. You wrote a story about football in a book about golf."

"Listen, Harvey, I really have to get out there and sell a few books. I'll talk to you tomorrow."

"Why don't I buy a couple of your books. How much are they?"

"$14.95 each."

Harvey mused a minute. "I don't want to be picky, but I was an accountant for CBS. How many words in the football story?"

I sighed. "Around 1,500 I would think."

"Wow! You are really well paid at $14.95. That's about a dollar a word. I guess that makes your Resolution book a real bargain with two stories in it. I'll send you a check for $30. How's that? What's your address?"

"Harvey, Match.com doesn't want us giving out our addresses."

"Shall I send the check to Match.com then?"

This man was really getting on my nerves.

"All right. I'll give you my address. But don't come stalking me."

"Stalk you? I'm going to marry you!"

"You are? All right. But first you have to buy my *Chicken Soup for the Soul* books."

"This is blackmail. Are you signing them for me, too? What are you going to write in the front of them?"

"Hm, let me think about that. In the Resolution book, how about, "To the most exciting man I never met?"

"That sounds good. And in the Golf book?"

"I'll write, 'The ball is in your court.'"

Harvey was thoughtful. "The word 'court' really applies to tennis, but we don't need to get technical. I'm writing the check now. Are you wrapping my books?"

"They're practically in the mail."

"That's great. And I'm practically on the next plane down there."

"In that case, why should I send them? Why don't I just hand them to you when you arrive?"

"Why don't you? And then I can write, 'To the most expensive date I never had!'"

***

He did fly to Florida, and I did marry him, and he did buy my *Chicken Soup for the Soul* books... all of them!

—Phyllis W. Zeno—

All Over Again

For 'mid old friends, tried and true,
Once more we our youth renew.
~Joseph Parry

I was the proverbial soccer mom, and all of my friends were married. At the time of the divorce, I hadn't dated anyone but my ex-husband in over twenty-five years.

I joined singles groups but still felt too raw to go on an actual date. Staying in a large group became one more way to hide out. The invitations came in, but every time, I said the same thing: "I'm sorry, but I'm just not ready to date."

A couple of years rolled by this way. Then one day, a name appeared in my Facebook inbox that was so familiar, it didn't seem out of place at all even though I hadn't seen that name in close to thirty years.

He'd lived on the other side of my neighborhood, so we were practically children together. What was I — fifteen, sixteen when we'd first met? My sister and her boyfriend had given him a ride somewhere and we briefly shared a back seat. I thought he was adorable and easy to talk to and I liked him immediately, but he had a girlfriend. I ran into him after they'd broken up and we clicked again as friends. Friends who dated on and off for years.

And now here he was e-mailing me after all this time. Did I remember him? Ha. I checked out his picture; to me, he looked exactly the same, right down to the scar I'd always loved because it somehow added a slightly rugged defiance to those almost-pretty features. He was always pleasant, easygoing, and fun. How I used to love his conspiratorial grin, the way he leaned in and sort of nudged me when we laughed, as if we alone got the joke. For years I'd found myself gravitating toward him again and again, drawn by his core of deep and solid kindness.

What I remembered most was the time he picked me up for a date and I asked him if he'd been to work that day. He answered no, that he'd only been mowing his neighbors' lawns. Wasn't that work, I asked? I still remember the way he said it. "Well, no — I mean, it's not like I'd charge them or anything," he shrugged. "They're old." As if that explained it. And it did. I believe I fell in love with him just a little bit at that moment.

Now here he was again, recently divorced, and although we'd both moved out of state, it just so happened we'd chosen the same one. He was only a few hours away. Would I like to get together? At first I panicked and stalled. I was thirty years older and twenty pounds heavier. What if he didn't like the middle-aged me? What if he did? I wasn't ready!

A couple of months went by, and I couldn't stop thinking about him. I also couldn't stop thinking how ridiculous it was to refuse to see an old friend just because I was scared. And worse, I was using the excuse that I wasn't ready to date someone new. Technically it didn't have to be a date, and he really wasn't someone new, was he?

So I picked up the phone and dialed the number he'd told me to call if I ever changed my mind.

All the while I couldn't help but hear my mother's voice in my head about never calling boys. Good thing he was no longer a boy! We were, after all, old friends, and we talked for ages, finally agreeing to meet in the middle for a simple, casual, easy day. When I started to panic about that upcoming date, it calmed me to remind myself that it really wasn't a first date at all. "Don't worry," my smart friend Mary comforted me. "He'll see you as he did back then. People do."

And guess what? I believe she was right. I know he looked the same to me. He was still cute. He still had the same walk, the same smile, the same gestures. The same conspiratorial grin, the same nudge. His gray hair still somehow looked brown to me. How easy it was, how simple, how natural, that we fell right back to feeling like we used to. When it was time to leave, before there was a chance for any awkwardness, he drew me in just as he'd always done and gave me such a sweet kiss, thirty years melted away under the warm summer sky. I giggled all the way home.

But what surprised me the most was the way all those years of living had made him even dearer to me. I'd forgotten how nice it was to be with someone who understood so much about where I'd come from. We'd both made some painful decisions at times, and we'd suffered some profound changes and losses, but we had eventually found our way to a better place. His core of goodness was as solid as ever. He had experienced his own struggles, and they'd given him depth and character. Wisdom.

Once again, I was drawn to his scars. I believe I fell in love with him just a little bit, all over again.

—T'Mara Goodsell—

The Robes of a Prince

*Love is like swallowing hot chocolate before
it has cooled off. It takes you by surprise at first,
but keeps you warm for a long time.*
~Author Unknown

never expected to be single when I was sixty. I certainly never expected to be dating at my age.

I was shy, unpopular, and socially clumsy when I was a teenager. Now I've had a lifetime of experience and I'm shy, unpopular, and socially clumsy.

It is hard to meet single men at my age. Dates are few and far between, so when I do have a date I try to make it a special occasion. On my last date I dressed up, applied make-up and put on enough perfume to smell like a flower garden. My date fell asleep during dinner and snored, which wouldn't have been so bad if we hadn't been in a restaurant. I finished my dessert and woke him up. He picked his teeth with a fork and left a fifty-cent tip for the waitress. I decided to give up dating forever.

My son Shane is very devoted to me, wants me to be happy, and is terrified that if I don't get married he'll get stuck with me. Shane arranged for me to meet his neighbor George who needed help writing his memoir.

I often help people write their memoirs. I think it is important for people our age to leave behind a record of who we are and our family history. When we die, our stories will die with us and be lost forever. Sometimes writing the story of your life seems overwhelming and people need a little help getting started.

I agreed to meet George at a nearby restaurant and took along a pen and notepad to record his memories. I felt like I was doing a favor for Shane's neighbor so I wore my second best dress and didn't bother to wiggle into my incredibly uncomfortable body shaper that pushed my belly into my kidneys to make me look ten pounds thinner. I put on some make-up and applied lipstick that was guaranteed not to run into the lines around my lips.

George was short and chubby, and like most men his age he was bald, but he did have a cute little white moustache. I was two inches taller than George and he wasn't my type at all, but that didn't matter because this wasn't a real date; I was just going to help him get started writing his life story.

George was wearing the ugliest shirt I'd ever seen. It was yellow with small brown flowers on it, and to make matters worse, it buttoned on the wrong side, making it look like a woman's blouse.

Since I didn't consider this a date, it didn't matter what he was wearing, and after introducing myself, I took out my notepad and began asking him questions. Where he was born, where he went to school, whether he had brothers and sisters, what kind of jobs he'd had—I carefully wrote down every answer. In a few minutes I knew the name of his dog, the name of his third grade teacher and that his favorite dessert was chocolate cake. He'd been widowed seven years, had two grown sons and four grandchildren. His hobby was building model ships and he'd retired from the post office five years earlier.

"See how easy it is?" I asked and tore five pages out of the notebook and handed them to him. "You just need to get started and before you know it your book will be written."

"What book?" George asked.

He wasn't writing a book. My son had used that excuse to introduce us. I'd just spent fifteen minutes giving George the third degree and writing down his answers to my questions.

Now he was convinced I was crazy, but after I explained what Shane had done we both had a good laugh. George was one of those people who laugh with their whole face; his blue eyes twinkled and the laugh lines around his eyes got deeper. Wrinkles in a person's face give them character. He had a nice laugh too, it wasn't a fake polite laugh; it was the kind of laugh that made you laugh too.

"I should explain about my shirt," George said. "My twelve-year-old granddaughter wants to be a famous fashion designer when she grows up. I bought a sewing machine for her and to thank me, she made this shirt for my date tonight. I had to wear it. I couldn't hurt her feelings. I thought about putting another shirt in my car and changing in the parking lot before I came inside but that seemed dishonest. If she asked me if I wore the shirt on my date, I wanted to say yes and that it was a fine shirt. I just couldn't lie to her."

I liked George so much at that minute I got tears in my eyes.

"Tell your granddaughter that your date liked your shirt very much and good luck with her career and that she is off to a good start," I said. "Tell her I said she could make robes for a prince."

I wanted to tell George that right now he seemed like a prince but I was afraid I'd sound stupid and it might embarrass him.

"Thank you," George said and squeezed my hand. "I knew you'd understand; your son told me you were one in a million."

I blushed. I hadn't blushed in years but I was definitely blushing. My heart was also beating faster and I hoped it was because George was holding my hand and not because I was having a heart attack.

I decided I didn't care if George was short and bald; he was a man with a good heart and integrity. He was willing to embarrass himself by wearing a hideous shirt on a first date so he wouldn't hurt his granddaughter's feelings.

"If you ask me for a second date, I promise not to interview you and ask dozens of questions." I gave him a big smile, which I hoped was flirty. I also hoped he'd think my teeth were really mine... well, they would be mine in three more payments.

"I didn't mind. I've never had a woman interested enough to want to know my whole life story and then not just listen to me but write

down what I said," he smiled back. "You're a nice lady."
And it was as complicated and as simple as that.
I met a nice man and I'm not alone anymore.

—April Knight—

Come Here

Grow old along with me! The best is yet to be.
~Robert Browning

It was a beautiful summer day in July. I had cleaned the house, bought the groceries and run the errands. Now I had time to walk the beach and unwind before the relatives arrived for Jim's anniversary mass.

I pulled on my bathing suit, shirt and shorts and headed for Cold Storage Beach, my favorite at low tide, because I could walk all the way to Brewster on smooth, hard sand with a view of the entire arm of the Cape.

A year had passed since the morning when I found Jim on the floor, struggling to tell me what happened. I called 911, and he was dead six hours later at Cape Cod Hospital. He'd had a massive brain hemorrhage.

It was a long and lonely year for me. I completed a bereavement group therapy course and cried a thousand rivers, yet I felt no relief. Despair was my daily companion, and life seemed so meaningless without my soul mate.

We had been married for forty-eight years! He was my anchor. Our four children were grown, and it was time for us to complete our bucket lists. He was my happy-go-lucky side and balanced my seriousness perfectly. Friends with good intentions tried matchmaking, but I was not looking.

"Damn you, Jim!" I cried out to the vast ocean in front of me. The surf splashed against my legs, sending my protests straight to heaven, but no comfort came. I followed the edge of the sea and walked until the incoming tide surrounded me and I was on an island far from shore. But I was oblivious to where I was and kept on complaining. I was purging myself of feelings I had kept locked inside, and it felt good to let them go. The water seemed deeper, and I realized I had to head for shore or swim. I took off my shirt and shorts and made it to shore before the tide overcame me.

How fast the tide came in, I thought, *and how foolish of me not to pay attention.* The late afternoon sun felt like a warm blanket. I stretched out and soaked it up. "God help me," I sputtered.

Looking to the west, I saw a man coming in my direction. We seemed to be the only two people way out on the flats. My friends always warned me about walking the beach alone. I walked into the water to avoid him.

"Nice day!" he shouted out to me. Then he said something else that I didn't hear.

"Excuse me?" I asked, not really wanting to engage in conversation with this man. I was too engulfed in my own misery.

"It's kind of spooky. You are standing where I threw her ashes."

Oh, my God, I thought. Then I faced him.

He was tall and thin with a graying beard. A golf cap and sunglasses obscured his face, but his body language was loud and clear. He was kind and not to be feared.

"I'm so sorry," I called out against the sounds of the surf. We looked at each other.

"Are you all right?"

"My husband died, too."

Then he opened his arms with such sympathy. "Come here," he said softly.

In a haunting fog, I walked from the water onto the sand and into his arms, and we shared a moment that changed us forever. It was a warm hug that said, "I'm sorry for your heartache. I know how you feel."

He took hold of my hand and led me to a rock where he had engraved his wife's initials.

"She died a long time ago when I was a lot younger," he said. "I live in South Carolina now. I'm here visiting a friend in a nursing home. He's not doing well, and I wanted to see him before he dies. I always come here and visit before I head back."

Then he told me how his wife had died of cancer and of his fulfilling her desire to be cremated. "The bay was our favorite place. We brought up a family here."

I asked about his friend, and when he told me the name of the nursing home, I realized that my employer, a doctor, was the director.

"I'm the secretary for your friend's doctor! What a small world it is," I said.

"I married again, but I learned the hard way that you just can't replace someone you loved. It didn't work, and I sold our house in Brewster and moved to South Carolina."

It felt weird being so close to him in such a secluded area. I took my cue to leave after revealing very little about myself.

How could I have just walked into his arms like that? I thought. *He could have been a serial killer.* Yet I felt something... a spark that both excited and scared me as I walked faster back to my car.

Weeks later, he called me at work. He had found the doctor's name and did some investigating.

"I'm the man you met on the beach. Do you remember me?" he asked.

"Of course, I remember you. How could I forget you? I thought you were an angel. And if I looked back, you would be gone — and I didn't want you to be gone."

"No one has ever called me an angel before," he said. "Can I call you at home?"

I gave him my number, and he called that night. We talked every day after that, realizing how much we had in common.

One night, he called as I was falling asleep.

"How old are you?" he asked in a panic.

"What?" I said in a sleepy fog. "How old am I? A gentleman never asks a woman her age!"

"I don't want to be arrested for courting a minor. I'm seventy-eight years old."

"Wow. You don't look seventy-eight at all. Do you have a pacemaker?"

"No. I'm very healthy. So how old are you?"

"Well, you're the math teacher." He had told me he was retired from teaching high-school math.

"I was married at nineteen in 1962. Figure it out."

"Sixty-nine," he shot back in an instant. "I thought you were much younger."

"Hooray!" I laughed again. "We're both old."

"I can't stand it any longer. Can we meet on the beach again at that same spot? I'm making plans to fly up."

In September, my phone rang. "I'm at the beach. Are you coming?"

I made sandwiches, packed them into a backpack and threw in a bottle of champagne. I was off in a whirlwind.

As he came into view, he walked toward me, arms outstretched.

"Come here," he sang, and I flew into them. When I pulled out the champagne, his smile turned to laughter.

As we sat on the rock toasting each other, three women walked by.

"Congratulations!" they called.

He hadn't proposed, but those women were prophets. We were two lonely people led to that remote area of beach by fate, but we were destined to spend the rest of our lives together.

— Sandra Bakun —

46

Peel an Onion

Cowboys don't go around breaking hearts.
~Missy Lyons

e leaned in and whispered, "You'll like me when you get to know me better. I wear well." I was speechless. *Get to know him better? Doesn't he know that I'm at the movie as payback for that favor he did for me? Get to know him better? Not in this lifetime, country boy. You are not my type.*

Not my type because he reminded me of my roots, which I had ditched thirty-plus years earlier. No more living in a small town. No more pastoral settings. No more boring weekends. My best girlfriend and I had headed to Columbus, Ohio — a metropolitan area booming with theaters, museums, and better job opportunities — the day after high-school graduation. We never looked back.

The first time I laid eyes on this man — John — he was wearing a white, short-sleeved T-shirt, paint-stained pants and Wolverine work boots. Bland. But it didn't matter; I was not there to see him. I was there to see his wife, Jan, who was housebound from undergoing a series of chemotherapy treatments for a recurrence of ovarian cancer. I was one of several volunteers from my church who made monthly visits to those no longer able to attend.

When I signed up for the program, I was already stretched as tight as a rubber band, yet I believed in it and wanted to serve. Never mind that I was a single parent of a twelve-year old boy and a daughter in college. I was taking classes two nights a week at a nearby college while working full-time at a demanding job.

The only times John and I connected during the two years I visited Jan were when I arrived at their house and when I left. His greetings were the same: Thanks for coming, and thanks for the visit. A broken record.

My visits with Jan were helpful to her and heartwarming to me. We chatted about our personal lives and her condition. During one of our visits, she asked if I wanted to see her hair, which had fallen out and was now growing back. Before I could respond, she ripped off her scarf and ran her hand over a head full of gray one-inch curls! She beamed.

I was at night school when John called about Jan's death. He left a message with my son. "Tell your mom Jan passed away this afternoon. She was so good to her; I know she would want to know," he said. I attended the viewing. That was in May.

In mid-July, I gave John a call to see if he would assemble the still boxed stove hood that my dad had promised to install but never did. I knew through Jan that John was retired and a handyman. He agreed. I gave him my address, and we set up a time.

By the time the job was finished, I was feeling sorry for the poor guy. He gashed his head twice while maneuvering the hood — even drawing blood — and he had to go home once for tools he had left there.

He seemed distraught after finishing the job, so I offered him a beer. Before he even sat down, he began to reminisce about the good old days when he was in high school and worked for a gentleman farmer who raised and bred Black Angus cattle. He was animated as he talked.

I wanted not only to change the subject but to encourage him to leave, so I piped up, "John, you might want to grab a friend and see the new movie, *City Slickers*. It's about herding cattle on a ranch out west — right up your alley." I headed for the door, hoping he would follow.

He didn't. Instead, he blurted out, "I don't know anybody." Then he added softly, "Would you go with me?" Still feeling sorry for the guy, I agreed. We set a date and time for a month away. I was hoping he would forget by then. He didn't.

We went to see the movie *Mr. Roberts* in August. *Okay, one date,* I told myself. *I don't want to encourage this country boy who is clearly not my type.*

In September, however, I received an invitation to a wedding for November. It was addressed to me "and guest." It was going to be a first-class event, and I wanted to go. I hadn't met any single men at work, night school or the ball fields where my son played baseball. I doubted if "country boy" could even dance, but I asked.

"Yes, I can dance, and yes, I would like to go," he said eagerly, then added, "but I don't have anything appropriate for an occasion as 'dandy' as this. Would you go with me to pick something out?" *Would I? You bet!* I had visions of him dragging out a beige 1970s leisure suit for the occasion.

At the reception, as we hovered over the canapés next to a three-foot ice sculpture in the shape of Cupid, John turned to me and asked, "Wanna dance?" I placed my plate of shrimp tails on a nearby tray and followed him to the dance floor. The navy blazer, taupe slacks, striped shirt and patterned tie we had picked out earlier gave John a "natty" image. Gone was the country boy.

I could smell the Perry Ellis cologne we had picked out together especially for the occasion. The longer the music played, the closer he held me. His palms were sweaty, and I thought I could feel his heart beating. Or… was it mine? Nah!

Six months later, I was admitted to the hospital, a victim of exhaustion. The doctors told me I was overloaded with responsibility. Too much work, too little play. I also needed to learn to set boundaries. The superwoman lifestyle had to go!

On the first Sunday after my hospital stay, I spied John's smiling face and 6'4"-inch frame at the back of the church. He was wearing the same clothes he wore the night of the big wedding. "Will you go to breakfast with me?" he asked sheepishly.

At the restaurant, before I could even pick up the menu, he took my hand in his. "If I contributed in any way to your collapse, I'm sorry. I didn't mean to. I just wanted to be with you," he whispered, and then added, "I would like to help make your life easier. Will you marry me?"

I did not hesitate. Beneath the T-shirt, gabardine work pants, Wolverine boots and country twang stood a man of substance — a loyal, responsible, kind man. He was right when he whispered, "You'll like me when you get to know me better. I wear well." Lucky for me, he was just my type.

— Rosemary Barkes —

47

I Almost Gave Up on Romance

First romance, first love, is something so special to all
of us, both emotionally and physically, that it touches
our lives and enriches them forever.
~Rosemary Roger

I t had been five years since my last real date. The post-divorce rebound taught me to be cautious, and looking online left me feeling empty, so I tried not to want a man in my life. Maybe I was better off single. Maybe the dogs, my most loyal companions, would be enough.

In January 2011, I promised myself I wouldn't look anymore, at least until my daughter graduated from high school in June.

Six months after I made that promise, on the Tuesday night after my daughter's graduation, I sat down at the computer in the hallway alcove. It had been another long day at work. My hands ached, and my eyes wanted to close as I scanned my in-box and then diverted to Facebook, hoping to relax.

A private message was waiting for me. I clicked the icon and stared at the name for several seconds as my weariness evaporated. My heart pounded as I read the message: *Greetings to you! After many years, I hope you are well. Take care and be safe!*

I looked at the name again, and then sat back from the computer. Could it really be him? My first love in high school? I took a deep breath. Maybe I was seeing things.

Like a skeptical jeweler studying a diamond, I moved closer and read the name again. I'd typed that name into the computer a few times, but gave up after seeing how many people had the same name as my first love. And besides, I was the one who wrote to him last in 1972, so it was his turn. Now, in 2011, he was finally getting back to me with this simple message that made my heart feel like it was going to leap out of my chest.

David was a good guy when we dated in high school, but so much time had gone by. A person can change a lot in thirty-nine years. But the timing was too much to ignore.

Wow! It's so nice to get your message! I typed, and then added a little about sweet memories and high-school friends. I sent him a friend request, figuring he was still far away. If he turned out to be a jerk, I could simply unfriend him.

As we progressed from Facebook to phone calls, David didn't sound like a jerk at all. He sounded very interesting. He worked as a firefighter/EMT in Connecticut, and he had three dogs. He talked about his dogs like they were family. Beep, his ten-year-old Australian Shepherd mix, couldn't climb the stairs anymore.

"Yep, I carry the old girl upstairs to the bedroom every night," David told me.

My heart wanted to melt, and my toes tingled at the image of him carrying his old dog upstairs at bedtime. "Must love dogs" had been on the top of my list, the one I made in case I ever decided to take a chance on love again. As David and I talked on the phone, a tiny ember of hope — almost forgotten after so many years — glowed in my heart.

Still, I kept reminding myself to stay grounded, to keep my ears open and my brain fully engaged. I asked a lot of questions, and he didn't mind answering them. "Nothing's off the table," he told me.

One night, David had a question of his own. He asked me what I was doing on Friday, July 15th. He said he had some time off that weekend and wanted to take me out to dinner. I was hesitant. Talking on the phone was one thing, but...

"Are you still there?" he asked.

"You want to come all the way from Connecticut to North Carolina just to have dinner with me?"

"Yep, with one catch."

"What's the catch?" I tried to sound businesslike.

"I'd like to spend time with you on Saturday, to sit and talk, to find out what has brought you to this point in your life."

I had to take the chance. I agreed. It was a date.

And a wonderful date it was! We ate dinner at a cozy restaurant near the river. As David talked about his career and the lessons he had learned, I realized he had become a man of integrity. After dinner, we walked along the riverfront, and then sat on a bench to watch the golden sunset. I leaned back against him and let his strong arms hold me gently. The natural scent of his skin, which must have imprinted itself on my teenaged brain, was intoxicating. His kiss awakened feelings I had not felt in a long time.

David was a perfect gentleman on our first date, and on all the dates thereafter. He flew down from Connecticut about once a month, and I flew up to meet his friends and family, including the dogs. We talked on the phone every night between visits, asking questions, giving honest answers, and sharing our hopes and dreams.

On December 9th, three days before my birthday, David joined me on a church outing to Brookgreen Gardens in South Carolina. After dinner, we strolled under the live oaks lining the walkway. Twinkling lights and luminaries transformed the gardens into a land of magic as musicians played holiday melodies on flutes and violins.

We meandered to a path less traveled near the back corner of the gardens where white globes on poles stood like giant lollipops.

"What do you want your future to look like?" David asked.

"I want you to be in my future," I smiled, wondering what he might have in mind.

"I want you in my future, too," he said.

We stopped to gaze at the moon, and then David turned to face me. I looked up into his blue-grey eyes and noticed the moonlight gleaming silver on his hair.

"Will you marry me?"

"Yes," I answered without hesitation, and then added on impulse, "but you have to get down on one knee."

"Do you want me to ask you again?"

"Yes."

He looked around. No one was watching except the moon. David granted my request and asked again, "Will you marry me?"

"Yes!" I laughed. "Of course, I will!"

One year later, after I'd almost given up on romance, I married my first love, my last love, the love of my life.

— JoAnne Macco —

48

Falling in Love Again — Maybe

*You didn't date someone to change him. You dated him
because you wanted him for the way he was.
Flaws and fears and all.*
~Jean Oram, Whiskey & Gumdrops

have a date tonight. It's the first date I've had in five years. A friend has arranged a blind date for me and her neighbor. Fred and I haven't met, but we've talked on the phone twice, and he sounds nice. We both lost our mates years ago.

I thought dating was hard when I was sixteen. I had no idea I'd be dating in my sixties, and it would be a hundred times worse. Every insecurity, doubt and anxiety is magnified.

The body I have now is nothing like the body I had when I was young. I have wrinkles, spots, lumps, bumps and stretch marks from bearing four children. I have scars from accidents and surgeries. I wear bifocals, and I'm thirty pounds overweight. If I laugh or sneeze, I have leakage problems.

Fortunately, the men haven't aged any better. They have potbellies; they are bald; they wear bifocals. Many have had surgery for various reasons. Some have pacemakers, and some have erectile dysfunction. Many can't drive after dark because they have poor night vision, so they can only have daytime dates.

We may look like the walking wounded, but we are survivors.

We might be old on the outside, but we are still sixteen on the inside, and still looking for true love. We still get butterflies over the first date, first touch, or first kiss.

I don't pretend to be anything other than the age I am, and I dress the way I feel is appropriate for my age. I don't want to go skydiving or skiing on a date; I might break my hip. I enjoy having a nice dinner and watching television. There's nothing wrong with being "comfortable."

If I invite a date to my house for dinner, I have to make sure I cook something safe: roast beef or chicken, nothing too spicy or with dairy that might cause him problems. I hide all my medication out of sight; my health is not something I want to discuss on a first date. I keep my calendar in my desk so it doesn't advertise my doctor and dentist appointments. I keep my photos of my kids and grandkids in my bedroom. Potential boyfriends don't see my children and grand-children as "cute"; they might see them as potential dependents if we ever get married.

If we fall in love, we have to think about our grown children and how they will react to their parents dating "at their age"! His children might think I'm a gold digger. My children might think he is looking for a nurse or a purse — someone to either take care of him or support him. Grown children worry if their parents remarry later in life because they might lose the inheritance they've been counting on. It could all go to this stranger, this intruder into their family circle. Most of us don't have much, but our children expect to inherit whatever there is.

We haven't lived this long without getting hurt, having our hearts broken, losing loved ones, and facing disasters, even death. Maybe these things make us softer, more patient, kind and gentle. We no longer expect people to be perfect.

So we keep trying. We keep looking for love in our sixties and seventies with the same hope and excitement we had when we had a date for the senior prom over fifty years ago.

I go outside and then come back inside as if I were a stranger. Does my house smell nice, or does it have the "old people" smell of BENGAY, bath powder and disinfectants? Everything is clean and uncluttered. It is welcoming and comfortable. The lights are low, but not so low he'll trip over the furniture. I wear a nice outfit, not too dressy, not too casual. I want him to feel I've dressed up for him and made an effort. I put out three different DVDs so we can watch a western, a mystery, or a comedy after dinner — his choice.

Yes, I've prepared my house, cooked dinner, and dressed up. I'm ready. This could be a pleasant evening with a new friend, or it could be the first date with the great love of my life.

I look at the clock, and it is 7:00 sharp. He should be here. I peek out my window and see a man pacing back and forth on the sidewalk. He opens a roll of breath mints and puts one in his mouth. He sucks in his stomach and holds his breath for just a few seconds, and then shrugs and lets out his breath. His stomach goes back to normal. He's carrying a bouquet of mixed flowers wrapped in the same purple tissue paper as the flowers sold at the convenience store on the corner. He's picking at the price tag on the paper and finally tears it off. He's nervous, and I find it endearing. He finally gathers his courage and starts up the sidewalk.

There's a knock on the door, and I open it. Fred is short and bald. He wears bifocals, has a potbelly, and is wearing khaki pants and a red plaid flannel shirt. He has a wonderful smile.

He's perfect.

— Kate White —

49

Chicken Soup for the Soul

Twice in a Lifetime

The past is behind us, love is in front
and all around us.
~Emme Woodhull-Bäche

"All our efforts to save him failed." A faceless doctor's words echoed in my head, as I sank to the emergency room floor in total disbelief. My fifty-six-year-old husband, Sid — my soulmate for almost thirty-eight years, was dead from a sudden heart attack.

After the shock of his death wore off, I struggled with the many stages of grief, including depression, anger and confusion. Grief counseling helped tremendously, particularly with issues that were so unexpected, like happiness guilt.

When I then met and fell in love with Tom, I was elated and confused at the same time. How could I love someone other than Sid? I felt like a cheating wife. My head told me that Sid would want me to be happy again, but getting my heart to accept that fact took a lot of time and work on my part.

One of the things that helped me deal with those guilty feelings was the realization that I was really a lucky woman. Many people never find true love once in a lifetime, yet I loved and was loved by two wonderful, very different men. Sid was perfect for the young, naïve, teenage bride, and Tom was right for the sixty-year-old more confident, independent woman I had become since my husband's untimely death.

Almost two years after Sid died, Tom and I visited his grave. I was in the arms of one man I loved, sobbing over another man I also loved. But oddly enough, it did not feel strange. And as we sat there, total peace began to surround me. I was comforted by Tom's loving embrace, but it was more than that.

That chilly November day, the wind was as cold as the large concrete bench that stately guarded the family plot. Suddenly a gentle warm breeze kissed my face and caressed my hair. I knew it was Sid telling me he was happy for me, and that he was with me — just a smile away. My heart would always hold those wonderful memories of love from the past. But also I had enough love in my heart to give to someone new. I felt the last remnants of happiness guilt float away, and I imagined those feelings assimilating into the fluffy clouds above us.

I sighed and rested my head on Tom's shoulder. "How blessed I am," I said. "I found true love twice in a lifetime."

— Melinda Richarz Lyons —

New Adventures

50

The Muscle Car

*Here's to freedom, cheers to art. Here's to having an
excellent adventure and may the stopping never start.*
~Jason Mraz

I have been married for forty-six years. People ask, "How do you
and Bob do it?" There are the obvious answers — trust, consid-
eration, honesty, patience and respect. But mostly, I think it's
because we have taken advantage of some unexpected opportunities and just had fun. Recently, for example, our relationship was
enhanced by an automobile accident when my car was "crunched"
by an attendant at a "free" valet service. I decided to rent a car for five
days — a Camaro.

We had, of course, heard about them since they came out. My
sister had a green '72 Camaro and loved it. My daughter always wanted
one with the flame effect — she never got it. I asked Enterprise if there
was a black one with red flames trimmed with gold on the hood, but
they said that was a little high-end for them. So I took a 2015 black
Camaro — a bit more subdued, but we liked it.

We were driving "the car of youthful dreams." I knew it was going
to be fun the first time I stepped on the gas. We seemed to explode
down the road.

What did we think of it? Well, first Bob and I had to get in it and
we were not sure we could. Both septuagenarians, we've lost lots of
flexibility, but we were ready for an adventure.

The roof was low, the seats narrow, and windows so long and

slender they seemed almost non-existent. Eventually we learned to enter it by simultaneously bending, swinging, and dropping. We got pretty good at it.

Vision from the interior was difficult, but the mirrors were terrific and so were the large doors. Closing them needed someone with seven-foot long arms, but nothing is perfect. By driving fast, we managed to look almost like we belonged in a Camaro. By the time admiring observers realized how old we were, we were gone.

San Diego County is about the size of Connecticut. Its mountains, over 6,000 feet high, are just forty-five miles from the silvery beaches of Coronado and La Jolla. We tried to cover as much of the county as we could.

On our first day, Bob and I drove up to Julian, a charming nineteenth-century gold mining town. The mountain road wound past pine and oak trees, boulders, fields, and cattle, all a blur as the tires clung to the curves in our "muscle car." The motor's roar was rich and low, the sound of strength; the pipes in back rumbled, pushing the vehicle forward with a surge of speed reminiscent of a black jaguar lunging at prey.

We strolled Julian's wooden walks and dirt paths on the side of the main street. There are no large grocery stores, no fast-food places, and only one service station; but it is crammed with restaurants and a wide variety of small stores for shopping. We selected Romano's, a longtime center for Italian food and community get-togethers.

On the way home, as the shadows lengthened in the afternoon's setting sun, we reflected on the variety and beauty of the valleys and mountains. The car hugged the road as we made our way to Interstate 8 and home. Our first adventure was over; but we were not finished.

We drove all week — the mountains; La Jolla with its tricky traffic; downtown San Diego. We toured, we shopped, we visited renowned restaurants.

There was the fun, excitement, and challenge that two elderly, long-married people can have but seldom do. There are always routines and schedules, but there are also new opportunities. When those opportunities arise, take them — at any age.

The long-term advantage Bob and I gained from that Camaro? We did not argue or bicker once during that week — even as Bob gave me vague and dubious directions through the mid-day crowded downtown traffic. As long as you are active and curious, and have a good sense of humor, you are not too old to speed down life's highway. We enjoyed each other as much as we did that Camaro.

— Janet Bower —

51

Trading Houses

You don't have to be rich to travel well.
~Eugene Fodor

When I tell people that my husband and I are able to travel so much by trading houses with strangers, I usually get one of two reactions: "Wow! I want to try that!" or "Ew! You let people you don't know sleep in your bed?" House trading is not for everyone; it takes a certain adventurous spirit, flexibility, and a bit of faith in humanity, but we've found that taking that leap of faith has been well worth it, both in expanding our travel options and opening us to new experiences.

My husband retired early, and I work part-time as a freelance editor. This gives us lots of time and flexibility but not a lot of funds. And while we have happily chosen free time over money, we do love to travel, and travel is usually expensive. Still, we've managed to take a lot of affordable trips, and the best way we've found to keep the cost down is by house trading.

House trading is not the same as Airbnb or renting out a room in someone's home; house trading involves no exchange of money. We connect with people in cities we want to visit who are looking to visit our area — and then we trade! While there are businesses that facilitate house trading, such as Homeexchange.com, made popular by the 2006 film *The Holiday*, and HomeLink, which has been in operation since 1953, we've found all our trades through craigslist's "housing swap" category or through friends of friends.

There are, of course, commonsense precautions you should take before handing over your house keys (and sometimes car keys) to virtual strangers, but we've had more than fifteen successful trades so far. After the initial contact through craigslist (we post an ad both in our area and in the area we want to visit, and we also browse those areas to look at other people's ads), we exchange photos and e-mails with our potential trade partners. If both parties feel comfortable (a lot of it is just gut feelings for me), and we come up with dates that work for both, we'll move on to a phone call or two to work out the details, such as how we'll exchange keys.

We've found a whole range of trade partner styles — from the young couple who left the keys to their San Francisco apartment in their mailbox for us along with a note that said "Enjoy!" to the family who provided us with a three-ring binder full of information. I admit that I fall more into the "binder" category. Along with where to find things in the house, I include maps, tourist brochures, and menus from nearby restaurants. While it's fun to stumble onto new places on your own, it is even more fun to have an "insider" tip about the little taco place around the corner or the pop-up ice cream vendor who shows up at the park on weekend afternoons.

With no money involved, house traders feel more like guests in each other's homes. My husband and I are generally relaxed about people using our things, and we just assume our trade partners will treat our belongings as well as we'll treat theirs. Staying in someone else's home creates a certain intimacy. I always enjoy looking at our trade partners' artwork and décor, the books on their bookshelves, and the pictures on the fridge. By the end of our visit, I feel as if I know these former strangers pretty well. We've been lucky enough to find some trade partners to do multiple trades with, and they have truly become new friends. On our very first trade, our trade partner welcomed us with a bottle of wine and a cheese platter in the fridge. We've continued that gracious tradition with our own "guests."

The best part of trading houses, besides the savings, is being able to experience a new city more like a resident than a tourist. Having a kitchen means we can do a lot of our own cooking, shopping at a local market for groceries. We often find a favorite coffee shop nearby, and it quickly becomes "ours" with repeat visits. We find that when we slow down and enjoy the new atmosphere, we begin to feel the unique rhythm of the city or town we're visiting. We are happy to spend a lazy morning on the patio reading the paper, not feeling that we have to rush to see the major attractions.

Yes, house trading did begin with our desire to travel on the cheap, but it's become so much more than just a way to save money. It's thrown us smack dab in the middle of the true sharing economy, reinforced our faith in the goodness of people, let us get glimpses of places we might never have explored otherwise, and confirmed our decision to choose a lifestyle that values time over money. We all learned to share by the time we were in kindergarten, right? It's not too late to rediscover that basic lesson on a whole new level.

— Marjorie Woodall —

My Nights in a Tent

How glorious a greeting the sun gives the mountains!
~John Muir

nce a year my husband and I enter that storage unit most of us have called the "garage," to revisit all those treasures we thought we just couldn't live without. He wants to throw out those bottles I have saved for the day I might make flavored oils. I want to toss those small jars he saves for that oddball screw, nut and bolt. We anguish a little, laugh a lot, and end up pitching it all.

Then there's that shelf with all the camping gear we never use. The Coleman stove for wonderful outdoor cooking, the coffee pot for hot chocolate, the special toaster that fits on the grill, the sleeping bags, and of course the tent made for two.

My husband grew up camping. His stories are colorful and fun. They are fun to hear, but I think my allergies act up just listening to stories about being one with nature.

Every year I feel guilty as he scans the shelf, looking at it with such longing. I immediately start planning our next vacation to Europe, Hawaii, Mexico, a cruise… anything to take his mind off that tent.

For many years I've dodged the word camping. Last year the guilt finally set in. I poured a glass of wine, took a deep breath and told my husband I'd love to spend some time in a tent with him. You'd have thought we were going on an around-the-world cruise.

For me it was an "open to buy!" I went to the 99¢ Only Store and bought a plastic container, filling it with tablecloth, silverware, knives, pans, detergent, sponges, etc. All the things I thought I might need to set up housekeeping outdoors. I do love to cook so I filled the cooler with chops, steaks, sausages and all the wonderful foods I felt we needed for our camping trip my way… "gourmet."

The hours my husband spent planning our destinations was a treat in itself. I knew I had made the right decision. I hoped and prayed I'd made the right decision.

Our trip was to be two weeks: some camping, some hotels thrown in because I was such a "great wife," and then some more camping.

Living in California we headed for Las Vegas. We stayed the first night with friends and hit the casinos. That wasn't bad. I was going to like this. Then onto Utah! It was September and all the leaves were changing. It was so beautiful. My husband found a wonderful campsite near a lake and set up my kitchen. As I prepared pork chops for dinner he set up our tent. The lantern was hung from a tree near the stove and as I watched the bugs fly around that light all I could think of was "how many are falling into this food?" Dinner was just as he had described, with everything tasting better over an open fire. I made s'mores and felt young again. We spent the evening huddled close, sharing stories of our youth. That night, our first night in a tent, was COLD. But it's amazing how warm two bodies are when they are snuggled in a sleeping bag.

We went to Fort Bridger and Fort Casper in Wyoming. We wandered Deadwood, home of Calamity Jane and Wild Bill Hickok. We marveled at the wonder of Mount Rushmore. We saw the progress of the mountain carving of Crazy Horse. We traveled to Little Bighorn and onto Yellowstone. Old Faithful was faithful and the geysers were a sight from prehistoric times. We picnicked in the fields below the Grand Teton National Park. We even cowboy danced in Jackson Hole, Wyoming.

That shelf in the garage holds new meaning for me. It's no longer a shelf I'm longing to clean out, but a shelf I love to visit, even silently by myself.

And I truly love that tent!

— Kristine Byron —

A Suitcase and an Adventure

*All life is an experiment. The more
experiments you make, the better.*
~Ralph Waldo Emerson

Our lives had always revolved around our son Bailey's activities. In the early years of child raising, our social calendar consisted of birthday parties, soccer, and homework... so much homework! During Bailey's teen years, when *his* social life gave us our first taste of alone time, we added in dinner dates here and there, but since he was an only child, he seemed to go everywhere we went when it came to vacations. This was a choice we made on purpose as we loved to see and experience new things as a family.

Then Bailey left for college and a new type of adventure began....

George and I made a point of reinventing who we were as a couple. We said yes to adventure whenever the opportunity allowed. We began snow skiing again, hiking, and saying yes to things we hadn't tried before. We found places offering trivia games in the evening and had social dinner parties and barbecues with old and new friends. Our "we time" allowed us to get to know each other as a couple, not just parents, and remember why we married each other.

We took an amazing trip to the Grand Canyon where we hiked it, flew in a plane over it, river rafted down it, and even rode mules around the rim. What an adventure we had. We said yes to invitations for horse races, polo matches, weekend scavenger hunts in different cities, a trip to the Caribbean and the Bahamas.

Then COVID happened! Life as we knew it completely changed. Like so many, we had to create new excitement. Puzzles and board games became the norm on our dining-room table. We began planning our dinners and cooking together and spending evenings enjoying the back yard and hot tub.

As the gyms closed, we had to find a new way to exercise. The "positive" of COVID we discovered, for us anyway (I am sure the golfers disagreed), was that the beautiful golf course in our neighborhood was closed. Sad for golfers but a welcome opportunity for us to use the beautiful golf course as our daily walking trail. We purchased bikes and took evening rides around the empty town, often ending up at a park just to sit for a time and enjoy our surroundings and each other.

As things started to open up a bit we began discussing a new adventure. We put our house on the market and it sold in twelve hours.

"Now what?" we asked ourselves.

We had lived in the same house for many years and somehow over the course of those years every room and closet had filled with "things." There were things we didn't even know we had. There were others that had no rhyme or reason. I mean, who really needs a clown costume? I realized we had had that clown costume for more than ten years and not once had anyone worn it. And how about those holiday decorations that I bypassed each year because I really didn't like them? Why had I held onto them?

I had every single piece of artwork our son had made and every report card. Was he ever going to look at them? And why if he had not lived at home for five years was his closet still full of clothes, soccer cleats, paintball guns, etc?

You know those old-school photo developer envelopes that contain twenty photos but none you need to keep? After all, the one good one made it into a photo album years ago. But we hold onto all the rest of the photos plus the negatives. How about the twelve wallet-size photos that came with the one 5x7 you wanted from the school photographer?

Who even keeps photos in their wallet anymore?

I worried the trashman thought we had lost our minds as we threw away almost the entire contents of our house! Each night I attacked an area or box and found more and more stuff we didn't want. The kitchen appliances and items we got for our wedding twenty-eight years ago — how many times had we fondued? It began to sink in that all these possessions were owning us and not the other way around. A weight lifted with each cupboard or closet that we emptied. At times it was overwhelming, but as I found places to donate the items that I knew would be useful to others a sense of pride came over me.

The Humane Society came to pick up my towels and pillowcases. The new senior center was trying to build a library, so they were excited to take the many books I had accumulated. You know the ones I'm talking about — the ones that you read and planned to someday pass on to a friend.

Now here's where it gets interesting. I sold all our furniture, too — as much as possible to the buyers of the house, and the rest on Craigslist. By the time we were leaving, George and I were sleeping on the couch we had sold to the new people! Our bedroom set was gone already.

Why did I sell the furniture? Because after looking for a place to downsize into in our town, we realized we didn't need to live in our town anymore. Our son's in medical school; he didn't need to come home to this town. He would come home to us wherever we were during his limited vacation time.

I work as the Associate Publisher of Chicken Soup for the Soul from a home office, and George is a firefighter/engineer with shifts that span days on end. We can live anywhere within a few hours drive from his fire station in Southern California. So we decided to try something completely unpredictable. We rented an Airbnb for six months in Lake Havasu City, Arizona. And we put our few remaining possessions in storage and drove to Arizona with just our suitcases!

We have discovered walking waterside and watching the sunset, new outdoor-dining restaurants, and the fun of experiencing a new town and new state after living within the same area for our entire lives.

While I do not miss the possessions and house I left behind,

I admit I am a bit homesick for what was familiar. When George is here we have days of uninterrupted "we time" to explore and hike and enjoy winter in Arizona. The days when he's not around are the challenge, but I'm "stepping outside my comfort zone," experiencing "the joy of less," and "making me time," to quote three *Chicken Soup for the Soul* book titles!

I am glad we took the chance — it has shown there is nothing we can't do as long as we do it together. Our adventure and story is still unfolding, so stay tuned… I am sure it will provide a lot of Chicken Soup for the Soul material in the future.

— D'ette Corona —

54

Land of the Rising Sun

Grandmother-grandchild relationships are simple.
Grandmas are short on criticism and long on love.
~Author Unknown

"'ll take you to Europe when you graduate." I believed my granddaughter needed a bribe to stay in high school. "Choose three European cities and we'll visit them."

But Mariel wasn't interested in Europe. "Can't we go to Japan?" Her fantasy life sprang from the cartoon dramas of Japanese anime and manga. Her social life revolved around the anime club at school. Outfitted in goth mode of black and metal, accessorized with black hair, lipstick, and nails, she belonged to the international culture of alienated teens.

Japan wasn't high on my list of travel destinations in retirement — it wasn't on my list at all. But if it nudged Mariel closer to a high school diploma? "Sure, let's go to Japan."

Nearly six feet tall, overweight and depressed, my granddaughter's moods flowed from sullen to charming to hostile and back in a flash. Ridiculed and bullied at school — "Grandma, not a day goes by that someone doesn't call me retard or fat pig" — she put little faith in others.

When Mariel began disappearing from home or school for short but alarming periods, my daughter enrolled her in a boarding school for overweight teens where she lost sixty pounds and earned a high school diploma. At her graduation I sealed our bargain with a copy of Lonely Planet's guidebook to Japan.

Mariel found a steady job, took some courses at the local community college, and claimed to be teaching herself Japanese. We signed up with an Australian company whose Land of the Rising Sun tour and philosophy of responsible travel appealed to both of us. We would move around the country in a small, loosely organized group, use public transportation, and stay in locally owned inns. Because our itinerary called for only one night in Tokyo, we arranged for three more there on our own before joining the group.

As soon as our plans were firm my worrying started. Was I up to the task of escorting my unpredictable granddaughter to Japan? With departure a few days away, my therapist neighbor spoke up. "You seem uneasy about this trip. What's the worst that can happen over there?"

Jane's calm, therapeutic tone helped me find words for my fears. "Mariel will disappear and no one will find her." I told Jane I was dreading the trip. Japan, especially Tokyo, had become a labyrinth of blocked passageways through which I searched in vain for my granddaughter. Perhaps I'd feel better about things if I'd learned some Japanese. But it was too late now.

Jane suggested meditation might help restore calm — both before leaving and on the trip. I was skeptical but willing to try. When my yoga breathing became slow and relaxed she introduced a technique for letting go of stress. "Find the place in your body that harbors the emotion… visualize it in a bubble… let the bubble rise and evaporate into the universe."

Like spectators welcoming royalty, cherry trees in full bloom lined the tracks as our train sped from the airport into Tokyo. Fearing our timing made us too late for the show, Mariel slapped my hand in a high-five to celebrate our good fortune.

"Grandma, you know I'm not just interested in anime and manga, don't you?" But I didn't know. We roamed the grounds of the Imperial Palace, attended a Classic Noh Theatre performance, and scouted out "the best ramen restaurant in Tokyo." With practice and a few missteps, we built confidence in Tokyo's subway system, pronouncing it superior to New York's in every way. And when we joined the crush of costumed young people in Harajuku, the weekend gathering place of Tokyo's disaffected youth, I noticed that Mariel absorbed the flavors of the scene as an observer, rather than a cult follower.

Throughout our days alone in Tokyo my granddaughter cupped her Japanese phrasebook in the palm of her hand. After rehearsing a question or greeting under her breath, she scanned the surroundings for likely recipients. Shy around adults at home, she didn't hesitate approaching them here, where courteous replies and deferential bows rewarded her efforts. When we lost our way in search of the ramen restaurant in Tokyo, her language dexterity, not my map skills, rescued us. "Thanks for bringing me to Japan," I said.

It was Mariel's birthday the night we met our traveling companions: six Brits, four Aussies, and our group leader from Romania. When Kata asked what brought each of us to Japan, Mariel replied, "I've been interested in Japan for as long as I can remember. I like its history and culture and how everybody respects you here."

That night, from the tower of an office building, we looked over the lights of the city spread for miles in all directions. "Your Japanese is very good. Where did you study?" Kata asked Mariel. Learning she taught herself from books and computer programs without ever having a conversation with a Japanese speaker impressed Kata even more. "Most Japanese don't understand beginners, especially Americans. But your pronunciation is perfect."

My granddaughter had a gift for the Japanese language. No one deserved it more. The pride and joy I felt at her triumph was tinged with regret at not having believed such a moment possible.

Later that night, some of us dropped into an English pub to get better acquainted and to help Mariel celebrate her birthday. Gifts of alcohol soon filled the table in front of her. A tankard of beer and a Grey Goose martini competed for attention with plum wine and shots of shochu. When slurred speech and spasms of laughter aroused my protective instincts, I snapped, "Slow down!" Poised to deliver a lecture on the perils of mixing drinks, I was interrupted by Andrew, a father from England. "It's not your job to tell Mariel what to do. Leave that to us. Your job is Grandma. And you don't want to spoil the relationship."

Inhaling a deep yoga breath, I found the place in my body where fears still lingered… visualized them in a bubble… and let the bubble rise until it evaporated into the night sky over Tokyo.

— Ann Barnett —

55

Cheerio Parties

Few things are more delightful than
grandchildren fighting over your lap.
~Doug Larson

ur tiny house often rang with the laughter and occasional cries of our many grandchildren. They knew where Grandma kept the toys, books and their favourite snacks. The ones old enough to talk proclaimed the big old rocking chair as "Grandma's chair." They loved to curl up on my lap, often two or three at a time, for hugs and stories.

One day my daughter and her family stopped by. "Mom, will you keep the kids when I go to the hospital for this next baby?"

Without hesitation I replied, "Of course I will. No problem. That's what grandmas are for."

Several days later, my son and his family came for a visit. He asked, "Mom when it's time for our next baby's birth will you keep the other kids please?"

I looked at the calendar. The due dates were about three weeks apart, so without much hesitation I said, "Of course I will. Shouldn't be a problem. That's what grandmas are for."

I don't know what the odds are, but a few weeks later, within hours of each other, both my daughter and daughter-in-law were admitted to the hospital. Seven grandchildren aged one to six arrived at Grandma's for the promised sleepover, accompanied by what seemed to be a truckload of necessities. Piles of winter clothing littered the floor close to the front door. Bottles and sippy cups competed for room in the fridge. Diapers and clothes were stashed in the spare room while special blankets dragged behind children as they emptied the toy box and bookshelf looking for their favourite things at Grandma's house.

My youngest daughter surveyed the busy atmosphere and clutter of the house when she arrived home from school. Her face betrayed a mixture of excitement and being overwhelmed. I phoned Grandpa and warned him of the hopefully imminent birth of not one but two new grandbabies and he arrived home from work with supper in hand.

The evening passed in a blur of activity. Bedtime routines were anything but routine when I needed to change a one-year-old, two two-year-olds and make sure the two three-year-olds went potty before going to bed. There were bottles and sippy cups to fill and lots of little ones all anxious to be cuddled by Grandma in that big old rocking chair. Finally quiet reigned.

After sleeping lightly, while listening all night for any grandchildren who might need me, I felt less than ready to face the new day when the alarm's incessant ringing filled my ears. But seven little ones in a tiny house do not sleep through an alarm. Our day began with a rush of activities. Grandpa needed to go to work. Auntie needed to be ready to get on the school bus at 8:00 and the five- and six-year-olds would be picked up by Great-Grandpa who had been enlisted as taxi driver for their ride to school. Hungry children demanded breakfast. I grabbed the Cheerio box from the cupboard knowing they could feed themselves this finger food. Sippy cups of milk were spill-proof — well almost anyway. I started making school lunches while urging the older ones to hurry.

Auntie grabbed the last couple of bites of breakfast and shoved them in her mouth to hunt for her parka and boots. She grabbed her stuff and rushed out the front door to the waiting school bus. Great-Grandpa arrived early. I left the five littlest ones in various stages of sogginess and mess to help the older ones sort through the pile of mittens, hats, scarves and parkas to find the matching sets I knew they had arrived with yesterday. Quickly running a comb through their hair and doing a cursory check of backpacks, I helped them bundle up to face the frigid winter weather. By the time they left for school the clock only read 8:30. I felt like a whirlwind had gone through the house. As I glanced around I noticed it looked that way as well.

I took time to put away the milk and stack the dishes into the sink for later. Five little ones needed changing, clothes on, and their hair brushed. While changing the diapers and Pull-Ups I noticed that something — a diaper, sippy cup or bottle — had leaked during the night. I pulled the sheet from bed to throw in the wash and quickly grabbed a clean sheet from the cupboard. Might as well get it ready for naptime, as if anyone would want a nap other than Grandma. Finally I threaded my way through grandchildren, scattered toys and diaper bags to sit down for a moment or two. I smiled as I watched these precious little ones play contentedly side-by-side on the living room floor. I grabbed the ever-present camera and captured this priceless moment to share with their parents. Peace and quiet, at least for a moment or two, filled the house. I took advantage of it for a quick bathroom break of my own.

I shut the door. Within seconds silence greeted me with the intensity that could only spell trouble. No one called for me or demanded their turn for the bathroom. No sounds of fighting, crying or even playing noises sounded from the other side of the door. I quickly washed my hands and dried them as I opened the door, wondering what disaster would greet me. Abandoned toys littered the floor of the living room but not one of the five grandchildren could be seen.

In the spare room I saw my three-year-old grandson squeezed into the now empty little toy box. With his cousin's little Mickey Mouse hat perched on top of his head like a crown, he surveyed the kingdom of toys spread before him. When he looked up at me a grin lit up his entire face. Being a dutiful grandma I smiled, grabbed my camera and snapped a few photos before searching for my granddaughters.

Camera still in hand, I headed to the only other place they could be — the kitchen. The three-year-old and two two-year-old girls sat nicely on chairs at the kitchen table. The one-year-old, with mischief glinting in her eyes, stood in the middle of the table. She reached into the Cheerio box that I had forgotten to put away and placed handfuls of cereal in front of the others before feeding herself. She looked up and a huge smile wreathed her face. Being a dutiful grandma I smiled and snapped a few photos prior to rescuing her off the table. None of them were too impressed when Grandma spoilt their Cheerio party by putting the box of cereal away.

The grandchildren stayed for a couple more days before those new babies arrived and were ready to go home. My house rang with laughter and an occasional tired cry. Looking after the grandchildren's practical needs was interspersed with lots of cuddles and story times in the big old rocking chair. We even had time for more Cheerio parties, Grandma's way. It all added to making memories together the way grandmas and grandchildren do.

— Carol Harrison —

Life Launch

*Twenty years from now you will
be more disappointed by the
things that you didn't do than
by the ones you did do.*
~Mark Twain

The kids grew up, moved away and left us in peace. Most evenings found us lying on separate couches in our living room. Television reflected crime scenes onto our skin, contrasting with our predictable home life. I'd fall asleep during the commercials and eventually stumble to bed with a book — where I'd fall asleep again.

We were snoozing ourselves into oblivion, and I feared this would continue. Our headstone might read, "Here lie the Paxtons — bored to death in the 21st Century."

How do you fix a dull life? We'd talked about driving Route 66, backpacking the wilderness, navigating coastal waters. All just talk. Secretly I wondered if we'd ever do anything exciting again.

Then, within a couple of months, life as we knew it changed. Denny's dad passed away, and our beloved fox terrier died of a mysterious ailment. Our daughter's young friend lost his life, and several of our peers had bouts with cancer. We turned sixty as our marriage turned forty. Alarmed, we noticed photos of people our age moving into the obits, and we launched a series of conversations about life's brevity.

As time slithered away, we revisited an old pipe dream and decided to buy a used boat. Experts recommended thirty-six to forty-two feet — a stretch for us kayakers — but comfortable for long trips or living aboard. In case a thirty-foot increase in boat length and twin diesel engines were not enough challenge, we acquired a puppy that needed to learn the art of polite peeing on a live-aboard boat.

Now, erase the picture in your mind of a trim sixty-year-old couple wearing captain caps, perched at the upper helm on an aqua sea. They maneuver neatly into a tropical port where dockworkers rush to gather the lines.

No, it looked more like this: "What if she refuses to pee on the boat?" asks the captain.

"I don't know," the first mate answers, not feeling seaworthy. "Heaven forbid she does her jobs everywhere, and it gets all stinky and such."

First things first, we began pee pad training at home before acquiring a trawler. Puppy Smalls refused to pee on the pad. A determined sailor, I fenced in the pad and offered it at desperate moments. Success!

So began our thrilling future. Captain Paxton scoured the web for used trawlers. I scribbled numbers on tablets, wondering how long our pensions, semi-retirement jobs and pieces of our children's inheritance could fund our dream. I had calculated one to ten years, just as my captain presented a list of twenty-five trawlers. We planned a Florida boat-hunt road trip.

Only our imaginations, our checkbook, and questionable sanity limited us. We departed the couches for west central Florida. We toured boats hugging the Gulf of Mexico, crossed the skinny state, and then boarded a string of trawlers in rivers along the Atlantic.

Stories flowed from vagabonds who had lived their sea dreams, elderly sailors now selling their dream vessels to new dreamers. "We lived aboard ten years," said one aging captain. "They were the best-lived years of our marriage. My wife is ill now." A tear glistened in his eye as we dabbed at ours.

We discovered our own love-boat with a brokerage in Fort Pierce and made an offer.

What next? Will we still work? How will we operate this thing?

We would make it up as we went.

Back on our Iowa couches, excitement lit our faces. "This was the best trip I've ever had!" I said. "I don't even care if we buy the boat."

A month later, we e-mailed an offer and counter offers, arrived at a price and headed back to Florida, where a professional boat surveyor would inspect our vessel. Then we'd hand over the money, fix small issues and sail away.

After survey day and a glorious cruise on a turquoise river, I lay coiled in fetal position on our El Cheap-o Motel bed. "I'm so sorry I killed our dream!" I wailed between sobs. I felt I'd just inspected a different boat — or the same boat through different eyes. Whichever it was, our love boat no longer looked like a place I'd love to live for nine months while navigating the intracoastal waterways. The surveyor detected my angst and counseled us.

"You don't have to buy this boat. If you see deficiencies you missed before, either counter offer and have the items fixed, or withdraw your offer," said the surveyor, my new hero.

We countered. The seller declined. End of pipe dream or nightmare. End of story.

Or so we thought. After a week of whining, we resumed our quest, navigating from couch to deck so we could enjoy the sunset. Each evening, we shifted puppy and books from lap to lap as we sailed through basic boating courses. Within another week, Captain Paxton presented a new list of old trawlers and a fresh road trip itinerary.

This time we started in Baltimore and drove down the East Coast, hoping past experience would help us find a sounder vessel at a better price, and it did.

Terrapin is a classy 1984 with solid mechanics, teak interior, and expansive deck. Our dream boat bobs happily in a slip at New Bern, North Carolina. This unplanned location suits us. We will stay six months or a year to enjoy the Crystal Coast and to sharpen our seamanship skills.

Back in Iowa for Christmas, our grown kids surprised us with a pirate-themed treasure hunt. At one point we were blindfolded, our hands tied together, using our feet to pull a line with a clue up a flight of stairs. Minutes later we lay on our frozen deck, fashioning a hook from a paper clip; we tied it to sewing thread and pulled a clue basket up from the snowdrift below. In the barn we uncovered a wooden chest of boating supplies Our captors made us down a shot of rum and sing a sea shanty.

Today, from the windows of our floating home, we have new perspective in a watery world. Our brains exercise as we explore new plumbing, new knots, and new docking maneuvers. We conquer cooking challenges in a tiny galley. Our boating community regales us with stories collected from smooth and stormy voyages. We soak it all up as we form new friendships over glasses of wine.

Adventures beckon: a trip to the pump-out station, a dinner cruise to a neighboring town, a trip to the Outer Banks. The Great Loop. The Bahamas.

As I type, Smalls slumbers on a couch in the salon. She's exhausted from a romp with Hank, her doggy pal from Dock C. Soon she will awaken and make the rounds on her floating doghouse, stern to bow. Smalls embraces her new-and-uncertain life with a vengeance. We hope to follow her lead.

— Kristi Paxton —

57

Run

Continuity gives us roots; change gives us branches,
letting us stretch and grow and reach new heights.
~Pauline R. Kezer

kay, so I would never jump out of an airplane. How could I ever trust that a piece of fabric with a million strings coming out of it wouldn't get tangled up and fail to work? I have plenty of friends who have done it, but I won't.

But I'm all for doing new and scary things, especially as I get older, because I recognize the value of saying "yes" and ensuring that my world doesn't get narrower and narrower. And I've been inspired by all the Chicken Soup for the Soul stories that I've read by people who were advancing in years and made a special effort to try new things. So last year, when I was facing the prospect of turning sixty, a truly surprising development, I renewed my commitment to trying new things, including the *scary* ones.

And that's how I found myself standing at the top of a 1,000-foot cliff in Oman, on my way to a beautiful beach resort on the Persian Gulf.

You might think that taking a beach vacation on the Persian Gulf was enough of a "step outside your comfort zone" experience, but *that* was easy. It was gorgeous and luxurious and they picked us up at the airport in Dubai and took care of getting us across the border into Oman. Oman is a beautiful country on the Arabian Peninsula, known for its craggy sandstone mountains that plummet right down to the sea. It's very dramatic to see those tall mountains with sheer cliffs right next to the water, occasionally with beaches running along the edge of the sea.

The challenging part was the approach to the resort, which is so remote that you have three choices for the last part of the trip: 1) arrive by speedboat; 2) drive down a narrow, winding mountain road with hairpin turns and no guardrails; or, 3) jump off that 1,000-foot-high mountain cliff and paraglide down to the beach. According to tripadvisor.com, the really cool guests paraglide in.

I decided, that as a very cool fifty-nine-year-old, I would paraglide down to the beach. I imagined some kind of fixed wing thing, like bird wings. That made aerodynamic sense to me. Wings that were already in place would be guaranteed to work—not like parachuting out of an airplane where the fabric might somehow *not* get itself organized into the right shape, or the strings might get tangled up.

So I was shocked when they were putting the harness on me and I turned around and saw a flimsy piece of fabric lying on the ground behind me—with lots of strings attached to it. That was when I realized that *para*gliding is *called* that because you use a *para*chute. For someone who specializes in words and clear language, I had truly been off my game!

But I didn't have much time to think about it because they were already strapping me in. Then they stuck a helmet on me. I don't know *what* they said this was for, but whatever they were saying, what I *heard* was: *to identify the body*. And then they told me that it was critically important that I run toward the cliff and absolutely not stop under any circumstances. Because if I didn't run right off the cliff, the flimsy piece of fabric with the one million strings wouldn't catch the air and I would plummet to my death.

Before I could change my mind the guide and I were running toward the edge of the cliff. And then, miraculously, that parachute filled with air and we were soaring, riding the air currents and flying even higher than where we had started. The guide was thrilled that the air currents were so strong, and that we could stay up an extra long time. Of course, I was only half enjoying it, because the other half of my brain was trying to remember what "wind shear" was and whether that was relevant. If the winds changed, could we just drop like a rock?

Nevertheless, we soared for fifteen minutes and then, finally, we flew lower and lower until we put our legs out and ran to a stop on the beach. *Mission accomplished, time for a stiff drink, and I never have to do that again!*

But it was empowering, and I'm so glad that I did it. I've tried plenty of other less scary things since then, because now I compare everything to paragliding. If I can run off a cliff in Oman, I can certainly ride a roller coaster back here in the States, or be a keynote speaker at a conference, or try a new kind of food. Everything seems possible now. And sixty doesn't feel quite as old as I feared.

— Amy Newmark —

58

Westward Ho

There is something about the presence of a cat... that
seems to take the bite out of being alone.
~Louis J. Camuti

started second-guessing myself as I drove into the evening in my dusty car. What the heck was I thinking dragging Libby across the country? After eight weary hours of driving, we had completed the first leg of the "Big Adventure," from Orlando, Florida, to the quaint, little town of Monroeville, Alabama. We were westward bound, exploring as many states as possible along the way.

One middle-aged lady in a Subaru with a cat.

I had settled into a lazy life of retirement at age fifty-six. Ten years after officially retiring as a Detective Police Sergeant, I had an epiphany. I was not living my Best Life. My whole purpose in retiring at such a young age was to travel. I wanted to explore foreign countries in far-flung places. I dreamed of road tripping the entire United States. National Park Geek would be my new nickname. It was time for a major life change, or I would be too old, too infirm, or just too afraid to do it.

I sold my townhome at market peak and paid off all my bills. It was now or never. I got rid of loads of junk and put my "must keeps" into storage. My two faithful dog companions had passed away within months of each other, so I could hit the proverbial road. No current relationships. No responsibilities. Nothing should hold me back. Oh, wait, I had been talked into adopting a skinny black-and-white kitten named Libby. Flash forward three years to a full-grown, sassy boss of a cat. How could I leave her for two months?

My sister said, "If you leave her with me, you will not get her back." Well, that was not an option. It was currently hip to travel with a dog everywhere — to the grocery store, public library, or even the doctor's office — so why not a petite, sweet feline as a trusted companion?

On the first night of our journey, anxiety flooded through my body as I lay on the hotel bed. I was exhausted from driving. It was a challenge carrying Libby's litter box and my overpacked suitcase to our room. I knew it would be the first night of many. *What if there were stairs?* I told myself. *Maybe we should just drive back to Florida and hang out by my sister's pool.* I asked Libby in a shaky voice, "Should we turn around and go home? What do you think?" Her response was a cool, green-eyed stare. The Queen had her own comfy, giant hotel bed. She was not going anywhere. I decided I would reassess in the morning.

The arrival of a new day ended all that paralyzing fear. Life was once again full of endless possibilities.

Away we went checking off items on our "must-visit list." There were national parks to explore, local delicacies to try, and delightful independent bookstores to visit. Libby settled in quite nicely. I had bought a giant Pet Tube that fit the entire back seat of my Subaru. It was a cylindrical, deluxe cat house fit for the Queen.

Each new stop was a plethora of weird smells and odd spaces to pad around. Hotel room windows became Libby's favorite perching spots. She startled a couple of young cleaners in a fancy bed-and-breakfast in Mississippi, who thought she was a cute stuffed animal until she skittered under the bed. She made many friends along the way, including vacation rental owners, pet-friendly hotel concierges, and delighted children looking for a break from long backseat travels. It was a toss-up as to whether people thought I was cool bringing my cat along on my big trek or a "Crazy Cat Lady." One of the best things about this trip was it taught me not to care about what people think.

Many times, self-doubt would creep back in, especially when we made it to Utah and I realized that I was more than 2,000 miles from home. Now we had to drive all the way back! I learned to focus on one day at a time, to live in the moment. Each morning brought fresh, new adventures. This was a trip of a lifetime, and I was doing it all by myself. Libby was the best of company; I never felt truly alone. She was my backseat driver, cuddle buddy and best friend. She was a trooper. If she could persevere through the insecurities of what came next, then I could, too.

We drove through majestic scenery that took my breath away. We traveled switchback roads through snowy mountains and dusty deserts where my palms sweated and my knuckles turned white. In many places, we lost our GPS and cell-phone reception. During these times, I would tell Libby, "We've got this, girl!" I'd receive a meow of approval from the back seat. Each new challenge made me feel strong, independent and resourceful.

Libby and I were on the road for forty-seven days. We traveled 8,443 miles through thirteen states. We explored five national parks, an ice cave, a volcano, and the birthplaces of Harper Lee and Elvis. We drove on Historic Route 66 and made side trips to funky museums. A sing-along with a trio of handsome mariachis was an unexpected highlight in Albuquerque, New Mexico. I got lost hiking in Sedona, Arizona for three hours on a trail misnamed "EASY BREEZY." I had no water or map but I never even considered panicking. I knew I had to survive and get back to Libby, who was window napping in our pricy, pet-friendly hotel.

Whenever my anxiety reared its ugly head, I would encounter friendly fellow travelers who shared experiences and tips for the road. In Bryce Canyon, Utah, a retired nurse gave me her spare pair of hiking boots because my worn-out sneakers were not cutting it through the snowy, rocky terrain.

With each leg of the journey, my self-confidence grew steadily. Yes, I could have made this fantastic trip all by myself, but it was so much better with Libby, my steadfast companion.

— Lori Shepard —

A Sticky Situation

Grandfathers are magicians who create wonderful
memories for their grandchildren.
~Author Unknown

Both of my parents worked full-time — my mother as a nurse and my father as a state cop. Sometimes, they worked the same shifts, which caused issues in the summer when we were out of school. My grandfather often stepped up and took us for those full days.

We never really knew what adventure lay before us at Grandpa's. It could be fishing in ponds we didn't have permission to be at. Or he could hand us each a $10 bill and take us shopping at the mall. Or we might hang around his place, the basement or garage that held so many interesting trinkets. The options were endless.

One day, Grandpa loaded the three of us into his Ford Escort hatchback, the ugliest yellowish-beige color you ever did see. I had never seen a car that color before, nor have I since. I have no recollection of where we were headed, nor do I know if we had a set destination in mind. All I remember was that the three of us were loaded up with Grandpa, and we were headed toward Broadway.

I remember coming up to 34th Street. Grandpa talked about gum and asked if any of us wanted some. My grandfather was the Gum King and always had multiple flavors stashed in his pockets. My sister, Charity, seated up front, took a package. Angie, my other sister, and I were in the back seat. We both voiced our desire to have

a piece, too. Grandpa turned around to hand us a package, and we were suddenly airborne!

Grandpa's Escort had climbed the curb. The passenger side was on the curb, and the driver's side was still planted firmly on the street.

My grandfather whirled back around and grabbed the wheel. I remember all of us, Grandpa included, screaming as we saw a SPEED LIMIT sign suddenly appear in the windshield. He only had moments to react. Just as quickly as we had gone up, we came crashing back down. We were headed back toward Broadway, miraculously avoiding a collision with a metal sign.

I remember Grandpa looking up in the rearview mirror at me and Angie as he said, "We'll hold off on the gum for a bit."

That right there would have been enough to call it a day, but we weren't through yet. We continued to travel up to Broadway and then turned to head east down the main road. We passed Casey Middle School and crossed the tracks approaching the stoplight that sat there. Grandpa turned around again, only for a moment, to pass back that ill-fated package of gum. I remember trying to reassure Grandpa that we could hold out until the stoplight, but Grandpa was not having it. His grandkids needed gum, and we were going to get it.

That's when we hit something. Something SOLID.

I looked up to see the Stan the Tire Man ad to my right. The woman in the ad was glaring down at us. And what was the solid thing in front of us? My grandpa had just hit a BUS! He calmly told us to "Stay put" and climbed out of the car. By this time, two men wearing cowboy hats had exited the bus and come to the back of the large vehicle. They approached my grandpa, and all three of them began talking. I watched from the back seat of the car, trying to get any of the conversation I could, but I couldn't hear anything. That's when my twin sister noticed something.

"Look!"

She pointed to the bus. The back window curtains parted a bit, and we saw someone looking out at everyone below. I could make out what appeared to be a female with long hair. A slight wave came from the window, and I watched my grandfather wave back. That's when I noticed something: a name ran across the back of the bus. It read… Loretta Lynn.

My grandfather had just rear-ended Loretta Lynn's tour bus!

I remember my grandpa shaking the men's hands and waving one final time at the window in the back of the bus. It appeared as if there was no damage to the bus and surprisingly no damage to grandpa's Escort. Grandpa opened the door to the car and slid in. He shut the door and then let out a long sigh. After a few moments of silence, he turned to all of us and smiled.

"So, who needed gum?" he asked, pulling out a package from the pocket of his shirt.

—Jeremy Mays—

Spontaneous Spirit

*I learned that courage was not the absence of fear, but
the triumph over it. The brave man is not he who does
not feel afraid, but he who conquers that fear.*
~Nelson Mandela

nyone going to an amusement park might have seen
the likes of me. I was the gray-haired lady with sensible
shoes. I held purses, cellphones and sunglasses while my
loved ones hurled themselves through space on roller
coasters. Afterward, flushed with excitement, they'd pose for selfies
to celebrate their latest flirtation with the Grim Reaper.

I admired their bravery, but refused to challenge my own limitations.
Sitting it out worked for me, and that's exactly what I had planned to
do on that pleasant spring morning twelve years ago.

To celebrate my husband's sixty-fifth birthday, we'd driven an hour
south to Skydive Miami in Homestead, Florida. As a young man in the
Army, Joe had logged hundreds of jumps with round parachutes, and
he wanted a closer look at the newer wing style. Watching those young
people swoosh in to a perfect, stand-up landing reignited memories
of his youth.

"Sure looks like fun," he hinted.

"Like the best birthday gift ever?"

His eyes twinkled with mischief. "Exactly like that."

"So much for the new tie," I laughed.

We high-fived and headed for the skydiving office. My mind was racing. I visualized Joe suited up on the tarmac. I would shoot video as the plane took off. Then I'd rush over to the drop zone to capture the landing.

Knowing my adrenaline-junkie husband, I wondered if this might become a recurring event. I saw our weekends planned out for the next few years. Joe would skydive while I took pictures. He would struggle to describe the sensation of flying, and my imagination would strain to fill in the gaps. If fear kept me sidelined, I'd never fully understand.

Not this time, I decided. I didn't want to hear about it. I wanted to see and feel it for myself. When he approached the sign-up window for an application, I squeezed his arm.

"Why not make it two?"

"You're kidding," he grinned. "You'd do that?"

"It's a once-in-a-lifetime offer. I want to share this with you."

Chuckling in disbelief, he held up two fingers. We filled out paperwork and signed liability releases. Joe paid extra for a video of my first jump.

After zipping ourselves into electric-blue jumpsuits, we filed into the training room. Using a mock-up of an airplane door, we learned to roll out, maintain a stable free-fall position, and lift our feet at landing. In the tiny, windowless classroom, everything seemed easy. I repeated the steps with my instructor, Pete. Joe beamed with pride at his remarkably confident wife. Our trainers dispensed altimeters, helmets and goggles, and strapped us into heavy black tandem harnesses. My videographer taped a pre-flight interview in which I laughed with ease.

When our flight was called, we boarded the small Caravan airplane where we sat cross-legged in pairs on the floor, instructors directly behind their students. Pete clipped his harness to mine as the plane roared down the runway. Through the clear, roll-up door, I watched the treetops fall away.

My stomach lurched as two realities hit me: This was actually happening, and I'd made a terrible mistake.

My mouth was dry as the Sahara, my palms sweaty. I couldn't do this. What was I thinking? I belonged on the ground taking pictures, not in the center of the action. I glanced at Joe, who was chatting away with his instructor. The animated look on his face did not calm my nerves. My husband was afraid of nothing. He'd done this hundreds of times without an experienced jumper strapped to his back. Crazy fool probably wanted to go solo.

At 13,500 feet, the jumpmaster gave a thumbs-up, and to my horror, the clear door slid up like a roll-top desk. This could not be right. Flying with an open door was dangerous! Didn't they realize someone could fall out?

Oh, yeah. That's why we were here.

On cue, Joe and his instructor shuffled like chain-gang prisoners toward the deadly aperture. I watched in disbelief as they nodded three times in unison and tumbled out. There are things in life we can prepare for, but seeing one's husband fall out of an airplane is not one of them. My heart was in my throat.

I was reeling with shock when Pete lifted me to my knees and nudged me toward the gaping hole. To steady myself, I clung to a metal bar overhead. Pete tried to pull my hands away, but I refused to let go of the one solid object between me and certain death.

As impatient jumpers piled up behind us, I realized I had a choice. I could refuse to jump and ride back with the pilot. I played it out quickly in my head. The waste of non-refundable money. Joe's face watching my instructor land without me. My shame at letting fear win out once again.

No way! That was not going to happen. I took a deep breath and released my death grip on the bar. Following our pre-flight instructions, I crossed my arms over my chest and arched my back. Pete rolled us out of the plane.

The sense of falling lasted only seconds until we achieved the welcome stability of terminal velocity. Pete tapped my shoulder, the signal to spread my arms like wings. Just as Joe had described, the wind resistance at 120 mph was so powerful, it felt like a cushion of air supporting us. The noise was deafening, and G-forces assaulted my face, making my smile feel more like a grimace. I remembered to make eye contact with the videographer flying directly in front of me, documenting my final moments for the next of kin. "Hi, Mom!" I mouthed, although in space, as they say, no one can hear you scream.

Pete checked his altimeter at about sixty seconds and then waved off the videographer. He reached back to deploy the parachute, and our free fall came to an abrupt end. Our bodies jackknifed from horizontal to vertical, legs flying out in front like two rag dolls as the harness held tight and the chute flared open. It was peaceful then. Quiet enough to talk. We drifted through the air like a giant butterfly. Pete pointed out landmarks on the horizon, and I admired the beautiful patchwork of the surrounding farmland. As we soared gently toward the earth, my only regret was that we couldn't stay up longer.

Skidding into the drop zone, I lifted my feet and let Pete nail the landing. When he uncoupled our gear, I ran into Joe's arms. Our celebratory embrace was captured by the videographer. The look of admiration on my husband's face said it all. On the way home, we both had stories to share.

Years later, reliving the memory still makes my heart race. When faced with an opportunity that scares me, I remember that open door on the airplane. "Why take a chance?" my doubting voice says. "Why jump out of a perfectly good airplane?"

"Because I can," my adventurous voice replies. It's my choice — sit it out or try it out. I choose to push through the fear and seize the adventure that lies beyond.

— Linda Barbosa —

Second Wind

What's Your Story?

Storytelling is a very old human skill that
gives us an evolutionary advantage.
~Margaret Atwood

hen my daughter joined her brother at college the year I turned fifty, I was finally an empty nester. My husband and I had been working from home — he on investments and various business ventures, and I on investments and several corporate board memberships. So this should have been our time to scale back our workloads, travel, exercise, and enjoy ourselves.

But no. Crazy us. We had learned earlier that year that Chicken Soup for the Soul was for sale by its founders, Jack Canfield, Mark Victor Hansen, and his ex-wife Patty Hansen. We loved the brand and thought that we could take the company to the next level, bringing the books back to their old level of popularity and relevance, and expanding into new areas where we could add value to people's lives.

The second half of 2007 and the first few months of 2008 were devoted to due diligence, and in April 2008 we and our business partners became the proud new owners of Chicken Soup for the Soul. We kept a couple of key people from the editorial staff in Southern California and opened our new headquarters in Cos Cob, Connecticut, in a tiny office over a CVS drugstore.

I had read 100 of the old *Chicken Soup for the Soul* books in preparation for the acquisition, and somehow I thought I knew, really knew, exactly what to do when we took over. It was like Chicken Soup for the Soul had been inside me all along waiting to come out. I hit the ground running as publisher, editor-in-chief, and author of the books, with a clear vision of what I wanted to accomplish and how I wanted to tell positive, uplifting stories to our readers.

Thus, at ages fifty-five and fifty, respectively, my husband and I returned to the world of full-time work, just when we should have been planning our exit strategy! It has been non-stop excitement ever since. The first "excitement" was that we managed to time our purchase perfectly for the start of the deepest recession since the Great Depression, one that led to Borders shutting down, independent bookstores closing, and consumers scaling back on discretionary purchases. But we survived that, managing to redesign our books and increase our sales and have a number of bestsellers among the 100+ new titles that we have published. We've also updated our popular pet food products, launched a new line of delicious food for people, created a new website, started a television production business, and signed to have a major motion picture made by a big Hollywood studio, using our stories as inspiration. And we've grown a lot, taking over more and more space in our little office building and creating a large staff of passionate, talented, friendly people who work as hard as we do.

The first thirty years of my career were all about business and finance. I was a Wall Street analyst, a hedge fund manager, a corporate executive at a high-flying public telecommunications company, and a director of several publicly traded technology companies. I must admit I was the "writer" in all those positions, writing the annual reports and press releases for my companies, writing voluminous persuasive investment recommendations, even doing whatever writing was required on my corporate boards. After all, everything in business is really about telling stories, whether it's explaining a company's mission, or leading an investor through recent results, or describing a new technology or product in a way that is understandable.

I wrote a lot of great stories in business and finance, as I made the complex understandable and passionately explained the reasoning behind my buy and sell recommendations. But it seemed like the two main emotions I dealt with in the world of public companies were the classic stock market ones: fear and greed.

Now, at Chicken Soup for the Soul, I get to deal with the whole panoply of human emotions, and it is a real treat. And reading and editing the stories submitted for our books has also made a difference in my own life. I've learned how to have better personal relationships, how to focus on what's important, how to stay fit, how to look for the positive in every situation, and how to put in perspective the daily ups and downs of life.

There is a saying that in order to be happy you should return to what you loved doing when you were ten years old. When I was ten I loved to walk in the acres of woods behind our house, wrote stories just for fun, and read books. And now I have a job where I read and write every day, I go for long walks in the nature preserve near my house, and I occasionally get to read books that I did not have to edit. So despite the fact that I am working seven days a week and am constantly in crisis mode, I am truly doing what I have always loved doing.

When I started at Chicken Soup for the Soul, it took me a little while to realize that I had actually done this before while in college! During my junior and senior years of college, I researched and wrote a thesis about popular, spoken-word poetry in Brazil, which involved living in Brazil for several months, traveling throughout its impoverished northeast region, and meeting with poets and writers to collect their stories. These stories were about every aspect of their lives, usually told in the form of chanted poetry, and were printed up as pamphlets and sold at marketplaces. These *folhetos* were the "literature" of the masses in Brazil. I'm delighted to have come full circle in my writing career — from collecting poetry "from the people" in Brazil as a twenty-year-old to, three decades later, collecting stories and poems "from the people" for Chicken Soup for the Soul.

Maybe "rebooting" our lives is not just about starting something entirely new. Maybe it's about returning to our core passions, to what makes us tick, to what we have always valued. My "reboot" feels a lot like coming home.

—Amy Newmark—

Ripe for a Change

Find a job you like and you add
five days to every week.
~H. Jackson Browne

For my fortieth birthday, my daughter gave me an empty glass jar on which she had written the word Happiness. "When you find what makes you happy, you can put it in here so you don't lose it!" she explained.

The gift nicely summed up the vast majority of my life: a search for happiness. I certainly was happy as a boy; I can't tell you how many times I've relived boyhood games in my mind. I reminisced about childhood so much that my wife even called me "Peter Pan." Even young adulthood was fun: I loved working at the grocery store, setting up the produce stand, helping customers select the perfect level of ripeness. It was relaxing and I loved interacting with the people I helped. If the real world hadn't beckoned, I could have worked there forever.

But when I became an adult, it seemed that everyone around me had found their correct life, and more importantly, had found happiness in that life. I always felt like I was still searching. I took a job in banking to support my family, but what really made me happy were my two young daughters. When they started growing up, however, I felt lonely and pointless again. My job and the long commute seemed absurd. Pushing papers and meeting deadlines without interacting with clients felt pointless; I'd come home and the girls would be at their friends', or at practice or rehearsal. And I wasn't there to see it.

Thinking about my job consumed more and more of my free time. Over the years, the banking industry had been heartless, and various mergers and acquisitions always left me questioning — and sometimes losing — my job security.

"Just leave work at work," my wife advised. "Come home, find something that makes you happy, and get absorbed in it."

Easy for her to say. She finds happiness in anything — reading, gardening, talking, cooking. In fact, there isn't much she doesn't find joy in — except for watching me mope around the house, miserable.

When the girls moved out, a new bank acquisition sent me away from the stress of New York City into the quiet cities of the South. At first we thought it was a blessing — and it was. My wife and I were now closer to where our daughters had moved. I had a shorter commute. And for a few weeks, I was happy.

But soon the doldrums came again, and my wife declared with frustration, "As long as you're working, you're never going to be happy, Peter Pan!"

A blessing in disguise closed the office, and the company offered to move us back to New York. My wife was horrified that I might accept the offer and frightened about what might happen if I didn't. We considered it carefully, and we decided we didn't need a lot of money anymore: our home was nearly paid off and our girls were out on their own. We could settle for a modest salary, health insurance, and proximity to our daughters.

I declined the offer.

I loved the first few months of being jobless. It was everything I ever thought I wanted. I repaired every problem with the house. I pruned the trees. I created built-in shelves in all the basement storage areas. Crown molding, recessed lighting... I did it all.

Once the adrenaline wore off, however, that tiny seed of worry sprouted in my soul. Why hadn't I gotten any calls from sending out my résumé? I knew the economy was bad, but I expected a handful of interviews by now.

"All the jobs are in New York," my wife sighed one night.

"I won't move back there," I insisted.

My wife understood, and she was glad for the decision, but she was starting to worry. She watched our checkbook carefully. She started cutting corners at the grocery store, buying store brands and skimping on her favorite treats.

Two years went by, and although my wife wouldn't say it, I knew what she was thinking: she wondered whether finally, now that I didn't have to work a job I hated, I was happy. I saw the anger growing in her face as she left for work each day and glared at me as I sat on the couch sipping coffee and watching television. I wanted to tell her that the joy of it had worn off after a matter of months. That I only continued repairing our home so that I'd have something to do. That now I felt useless and old. I had run out of job prospects and home-improvement projects, and the days blended together.

I wanted to work.

I wanted to be happy.

It took two years of résumé revisions, of unemployment workshops, of promising interviews that for one reason or another just "didn't pan out." My cover letters were lackluster. I realized the drive that had helped me through my early career had been my desire to provide for my family. Now, they were provided for. My epiphany came when I realized that, for the first time in my life since childhood, I could worry about ME.

One day at breakfast, my wife eyed me over her coffee. "You know," she said, "when we were younger, you always used to tell me that your favorite job was working at that grocery store, stocking produce. A few times you even mentioned that, money aside, that would be the only job that would make you happy. Do you remember?"

I smiled. "Of course I do. I can still see those lettuce heads, those glistening apples. I still remember the particular weight of a cantaloupe just begging to be sliced and enjoyed, the feel of a tomato that will be ripe in time for dinner. Helping people instead of pushing paper..."

My wife smiled. It was a relaxed smile, a smile I hadn't seen in a few years.

"What made you remember that?" I asked.

"I saw they're opening up a new supermarket in the next town over. It just made me think of — well," she said, trying not to be too blunt, "I saw an advertisement for a produce department manager. I just thought — "

But she was too late. I had already retrieved a cover letter and résumé from the kitchen desk. "I sent this in three weeks ago," I said. "I've already had a phone interview with the store manager, and he says there are a few positions he'd like to see me fill. My interview is next Tuesday."

Weeks later, happily in my new position, I gazed at the "happiness" jar on my dresser. It was now filled with all my favorite snapshots from my life, from the birth of our daughters to their graduations and weddings.

I may have lost it, but I found it once again. "The love of family," I think to myself each night before bed. "That is what my happiness has always been."

And tomatoes.

— Martin Walters —

63

Yuletide in Florida

There's nothing that makes you more insane
than family. Or more happy. Or more
exasperated. Or more… secure.
~Jim Butcher

'Twas the week before Christmas, and at JFK
My sisters and I flew off to Del Ray.
We've traveled each year since two thousand and one
To visit our aunt and sit in her sun.

We tell her each time "We want nothing to do
But sit by the pool and hang out with you."
And yet on arrival, agenda in hand,
Our aunt told us all of the fun she had planned.

Monday we visited her friends to play cards,
Their condo was gated, the entrance had guards.
They're serious players, we anted up nickels
They served us egg salad on rye with some pickles.

On Tuesday a bird walk where we saw a flamingo,
On Wednesday a free film, On Thursday, yes! Bingo!
But Friday's the night that my aunt liked the most
A party for forty where she starred as the host.

She hired some helpers who knew what to do,
The house looked like Christmas when they were all through.
And what to our wondering eyes did appear,
But a wet bar set up with wine, scotch and beer.

The hors d'oeuvres were plated and the room was all set,
Guests were arriving, all people we've met.
The Kellys, the Weinsteins, the Dailys, of course,
And Patty, the neighbor, who just got divorced.

Then Morris, who had to replace his left knee
Topped by Henry who just replaced hip number three.
Enter Myrna and Hilda and Rosie and Gwen,
There seemed to be far more women than men.

The men had on shorts and a Polo or Tee,
But the ladies were dressed as if diamonds were free.
Their eyes how they twinkled, 'tis Botox for many,
While others had crow's feet and wrinkles aplenty.

The bedroom TV was playing the game,
So we lost half the men, which was kind of a shame.
But there was a piano and this guy, Tommy Farrell,
He played all night long and taught us to carol.

There were cheese balls and salsa and hummus and dips,
Scallops surrounded by sweet bacon strips.
Chicken piccata, roast beef au jus,
Cheesecake and cookies and tiramisu.

Strawberry daiquiris and wine, white and red,
Went into my stomach and straight to my head.
By now the clock said it was way past eleven,
Going to bed became my kind of heaven.

Those octogenarians sure knew how to party!
I started to dance with this old guy named Marty.
He cha-cha'd away as the music grew loud
While I quietly slipped away from the crowd.

In all it was such a successful affair,
But as I fell asleep I whispered this prayer:
Auntie, at eighty you're still pretty cool,
But next year can't we sit by the pool?

—Eileen Melia Hession—

64

The Power of Positive Pigheadedness

A dream doesn't become reality through magic;
it takes sweat, determination and hard work.
~Colin Powell

"I'm too old," I wailed. "No one wants to hire a middle-aged woman. I'm doomed. What am I going to do?"

As dramatic as it sounded, I was dead serious. After my divorce, I felt so defeated and hopeless I really believed I would end up destitute.

The jobs I qualified for wouldn't pay enough to support a household, and I was past the age where moving up the ladder was a likely option.

"You should start a business," a friend advised.

"Doing what?" I was still mired in self-pity. During my married life, I'd focused on raising my children, supporting my husband's endeavors and publishing a few books and articles on the side. I knew I could write well, but even though I'd been publishing for decades, I'd never made any real money doing it.

She shrugged. I realized no matter how much she wanted to help, I had to find my own solution.

As I saw it, I had two choices: wallow or get creative.

I tried wallowing for a while. It didn't suit me. Too passive.

So, I took an inventory. What did I have going for me? I sat down and made a list of my existing talents and abilities. I included my curiosity, love of learning and stubbornness. My pig-headedness was legendary. Silly me, for years I thought it was a fault. Little did I know it would be the secret ingredient that would take me from despair to destiny.

Personality assessments helped me identify my strengths. One test said that my smartest career move would be "any job where you're paid to be opinionated."

I looked in the paper but didn't see anything that met that criterion.

I could get paid for my opinions if I had my own business, but if I wanted people to listen, I had to have information worth hearing.

It wasn't a straight line from where I was to where I wanted to end up. My long-term goal required training, and the short-term goal, survival, demanded an income. Fitting both into my days wouldn't be easy.

I tried different combinations of paid work and study time. I sampled jobs the way Goldilocks tried porridge. One was too hot, another too cold. In the background, hungry bears hovered, ready to eat me if I didn't keep moving forward.

I tried real estate, then retail sales. The Christmas chaos renewed my commitment to make a change.

My marketing and advertising background was an asset, but times had changed. To catch up, I would dive into this new world, reading and doing research, taking online classes and soaking up knowledge. I got a job with a software company managing their social media. This was a while ago, when social media was still a new concept. It was a disaster.

The experience made me want to understand what went wrong.

If it's true you learn more from your failures than from your successes, I was on the fast track to becoming an expert.

I took a novice class on how to build websites.

Yikes! There was so much information. Most of it was over my head. I struggled, fell behind and dropped out.

At this point, my secret ingredient, politely referred to as tenacious determination, kicked in. I refused to abandon my goal.

This was not going to defeat me.

A few months later, I took the course again. This time I kept extensive notes and did every assignment.

Things were beginning to make sense.

I made websites for family members and for myself. They were pretty simplistic, but gave me a chance to practice. I experimented, crashing my own sites, then figuring out how to fix them.

Tackling and solving problems increased my confidence.

I took an advanced website development course. Again I found myself over my head, so I repeated it until I got it.

The next step required finding real clients.

Terrified and tentative, I forced myself to go to professional mixers and events, where I tested out my elevator speech.

Initially I led with my identity as a writer. This usually ended the conversation.

I reframed my introduction.

"I build websites," I told them. "And help companies and individuals with marketing and promotion."

People hired me.

I'd done it!

I built a business from scratch. Taking what I knew and expanding it, ignoring the negative little voices along the way that insisted I couldn't do it.

It's been five years now and I've settled into my niche. Websites and graphic design keep the hungry bears satisfied, and I write every day. I've found a balance doing work I love.

Rebooting a computer clears out the old cache, eliminating those things that prevent it from functioning well.

Rebooting a life does the same. It's a fresh start, bringing together who you are, what you know, what you're willing to learn, and where you want to go.

And don't forget the power of positive pig-headedness. It's the final ingredient that can make all the difference in your success.

— Lynn Kinnaman —

A Not So Trivial Twosome

*Regardless of differences, we strive shoulder to
shoulder... [T]eamwork can be summed up in
five short words: "We believe in each other."*
~Jerry Smith

Т he announcement in the newspaper enticed me: "*Trivial
Pursuit* Competition... $500 First Prize."

The competition, for teams of two, was to be held at
a nearby mall. My wife Carol and I loved playing the game
with friends, but this competition would be in full view of the general
public. I waved the paper at Carol. "Did you see this?"

"Yes, and the answer is no! Ask Clive!"

Trivial Pursuit, a board game that tests your general and pop culture
knowledge, was the latest fad and had become an "intellectual hula
hoop" for adults. To be crowned the local champion would bring us
glory and gold.

But there are in life some things that loving couples should avoid
doing. Partnering to play a game based on knowledge and memory,
in a public forum, is on that list of relationship testers. Thus Carol's
firm answer to my query.

My friend Clive made a good fit. We were prepared and eager, but
just hours before the Wednesday night qualifying round, Clive took
ill. Now on the cusp of the competition I needed a replacement. This

called for desperate measures… "Carol!"

We arrived and found Table 8 set to accommodate eight couples. Although Carol was clearly uncomfortable, we took our places, nodding greetings to those present. A group of spectators had gathered and that made her all the more nervous. An announcement was made and play began.

The first couple started strongly, answering correctly and acquiring a few "pie wedges" in their scoring token before missing a question. The following two teams had very brief runs before losing their turns. Next up, we did well, garnering two wedges, but an Art & Literature question confounded us and we became spectators again, hoping for another chance. As the games continued, we could hear cries of joy and groans of despair from the other tables. Our table played on and elimination loomed; however none of our opponents filled their game pieces and we got a second chance. We did not waste it. Thanks to some favourable rolls, Carol's knowledge of birthstones and anniversaries, and a run of correct answers, we won our table and earned a spot in the finals. All the talk afterward was about the couple at Table 3 who had run the board on their first turn, answering over 100 consecutive questions correctly to sweep into the championship. We would face them on Saturday at "high noon."

Saturday's table was centred in the mall's rotunda. We were seated side by side in the eighth spot and selected a green (for Forrest, our last name) playing piece. The team that had been perfect on Wednesday sat almost across from us. This was a promotional event for the mall, and spectators surrounded us, standing three deep. The media was well represented and the local cable TV channel was taping the event. The judge called us to order and the questioner began.

Team 1 got off to a shaky start. They only answered four questions before missing one. Team 2 did better and half filled their game piece with wedges before faltering. Team 3 took the die and lived up to expectations. A mixed female/male team, she took the lead in answering and they seldom conferred, rolling strategically and answering about seventy consecutive questions. Without missing an answer, they ran the board. Technically they had won the game, unless another team could match their performance and force a playoff. The next four teams were clearly intimidated and unable to mount a serious run. During play, I watched the couple as their confident smiles became almost smug.

We were up last and started quickly, rolling on to the required squares and acquiring about half the wedges needed. Even though one of us thought we knew the answer, we always conferred before replying. Then, we ran in to a stretch of rolls that forced us to answer many questions without acquiring wedges. Every question threatened sudden death; but eventually we made it to the centre and then nailed the final question. We had done it — run the board to force a playoff.

Team 3 was up first, knowing as well as us that a single miss could mean defeat, yet they seemed quite calm. The audience had increased and even they too were tense, often being warned to silence by the questioner. Picking up where they had left off, our opponents breezed along, acquiring wedges quickly. Then an Entertainment question drew blank looks from both. They conferred and argued and then answered… incorrectly. The audience groaned. Our hearts, already in our throats, began to pound. We were up.

Frankly, I doubted we could run the board again, but it was do or die. Initially it seemed the game gods had deserted us. Our dice rolls were not placing us on the required spots to acquire wedges. That meant answering many more questions, with a single miss meaning failure. But with hands held and knees knocking, we pressed on and our luck turned. By the judge's count, on the one hundred and third question, we gained the centre of the hub. The scene became deathly quiet. The pressure was almost unbearable as Team 3 considered the deciding category and chose, Art & Literature. The tension increased and we held hands tighter. The audience buzzed, then hushed as the question was posed.

"In *Alice in Wonderland*… What did the Knave of Hearts steal from the Queen of Hearts?"

Carol shoulders slumped and she sighed. We conferred. She knew the answer. I agreed. We delivered it together… "Tarts!"

"Correct!" The audience exploded in cheers. We hugged in relief, first like shipwreck survivors and then in joy at achieving both fame and fortune. Our opponents congratulated us, the cheque was presented and the media interviews followed.

At home I poured a celebratory drink and toasted Carol. "Here's to you; thanks for stepping up, honey! You were a rock and saved us many times."

"At least it was worth it!" Carol replied.

Years later when telling the story to friends or family, they always ask the ultimate trivia question, "What did you get?"

Carol had that answer too. "John got the glory and I got a granite countertop!"

— John Forrest —

Would You Like to Dance?

This above all; to thine own self be true.
~William Shakespeare

I am waiting for the boy to ask me to dance. He is the best at doing the jitterbug. He doesn't ask.

My feelings are determined by junior high school boys, and I am not popular. I *will* be in high school, but not now. My pride is in the hands of these boys.

That dancer, the most popular boy in school, lives across the street. He is a basketball star, too, although he has not yet grown into a man's height. He tends to dance with the girls who will also kiss him. He knows how good-looking he is, even at twelve. Many of my classmates are competing to dance with him, to be his girlfriend for a night, a week, a month. He is a sassy charmer. He knows he is number one.

I am not one of the girls who want him, but I love to watch him dance. He is a great dancer who has impeccable rhythm and knows all the latest steps. He is dazzling on the dance floor.

One day, I am twelve, and the next I am sixty-three. The decades have brought me the marriage of my dreams, three incredible careers and a life in which I have been myself. One of my greatest passions is dancing.

My childhood girlfriend is coming into town to attend the fiftieth anniversary of our high school. She talks me into going. I am not sure why she has to talk me into attending because I loved high school. I was president of my junior class and spent four years being part of many activities.

I am not sure that this type of party, which is open to graduating classes spanning fifty years, will offer quality time to reminisce and visit. I receive some phone calls from old friends who have come to town. I decide to go.

A small group of my classmates attend, maybe fifteen or so. Most of these classmates were with me in junior high as well as high school. I am thrilled to see them. One man walks up to me and says my name. I struggle to recognize his face. He then says his name and smiles. It is the star dancer of my adolescence, my former neighbor, the jock my preteen girlfriends lusted after.

We catch up. As others arrive, I greet them and am greeted warmly. Everyone looks great. Sixty-three never looked better. These are the people of my youth. Their place in my life is special. The memories we share are our beginning years.

The band is getting ready to play the oldies. As the music begins, I walk toward the dance floor and turn. He catches my eye as I extend my hand toward him, motioning for him to join me on the dance floor. The best jitterbugger in sixth grade takes my hand, and we engage in a graceful and wild ride, singing the words to every song. He is still a great dancer.

When our dance ends, I motion to another childhood friend and then another. Each man joins me on the dance floor, one at a time. I had never danced with any of them back in our schooldays. Now I am enjoying their individual style and movements. On that dance floor, they are meeting me for the first time. And it is I who has asked them. I chose and picked the men with whom I wanted to dance.

One of my sisters is also there. When I talk to her at the end of the night, she tells me how wonderfully I danced, and how exciting it was that all the boys/men wanted to dance with me.

I smile to myself. I will always love the girl who was twelve and watched the dancers, but a woman of sixty-three never felt better on the dance floor.

— Elynne Chaplik-Aleskow —

67

It's Not Over Until I Say It's Over...

*The right way is not always the popular and
easy way. Standing for right when it is unpopular
is a true test of moral character.*
~Margaret Chase Smith

I was the last person who ever expected to have a problem with sexual harassment. I was a forty-five-year-old widow with four teenage children. I was an average-looking woman, and on a sexually attractive scale of one to ten, I'd have rated myself a two. I was thirty pounds overweight, wore bifocals and didn't wear make-up.

I'd been a widow for ten years and had worked a variety of jobs to support my family. I didn't have any college or special job skills, and I took whatever jobs I could get. I'd been working two jobs, cleaning houses and working as a clerk in a small gift shop. When the gift shop closed, I needed another job to keep supporting my family.

I applied for twenty-three jobs and couldn't believe my good luck when I was hired at a jewelry store at a salary that would allow me to quit my job cleaning houses. Having only one job was almost like being on vacation.

That lasted six months, and then my boss started asking me odd questions about my personal life. Was I dating anyone, and why not? He was a sixty-five-year-old widower and had been pleasant to work with until then. Two men in their forties and three women in their twenties also worked in the store.

My boss began asking me out to dinner, and I refused. I explained I had four children at home and wanted to be home in the evenings with them.

A sexy novel and suggestive cartoons appeared in my locker at work. I couldn't imagine anyone else at work would have put them there other than my boss. Things escalated. He hinted I might lose my job if I wasn't nice to him. I began applying at other places for a new job. One day, he cornered me in the stockroom and tried to kiss and grope me. He said he would make me assistant manager if I'd "be friendly."

I called a lawyer, and he took my case on a contingency. If I lost, I wouldn't have to pay him anything. I told my children I was filing sexual-harassment charges against my boss.

My children's first reaction was: *How could any man be sexually interested in you?* Then they were embarrassed I was making this public. What if their friends heard about it? And finally, if I lost my job, how would we survive?

I was crushed. I hadn't exactly thought of myself as an innocent damsel in distress defending myself against the villain, but I had expected my kids to be sympathetic and supportive. Maybe they were right. Maybe I was making a fool of myself and humiliating my family.

Things were worse at work. The boss stopped coming into the office and appointed one of the men as temporary manager. The two men who worked at the store laughed at me and would ask me how my love life was. The women stopped talking to me at all. To say things were chilly at work was an understatement; it was like the North Pole. There was gossip about me, but what did I do to cause it? How far did I go with the boss? Had I encouraged or seduced him? Was it about the money?

I was fortunate to get a nice lawyer, but he was very young. I even wondered if I was his first case. He told me I was the perfect victim. My boss had seen that and taken advantage of me. I was middle-aged, needed the job, and was the sole support for my four children. I didn't have any real job skills or training to make it easy to get another job. I was also quiet, shy and easily intimidated because I'd been bullied and abused as a child.

I told my lawyer that maybe it wasn't worth it. Maybe I should just give up. But he said he was sure my boss had abused countless women before me, and if I didn't stop him, he would abuse many after me. He said I had to be the champion who looked my boss straight in the eye and said not just "no," but "hell no!" He said he'd fight to the end for me, and it wasn't over until he said it was over.

My lawyer also got some good counseling for me that shed light on how I'd been timid and afraid my entire life. I'd tiptoed through life trying not to upset or offend anyone. I was feeling stronger and, in spite of the way I felt inside, I became brave on the "outside." I'd go to work every day whether anyone spoke to me or not. I would do my job and then go home to my children. I would see this through to the end, regardless of the outcome.

The case went to court. My boss did not show up, and the judge awarded me an amount of money that would have been equal to my wages for five years at the store.

I thought it was over. I'd survived. My lawyer said "no," it was not over, and I deserved more money. He wanted a written letter of apology and a good recommendation from my boss. It wouldn't be over until he said it was over.

I told my lawyer I didn't care about more money or the letter, and he said *he* cared. The judge contacted my boss and ordered him to produce a letter of apology and a recommendation, which he did.

The next week, my boss filed for bankruptcy — not because of my lawsuit, but because he hadn't been paying any of his debts for the past year and owed a fortune for jewelry, rent and income taxes. The store was closed and the inventory seized. My boss moved across the country. The people I'd worked with still wouldn't speak to me and blamed me for the store closing, even though I had nothing to do with it.

Going through the ordeal had been painful, embarrassing, exhausting and scary, but I came out of it stronger, smarter and no longer a victim. I faced the giant, and I won.

My boss died two years later, and my lawyer filed against his estate. Four years after I first filed my complaint, I got a check in the mail with the rest of the money I was originally awarded. There was also a note from my lawyer that said simply, "Now it's over."

— April Knight —

68

Caged

*It is precisely the possibility of realizing a dream
that makes life interesting.*
~Paulo Coelho, The Alchemist

efining moments are not supposed to occur in the local fish market. Rather, they should be created on a wedding day, during the birth of a child, or at a long-awaited graduation. In addition, these life-altering experiences are supposed to be planned for, anticipated, or at least somewhat expected.

However, as I walked to our neighborhood fishery with my husband of twenty-five years, a sense of foreboding hung over me. I kept thinking, "Something is up, and I don't think I want to hear it." As seagulls squawked overhead and water lapped against the shore, my husband told me that he wanted to leave his job. Even though he was concerned about leaving the security of a pension, health benefits, a terrific staff, an expense account, and other perks, this was something he had to do.

My stomach churned. At fifty-something, I had assumed we were finally at the point where, financially at least, things had eased up. For two decades, I had paid my dues by clipping coupons, shopping sales, and taking public transportation. Over the years, I had also pre-paid our mortgage, kept a tight rein on our credit cards, and funded our IRAs. Finally, I could treat myself to a manicure without guilt, hire a cleaning service for the heavy household chores, and employ a local teen to maintain the lawn and shovel the snow.

Standing in that fish market, I could see my carefully constructed life begin to evaporate, just like the steam escaping from the enormous pots of chowder. Then, my eyes traveled to the lobster tanks against the wall. Like the unfortunate inhabitants, I realized I too would be imprisoned within my current career as the primary breadwinner. I would also be responsible for providing our health benefits. I resented my husband for putting me in this position.

The look on my face must have been telling because he suddenly looked like a remorseful five-year-old kid. "Oh, no, I'm sorry. Forget I even mentioned it," he said. "It was just a stupid dream I had. Just forget it." And he tried to force a smile.

But somehow I knew it wasn't just a stupid dream. It was real. And it was something he had been working up the courage to tell me for quite some time. I looked at him carefully. I knew the way I handled the next few minutes would have an impact on the rest of our life. I tried a weak smile.

"I've crunched some numbers," he said tentatively, "and while I know that initially, the financial burden will fall on you, I really believe that in one year, I'll recoup my current salary. Then, I'd like you to cut back. Maybe part-time?"

Part-time? That did sound nice. Before I could respond, the clerk behind the counter was asking for my order. "The usual right, Ms. B? Two pounds of flounder and a quart of chowder?"

"No, give us two of your best lobsters, and throw in a dozen shrimp." I smiled. "I have a feeling we're coming into a windfall."

And somehow I knew we would.

— Barbara A. Davey —

A Future to Step Into

We must be willing to get rid of the life we've planned,
so as to have the life that is waiting for us.
~Joseph Campbell

I had always envisioned the "Golden Years" as a time in our lives when my wife Lynn and I would have the free time to explore the country in our custom motorhome, going from place to place like two leaves in the wind. This was not a "bucket list fantasy." This was a well thought out season-of-life game plan.

Lynn and I had met thirty years before and instantly became best friends, soul mates and later, husband and wife. Lynn was an artist and photographer. She was as wonderful as wonderful can be and allowed each day of her life to unfold as magic moments.

I was a young attorney at that time, building my practice in the Midwest. Lynn would come with me to the law library on weekends and was my cheerleader and confidante. About seventeen years into my law practice I was offered a once in a lifetime opportunity to become the CEO/President and General Counsel of a company that is America's leader in the field of self-help and peak performance strategies. This opportunity required that we move to Southern California. This was such an exciting time for us both.

This new role brought us the opportunity to travel the world together and to experience a lifestyle we previously would not have imagined.

We found our dream home in a beach community, and with our

six dogs and two parrots lived every day experiencing the joy and happiness of our life together.

And then Lynn was diagnosed with a medical condition that changed the course of our life. This disease had the ruthlessness of a home invasion robbery. The cancer had metastasized throughout her body. We approached it scientifically, medically, spiritually and with tenacious abandon. It was devastating for me to know that each day was one day closer to her end. For the entire year we were side by side during the ineffective yet hopeful regime of treatments.

On January 16, 2011, Lynn passed away with the same style and grace that she lived her life. On that day I joined 7,500 other Americans who also lost a loved one.

It was Friday, January 21, 2011 and the last of about twenty people were leaving our home. Father John, our parish priest, lingered behind and hugged me. He said: "Hang in there, this is God's will, may her memory be eternal."

As I watched his car pull away, I closed the door. I heard a new kind of silence and looked around. All of the dogs had circled me as if by design and we froze together in the moment.

This was going to be a time to thrive or a time to be smothered by the dark clouds of grief and despair.

We did not have children. We did, however, have a close community of friends who all stepped in and reached out to me in wonderful ways. Hospice introduced me to grief counseling and a counselor met with me weekly with assurances that the deep physical and mental pain of this journey would ease with time.

I realized that friends and associates were without words. Some disappeared from the radar. I was forgiving of that and was clear that this journey was mine alone.

Grief has a life of its own. We have all had our disappointments and loss of others. I was totally unprepared for this.

During the following year I went through the motions of work and life. I stayed close to home, and the dogs and parrots became my nuclear family. I did very little to our home other than find worthwhile places to donate Lynn's things.

I decided to take up poker and began to commute back and forth to Las Vegas. Poker gave me an opportunity to keep my mind engaged and to socialize in a new way. Eight weeks after learning the game, I played in my first World Series of Poker. Little did I realize that my time to thrive was unfolding in front of me and the healing process that protects us was in full swing.

Without a design or conscious game plan, my life was changing. It was little steps and I barely noticed it myself. On the first anniversary of Lynn's passing I was at the cemetery for my weekly visit. I can barely describe what occurred, which was a feeling of lightness and euphoria. I could hear the wisp of what I sensed was the dark cloud catching a wind and beginning to disburse. I felt guilty that I was feeling lighter.

The following week I was in Vegas. By chance and circumstance I met a woman who has become a great friend and companion. I got a stunning high-rise condo on the Las Vegas strip and began to split my time between Las Vegas and California. For the next two years I began to spend nearly all of my time in Vegas, experiencing a lifestyle change that I had never dared to dream.

Back in California there was unfinished business. The home I shared with Lynn remained untouched. I also still had a full-time high-pressure job to maintain. Somehow I made it all work. I had a house sitter and housekeeper take care of my home and my pets around the clock. This went on for three years. I would go back and forth for visits. The house was full of memories of Lynn and me and I would fast-track back to Vegas. My job could be supported virtually and I had a stellar team at the home office dealing with day-to-day matters. Where there is a will, there is a way.

I closed my eyes to the fact that something had to give. Of course what I was avoiding was letting go of my house and my pets and thirty-one years of the most wonderful memories. In my mind, that would somehow end my relationship with Lynn and I simply was not able to fathom that.

It was approaching the third anniversary of Lynn's passing. My poker coach, Kenna James, put it on the line. He said, "Poker and life have many similarities. You can only lose what you are attached to and until you can give up those attachments the game will control you instead of you controlling the game." Something deep inside me began to stir.

That month I returned to California. I got our home ready to list. With the help of Gale, a dear family friend, I found homes for all my pets. What a heartache that was. I realized that to thrive I needed to let go of it all. I made a decision to begin my life all over and to invent a new future.

I got rid of everything I owned. I sold six Harleys, my motorhome, all my cars, all my furniture, collectables — everything went.

The house was impeccable, and on the first day it was listed I had six full offers.

It closed on Lynn's birthday. I went to the cemetery and there were no clouds. I knew Lynn was orchestrating things. It was all too smooth and effortless to be coincidence.

I bought a new Corvette Stingray and returned to Vegas with only my clothes and a box of photos.

I then met with the Chairman of the great company that had given me such opportunity for the past two decades and we agreed on and announced my formal retirement.

Yes, I gave it all up.

I am a private kind of guy. I decided to share this story because I want anyone who finds themselves in these circumstances to know that life is guided. You unfold the future — the future does not unfold you.

There is such a thing as a time to thrive.

— Sam Georges —

So Much to Give

Becoming a Second Generation Parent

*Life is what happens while you
are busy making other plans.*
~John Lennon

M y husband Paul and I sat across the courtroom from his son Andrew and his girlfriend Tammy. Our lawyer sat beside us, the familiar yellow legal pad and expandable folder in front of her.

Andrew's extremely short hair was dyed black. Small sores and scabs peppered Tammy's arms and face; she'd been scratching at imaginary insects crawling on her skin again.

These sights did not compare though with the smell... their water had been shut off for almost an entire year. How they had lived in those conditions for so long was incomprehensible to Paul and me. The stench slapped us in the face the moment they entered and I stifled a gag as we rose to our feet as the judge entered.

After a small recess, the judge made his ruling. Two and a half million grandparents in this country are raising their grandchildren. Paul and I had just been added to those numbers.

Three years ago, I had my life planned. I was finishing my teaching degree, a dream I had had since I was a child. I had married a wonderful man whose children were already adults, and I had my daughter, Sarah, a high school sophomore. Life wasn't perfect but it was going along at a steady pace.

And then we got the phone call.

Andrew was Paul's older child and since we had been together, Paul had battled with Andrew over his substance abuse. We knew Andrew had a problem, but until he wanted to change, there wasn't anything we could do. It seemed as though he was getting his life on track that year; he had a decent construction job and he and his long-time girlfriend Tammy, had just had a baby boy.

Unfortunately, we only saw Andrew and Sam a couple of times in the next few months. Andrew would give us excuses as to why we couldn't come by or take Sam for a visit. As new grandparents, Paul and I were hurt but optimistic that we could mend the rift in our family over time.

In February of 2007, I got a call from Child Protective Services. What they told me still makes me shudder, thinking of how Paul and I had been so oblivious to all the signs. The caseworker told us that Sam had tested positive for methamphetamines and THC (the drug in marijuana) at birth and had been taken away from Andrew and Tammy. Andrew hadn't even mentioned that Paul and I existed, and instead signed over temporary custody to Tammy's parents.

That same month everything changed when Tammy's parents tested positive for substance abuse as well. "We can either place Sam with you, or he will go into foster care," the caseworker told me in a matter-of-fact way.

I stood there with the phone clutched tightly in my hand staring at Paul's questioning face. "I understand," I choked out. "Could I call you back after I speak to my husband?" I hung up and turned to Paul. As I explained what she had told me, I could see Paul's heart breaking. "What should we do?" I asked him quietly.

"We really don't have any other choice but to bring him home with us," he answered, echoing my own thoughts.

A week later, we stood outside a small two-story house in the bitter north Texas wind. The yard was strewn with broken toys and trash. Dead weeds scratched against the side of the porch. The door's paint, blistered and peeling, reminded me of a three-day-old sunburn.

I had never been to Tammy's parents' home, and its condition shocked me. This is where our grandson had been living?

As we entered the front room, my eyes quickly adjusted to the sight; a full-size bed, two playpens, and a small bassinet cluttered the small area. In the bassinet, shoved up against the television, a small bundle was squirming. I looked down into the crib to see Sam's blue eyes smiling up at me. "Why hello there, little one," I greeted him, and was quickly rewarded with a huge smile. I knew instantly that I would do whatever I could for this precious child.

We couldn't take him with us that day, which tore Paul and me to pieces. Over the next two weeks, along with my class schedule, Paul's work, and Sarah's school activities, we were also meeting with CPS, scheduling our own drug testing to prove we were clean, and trying to remember all the necessary items needed for a baby. At the end of March, just before Paul's birthday, Sam came home with us.

Andrew and Tammy had signed over temporary custody to Paul and me, and our hope was that this crisis would be the shock they needed to get straight. However, by June it was evident that they had no intention of changing their lifestyle or getting clean to get Sam back. Our CPS caseworker suggested we find a lawyer and Paul and I agreed.

In May of 2008, the judge awarded us full custody of Sam. Through research, I discovered that babies born to mothers addicted to meth can seem sluggish and have uncontrollable tremors. I learned that these babies have a higher risk of stroke before being born. Luckily, Sam is relatively healthy, and Paul and I monitor him closely for any signs that his development is lagging behind that of other children his age. While his development was slow in the beginning, he is now an active, happy three-year-old. Unfortunately, not enough research has been done on the long-term effects of methamphetamines on children.

Thankfully, Paul and I managed to weather this storm without any major damage to our marriage, but getting Sam came at a cost. Paul, who had dreams of retiring once I began teaching, had to change jobs to support the costs of a new baby. I had hoped to finish college in 2008, but I wasn't able to take summer classes and care for Sam at the same time. While our life hasn't worked out the way we planned,

Paul and I would not have it any other way. We are amazed at how this little guy makes us feel both old and young at the same time. And while we might have to postpone our retirement plans of travel and relaxation, our new adventures with Sam will be priceless.

—Christine Long—

Lunches for Christmas

*Christmas is not as much about opening
our presents as opening our hearts.*
~Janice Maeditere

"I have no idea of what to get you for Christmas this year," my husband Larry lamented in early December.

My lips turned up in a rueful smile. "Same goes for me in finding something for you."

Though we knew that Christmas was not about presents, we still liked to remember each other with small gifts and we had reached the stage in our lives when we didn't need more things. In fact, we were actively downsizing, cleaning out and getting rid of unneeded and unwanted "stuff."

Then an article on the Internet caught my attention. It was about schools having to turn away needy children from receiving lunches because the children were in arrears in paying for their meals.

I shared the article with Larry. "Let's each give money to the school lunch program for our Christmas presents to each other," I said. "We'll pay for children who can't afford lunch."

Larry smiled widely. "That's a great idea. It's a way of paying it forward."

Many years ago, when our children were small, we went through a hard time when Larry was unemployed. We lived on rice and beans and a whole lot of faith. Finally, we had to humble ourselves and ask for help. It wasn't easy for either of us as we had been brought up on principles of self-reliance.

Now that we were in comfortable circumstances, we wanted to give back.

I visited our local elementary school, the same one our five children had attended years ago, and explained that we would like to pay for lunches for children who couldn't afford them.

The secretary at the front desk looked first surprised and then pleased. She directed me to the cafeteria to talk with the coordinator there.

The lady in charge accepted our gift of cash with effusive thanks. "This will make a big difference to so many children," she said. "Thank you. Over and over, thank you."

There weren't as many presents under the tree that year, but it was one of our best Christmases ever.

—Jane McBride—

Memory Meals

What is patriotism but the love
of the food one ate as a child?
~Lin Yutang

"**M**om, thanks for making barbecued meatballs and rice before I left," said Betsy with misty eyes. She hugged me goodbye while her dad finished loading the car with packed boxes. My daughter was moving from our home in Florida to her apartment in Washington, D.C. to begin her new job. "I'm really going to miss your cooking," she added.

Betsy's comment about home-cooked meals gave me an idea. I decided to make special gifts for my three grown children, who were in various stages of leaving home for college and careers.

After Betsy waved goodbye, I drove to the store and bought three yellow recipe boxes and decorated index cards. For several days I copied family recipes from my food- splattered cards, including Betsy's meatballs, the traditional bunny cake Lori requested each Easter, Steven's special lasagna, and the family's favorite, fresh apple cake.

I included precious recipes I had gathered from country neighbors when our family spent summers on our farm in Missouri, knowing they would rekindle fond memories. I chose Cousin Donna's recipe for the beets she pickled, after she harvested them from her picture-perfect garden. I copied Lestie's tangy freezer slaw ingredients she had scrawled on a used envelope years ago. I made note that Pat's instructions for making her outstanding homemade rolls included driving thirty miles for fresh yeast.

When the handwritten cards stood alphabetized in their boxes, I closed the lids and set them aside until I would be with my children again. When the time came, I presented each one with the recipes and enjoyed their wide grins and shrieks of delight as they thumbed through the cards.

"I remember making this bread in my second grade class," remarked Steven.

"Oh, this is the best macaroni and cheese ever." recalled Lori.

"Look! Here's one for the homemade ice cream we churned on the farm each summer!" squealed Betsy.

Over the years the boxes of recipes continued to be popular resources in their kitchens, reminders of the food and love they were served during their childhoods. Now, with children of their own, they explained the stories behind the recipes to my nine grandchildren, and inspired them to become young cooks.

One day, a video arrived on my computer. I watched my animated, eleven-year-old granddaughter, Amy, as she pretended to be Julia Child and demonstrated how to make an omelet. When she finished, she held it up to the camera and imitated the famous, "Bon appetite!"

I think it's time to give Amy her own small box filled with handwritten family recipes.

— Miriam Hill —

73

Going to Full Lengths

Only those who will risk going too far can
possibly find out how far one can go.
~T.S. Eliot

The State of California has offices throughout the state. I worked in one of them. It was a cubicle maze with many of the attributes of a *Dilbert* cartoon, and it contained just as many absurdities. And none of them were about to change due to our dismal budget.

I had enough when, for the third day in a row, a woman in my office walked back from the ladies room with her skirt tucked inside her pantyhose. Of course, she didn't know she was flashing her derriere to the rest of the office until someone told her.

As I sent yet another e-mail to management requesting a full length mirror, I wondered what I could possibly do to correct the situation.

Our newly remodeled ladies room was indeed beautiful. It was much closer than our prior one. It sported a handicapped stall and a partial handicapped stall along with many additional stalls. We no longer had to wait in long lines. But the only mirrors were placed above the sinks.

My e-mails had progressed from merely requesting a mirror, to offering to pay for it myself, to now stating that the women in the office were willing to go in together to purchase a full-length mirror. Management replied negatively to all my requests if they replied at all.

I was ready to take on the world. A co-worker stopped by my

desk; Ray was known as the local union steward. He had a way of asking just the right question. He asked me one that day. His question completely changed my life.

As I explained the situation to him, he listened politely and then asked, "You have a very valid issue. What are you going to do about it?"

As I turned back to my work, my mind replayed the question. It was a turning point. I realized that if anything was going to happen I was going to have to make it happen. But how could I do that?

Perhaps management would give more weight to my requests for a mirror if I provided a valid reason. Was that possible?

The handicapped stalls in the ladies room seemed somewhat out of proportion. I started my investigation right after work on the Internet. After several nights I found the solution I was looking for.

Federal American Disability Act (ADA) regulations stated that the door to the handicapped stall could not swing out into the path of another door. If it was located at the end of a row of stalls, that door was supposed to swing inward.

I had found my first valid legal issue!

I kept searching. ADA regulations stated that the sink actually had minimum and maximum height requirements if there was a handicapped stall. The next day I measured and found my second valid issue. Our sinks were too high and so were the soap dispensers!

On the third night of reading federal regulations I found the small print I needed. If there was a handicapped stall, a full-length mirror was required.

My next e-mail to management outlined the three infractions. I provided the Federal Regulations number and the website so they could read it for themselves. I asked for a meeting to discuss these items.

I did not get a response to this e-mail.

However, about three days later, the ladies room was closed for repairs.

The door to the handicapped stall was reversed so that it swung into the stall.

The entire row of sinks was reinstalled and lowered along with the mirror above it.

There was a full-length mirror placed on a wall so that a person would get a full view of herself as she exited.

I thought the problem was solved. I was finished. I could rest and get back to work. But that isn't quite what happened.

A few weeks later a visitor in a wheelchair came to my cubicle. I had seen this lady exiting the paratransit bus as she arrived at work each morning.

"Are you Linda?" she asked.

"Yes."

"I want to thank you," she began. "I've worked here for seven years and I have never been able to wash my hands in the ladies room. I understand you are responsible for that." She had tears in her eyes and she reached a tentative hand out to me.

I then thought about the other people I had seen in the office in wheelchairs.

"Oh my!" I replied as I grasped her hand in mine. "I am so glad I was able to help."

Sometimes we see only ourselves in the mirror. My tenacity in fighting for a mirror opened the door to many ladies rooms. When I retired from my job working for the State of California I went on to fight for ADA requirements in other state offices.

The question Ray asked changed my life.

The mirror changed how I looked at things.

— Linda Lohman —

74

A Ham Is Born

You will do foolish things,
but do them with enthusiasm.
~Sidonie Gabrielle Colette

y son Levi went off to college and never looked back. Yeah, I know, I should have been happy that he was independent and doing so well. But when even my very subtle reminders about the nineteen hours of labor I endured to bring him into this world failed to get him to phone home, I realized it was time to get on with my own life.

The day-to-day part of raising a kid was done. All that creative energy, all that passion, all that focus — they had to go somewhere.

And then.

Our family joke is that I have always been Lucy to my husband Bill's Ricky — the wacky redhead who is always trying to get into her husband's shows. Bill sings, acts and writes musical theater. Levi has inherited his gifts. I, however, hadn't appeared on stage since my remarkable debut as Aunt Polly in my sixth grade production of *Tom Sawyer*. Whenever Bill produced or performed in a show, I pretended to campaign for a role. "Why can't I play Othello? I'd be brilliant!"

Now that my days weren't full of have-you-done-your-homework, have-you-written-your-college-essays, get-off-the-computer-and-go-to-sleep hysteria, I thought maybe I shouldn't pretend anymore. Why not give acting a shot?

Bill challenged me: Our local theater, Curtain Call, was doing *Waiting in the Wings* by Noël Coward. Set in a home for retired actresses, it had a large need for "women of a certain age." "If you audition, I will too and we can do it together," Bill offered. It was put up or shut up time.

I'd given lectures and readings, and had always felt comfortable on stage. I'm pretty good at feeling a mood and getting an audience to come with me. But that was me as me, saying my own thoughts. Could I assume the role of someone else? Could this aged brain actually retain lines? I read the play and saw a teeny tiny part that lasted a whole three pages. I could audition for that. "Sure, what the hey," I said.

Flash forward and guess what? I was cast. Initially I was sure they did so because they knew it was the only way they'd get brilliant Bill. (He made it clear that we were a package deal.) But I was cast in a much larger role than the teeny tiny one. I was Almina, an eighty-five-year-old obese former vaudevillian. Huh.

Bill and I were out together every weekday night at rehearsals for two months. When 7 p.m. rolled around, we both thought, "Uck, we're too tired to go out." But once we got there, we were energized by the creative process and the camaraderie of the cast. I felt as if I were back in college — making friends, laughing, discovering, and gossiping. I loved the inside jokes. I liked challenging myself to get inside someone else's skin.

I had few lines but for some reason was on stage the entire time. I couldn't figure out what I was supposed to be doing. "Do whatever you feel like," said the director. "I'll pull you back if it doesn't work." Wha? On the Internet, I found one review of a former production that said Almina stole the show every time she was on. Okay, I thought, she was doing something out there. It was up to me to find it and go for it.

At first I did a little mugging and sighing and eye rolling. The director said nothing. So I went broader: I hid food in my purse and pockets and stuffed my face constantly, actually making a bit of sorting through jellybeans. For the Christmas scene, I took a bird ornament and fashioned it into a barrette for my hair. (We were performing in a dinner theater in the round. During one performance, the ornament took a swan dive into a patron's dinner. I turned around and asked, "Can I have my birdie back?") By the final performance, I had become fearless. I was singing, dancing, pretending to sleep and snore, shamelessly scene stealing. This is what used to be referred to as "making stupid." Directed to take a small drink of rum, I grabbed the whole bottle and pretended to guzzle it. I did everything short of roll on the floor and pull my dress up over my head.

A ham was born. (Did I mention that the bows were my favorite part? Yay for me! Everyone clap for me!) Was I great? No, but was I really kind of okay? Yes. And did I enjoy it? Oh, yeah. While seasoned trained actresses in the cast were practically throwing up before every performance, I calmly did crossword puzzles.

I no longer sit home, waiting for Levi to call to fill me in on what's going on in the world. I am finding out for myself. Although I still can't believe how fast parenthood flies, from the umbilical cord dropping off to your kid dropping off laundry on his way to somewhere else, I have learned that the empty nest can actually be a blessing. It gives me time to find out who I am when I am not Levi's mom. And apparently, there are many different "me's" who are waiting to make their entrance.

Do it again? I already have. (I believe audiences are still talking about my definitive Sarah the Cook in *The Man Who Came to Dinner*.) I have learned to sing and dance — at the same time, mind you — for *Fiddler on the Roof*. The head of the company has talked to me about upcoming productions that call for over-the-top comedy. Or as he so delicately puts it, "whacked-out nut jobs." I've never been so complimented.

— Beth Levine —

A Senior Dog Named Ernest

A really companionable and indispensable dog is an
accident of nature. You can't get it by breeding for it,
and you can't buy it with money. It just happens along.
~E.B. White

The big, scraggly Golden Retriever burst into our home, pulling the rescue worker at the end of the leash. He shook his head vigorously and lunged toward everything he set his sights on. Clearly, he hadn't had a bath in years. His dingy reddish-gold hair lay matted on his neck and back. His warm eyes and goofy grin, however, stole my heart. I glanced at his graying muzzle. Another senior dog. Could we really do this again?

Years ago, my husband Mike and I had adopted our first senior dog — an eleven-year-old Golden Retriever. He'd been abandoned and on his own for who knows how long. I'd hesitated. What if he had expensive medical concerns? What if he had behavioral issues we couldn't correct? And… what if we fell in love with him and he broke our hearts?

But we took a chance. We adopted him and we did fall in love. And he did break our hearts. But then one day, another senior dog who needed a home found us. And another. By then, we realized that our first old Golden had come to us in order to open our hearts and set us on our mission of rescuing senior dogs.

We discovered that there is so much we love about senior dogs. They are already housebroken. They lounge at our feet in the yard and are happy with our leisurely pace when walking around the block. Sunday strolls are just our style. Senior dogs are happy to nap while I work at my desk. And they are eager to please and already know the rules. Living with a senior dog fits our lifestyle.

Then we lost two beloved old friends within a week of each other. Saying goodbye to them was one of the most difficult things I've ever had to do. We missed them terribly, but we also didn't want to wait too long to fill our home with a dog to love again. I barely knew how to navigate my morning without a pooch to let out the back door and a bowl to fill with kibble. It was too sad coming home from an errand without a furry friend greeting us at the door, jumping for joy at our arrival. There was no warm companion to snuggle with me on my living room chair. Still, my heart reminded me, loving and losing are hard.

Then this big, messy Golden Retriever bounded into our home. "He's been kept in a cage," the rescue worker said, shaking her head. "He's a little wound up!"

"Kept in a cage?" I asked. "How did this happen?"

She told me that the previous owner had no interest in the dog, so she kept him caged up. "Fortunately, she finally agreed to surrender him. She told us, 'I didn't take good care of him, but who cares?'"

I gasped. How could anyone feel that way about another living thing?

"Can you imagine, she let us lead him away... didn't even say goodbye."

The dog sat down and scratched hard at his neck. Poor guy was uncomfortable. Then he ran up and pushed his head under my arm to pat him. As I rubbed him all over, I discovered that he'd been let outside just enough to become covered in ticks.

"Looks like he needs us," Mike said, and there was no question in our minds that this unruly, unkempt, sweet dog was our new best friend.

We named him Ernest because he seemed so sincere. We always re-name a rescue dog when we get one — new life, new name. We didn't want him to associate his name with anything negative. We gave Ernest a good grooming, removed six ticks, and trimmed his nails. Ernest just looked at us, grinning the whole time.

Ernest was so excited to be out of a cage that he ran around the whole house and yard. "You don't have to worry about being locked up now," I said. He was so happy to be free; he couldn't get enough of the human touch. He loved to be patted. He loved it so much that he developed a bad habit. Any time we stopped patting him, he barked, loud. The minute we resumed, he relaxed and remained quiet. I figured it would just take time for him to feel secure that we'd always pat him whenever he wanted. I was right. After several weeks, he stopped the barking habit. But he still loved to be patted all the time.

I knew right away that Ernest would make a great therapy dog. Sometimes, when a dog we adopt seems like a good fit, we take him for therapy-dog training. Ernest seemed perfect.

He walked into class calmly, unlike the first day when he had bounded into our house full of pent-up energy. He was friendly to people and polite around other dogs. He didn't react to loud noises and sudden movements. He wasn't afraid of wheelchairs and walkers. Ernest passed his test with flying colors. He's now certified with Therapy Dogs International and proudly wears his red therapy-dog bandanna. He works at nursing homes, libraries, colleges, and elementary schools. He even went to the New York State Capitol to help employees there during stressful times at work.

Rescuing Ernest hasn't been without its challenges. Sometimes, he has trouble managing the stairs when he's tired. He's had issues with food and seasonal allergies. And he was diagnosed with cancer, but he had surgery and is more than two years cancer-free!

Living with and loving a senior dog aren't always easy, but we've realized we wouldn't have it any other way. Ernest fills our hearts with love and is living out his golden years with a family that cares about him. The dog who lived most of his life locked up in a cage is now free to enjoy the life he was meant to live. And he gets patted just as much as he could ever want.

— Peggy Frezon —

76

Take Your Husband to Work Day

One moment the world is as it is. The next,
it is something entirely different.
Something it has never been before.
~Anne Rice, Pandora

When I retired, I planned to do more of the things I loved and try new things I never had time for. But after six months, tennis and writing grew stale from overdoing them. Expanding the garden created so much extra produce that I couldn't even give it away. As for new things, well, kayaking hurt my back, golf seemed pointless, and a year into retirement, I had completed every project on my home improvement list.

I began watching more TV, taking up sudoku, mowing the lawn before it needed it, and even asking my wife if she needed anything done. I sighed and snacked a lot.

One morning, Carol announced, "Today is Take Your Husband to Work Day."

"I never heard of that."

"Because I just invented it. Get dressed — nicely."

I started to protest, but I had nothing. Could I say that I planned to watch *Mutiny on the Bounty* at 10:00 a.m.? I shucked off my baggy jeans and sweatshirt. Khakis and an unwrinkled shirt felt pretty good.

She was on the road visiting clients. I could carry supplies if I wanted to be more than a useless lump. Carol is a retired therapist. Since giving up a salary, however, she's volunteered with the same agency to do therapy, organizational counseling, social work, grant writing, data input, program assessment, and speech making. She latches onto new challenges like a bulldog.

Our first stop was at a rickety boarding house for men. They shared a common kitchen and bathroom, and each man had his own room. The porch steps bounced under my weight. The house paint was curled and cracked. "Have you been here before?" I asked. It was hard to picture my classy wife in such a house.

"Oh, yes. Pull up your socks and roll down your cuffs," she replied. "You don't want anything jumping aboard."

She marched through a dingy hallway and banged on door number three. My skin prickled. I knew she dealt with poverty, but this seemed dangerous. "You shouldn't be alone in places like this," I said.

She shrugged. "I go where the people who need help live."

"Who's there?" a grizzled voice said.

Carol announced herself, and the door creaked open. "I brought you some things."

"Okay." Perhaps sixty, the man was unshaven and wore a sleeveless white undershirt. The room was maybe ten by ten with a card table, two chairs, a TV, and a bed dripping its blanket on the floor. The one window faced the wall of another building.

"Did you get a can opener?" he rasped as he pawed through the box I set on the card table. Eventually, he pulled out a hand-crank opener with a triumphant "Hah! What good's a food pantry if you can't get into the food?"

As we were leaving, I thought Carol's efforts were hopeless. It all drained into a sinkhole. Then the man called after us. "Hey, Mrs. B. That guy you told me about, he's got landscaping work for me. Thanks!"

Back in the car, I said, "I can't believe you go into places like that."

She shrugged. "Someone saw him trying to open canned goods with a brick. That can opener is the difference between whether he eats tonight or not. One thing this job does is make me grateful for everything we have. When I get home at night, I feel like a princess."

I grinned. "Really?"

"I'd feel like a queen if dinner was waiting."

"Uh-oh."

"Another thing. In this job, I'm never bored. Here, use the sanitizer."

Our next stop was at a small but neat house. Carol said, "Two elderly daughters are caring for their mother, and I need to set up respite care to give them a break."

The daughter who greeted us was in her seventies. In the living room, a hospital-style bed with steel sidebars was set up. An ancient woman slept there, snoring. The daughter wept as we watched the mother's chest rise and fall. "Mom's dying, but she just won't let go. She's had such a full life. Seventeen grandchildren, fifty-two great grandchildren, a few dozen great-great grandchildren, and then I lose track. See the picture over her bed? Mom's last birthday — her 99th." A panoramic shot was filled with a huge, waving crowd. I was awed. This woman was like a spring that had expanded into a river of humanity. She was like a biblical matriarch.

Right before Carol took the daughter aside to counsel her and discuss practical matters, the daughter told me, "If Mom stirs, just hold her hand. She'll think it's one of the family." Me, hold this stranger's hand? A few minutes later, the mother began to moan, and I tentatively touched her hand. She clutched my hand and held tight. Such strength! Such passion even near the end. And I struggled to fill empty hours? I squeezed back to let her know that someone was here, as she had been for so many others. I felt as if some part of myself that had been shut away was stirring, that this unexpected intimate moment with a stranger was the most worthwhile thing I had done in quite a while. A few minutes later, she relaxed and slept.

In the car, I said, "That was amazing! Think of all the people she's leaving behind, the history her descendants will make! The nurturing she's done. One person can change the world."

Carol nodded. "There's plenty to think about on visits. I never know what I'll face." She shrugged. "Sometimes, it isn't pretty, but it's real life. I need to contribute while I can. You never know what difference a small contribution can make. Don't get me wrong, I like snuggling up with an old movie. And snuggling up with this same old guy I've been with all these years. But dealing with the unexpected makes our quiet moments even more precious."

Take Your Husband to Work Day was a success. I signed up to volunteer that week. Otherwise, Carol would have made me cook dinner.

— Garrett Bauman —

77

The Wooden Bench

There is no exercise better for the heart than
reaching down and lifting people up.
~John Holmes

I was sixty-eight years old and retired, and I was sitting on a wooden bench in the county jail, hoping I would be rejected. The gray tile floors echoed the sounds of the officers' shoes as they went from one room to another. People came in from outside, and the scent of greasy take-out food wafted through the facility. Then they called my name.

A guard took me to the middle room where I was searched and patted down. My nametag was checked, and the officer signaled the tower to open the gate. There was no turning back.

I was still wondering how I got there. Our church had joined a jail ministry group, and the pastor had asked me to think about being a teacher. I had said, "No." Instead, I volunteered for the Angel Tree ministry, taking Christmas gifts to children of the inmates. Then I was invited to go with the jail ministry team to tour the jail and be educated about what was expected of the inmates as well as the teachers. On that tour, the clanging metal doors sent chills through me. I knew I couldn't handle being locked behind those doors, even as a volunteer who knew she was getting out. I did not feel safe, even though we were with the guards.

Then a woman named Margo started talking to me about being her partner. She was young and full of energy. She had prior experience volunteering in a prison, and she felt she could speak to the women's needs and be a good influence. I enjoyed being around her, and her positive attitude was contagious. The more she shared with me, the more the idea didn't seem so crazy.

I talked about it with my daughter. "Am I too old to begin something like this? I am not comfortable with the idea."

"Mom, you could be like a mother figure or grandmother to those women in jail. They would appreciate you."

When I asked my husband, he suggested I give it a try.

My confidence began to build, and I finally told Margo I would be her "buddy" and volunteer with her. She was so excited.

That was how I found myself sitting on that wooden bench waiting to be approved to go to jail.

After I was approved, Margo and I scheduled our first visit. I was nervous. I pictured the room we would be in, with the metal stools fastened to the floor and a buzzer to push by the door if we needed to summon a guard. I packed my jail bag with the soft-covered Bible, unstapled handouts and my pencil with no eraser. I also put in a little packet of tissues.

We arrived at the jail and sat on the now familiar wooden bench after signing in. The guard came in, and I felt my heart race. But then he said, "The women are not coming out tonight as there is a problem in the pod."

Margo was so disappointed. "I can't believe, after we got everything ready, that they can't come out."

"We will try again next week," I said. I tried to sound disappointed too.

We were back on that wooden bench the next week. The guard came out and said the women did not want to come out for the service. Apparently, there was a good television program on. Margo wiped away a tear, and I felt guilty at the relief that I felt.

"I don't think I am supposed to be part of this ministry," I told Margo. "I don't feel your disappointment when they don't come out. Frankly, I am relieved."

"You can't quit now," she pleaded. "Give it another week."

I agreed.

The next week I arrived at the jail first and signed in. I sat on the wooden bench. The phone rang, and the secretary called me to the window and told me Margo had called and said she couldn't come, as her child was ill. I turned to get my bag and head out the door when the guard came out.

"Ready to go," she motioned me forward.

"Alone?"

I was checked and patted down, and then followed the guard through the clanging metal doors. The echo of the door mechanically unlocking made me jump. I was in the room, and soon the women would be filing through the doors. I prayed.

One by one, the women in orange entered the room. I was stunned. I saw daughters, mothers, and grandmothers. They had all made bad decisions for one reason or another, but they wanted a better life. I felt no fear, and suddenly I couldn't wait to share encouraging words with these women. Before I knew it, our session was over and the women were thanking me for coming.

Fifteen years have passed now. This ministry I once feared continues to draw me weekly to the jail. I have seen thousands of women and heard their voices echo, "Thanks, Granny Bev," as they follow the guard down the hall to their cells, and I go through the clanging doors in the opposite direction.

— Beverly LaHote Schwind —

78

The Power of Giving

Christmas is the spirit of giving without a thought of getting. It is happiness because we see joy in people. It is forgetting self and finding time for others.
~Thomas S. Monson

The e-mail came from a friend who is always doing something interesting, unusual or rewarding. This time, it was an invitation to participate in a Christmas Day visit to a Lutheran assisted-living facility in our community. The mission: help the staff in whatever way we could because, as Jewish families, we don't celebrate Christmas ourselves.

Christmas can, in fact, be a somewhat odd day for those of us who are Jewish. Most years, the formula is familiar: a newly released movie and Chinese food.

We almost said no. We'd already made plans, and this suggestion sounded a bit daunting, as the unfamiliar often does.

But after some conversation, my husband and I decided to take on the three-hour shift together at the familiar building on our town's Main Street, a building we'd walked past often.

Of course, the motivation was not only that we could be of help to the staff; we also could hopefully interact with some of the lonely souls who were not slated to have visitors on Christmas Day.

My husband always had the gift of easy communication and connection. As a long-time writer I, however, had been shielded behind the written word.

I'm a tad shy, and I was more than a tad nervous about this Christmas Day visit.

"These are strangers," I reminded my easygoing husband. "We're Jewish. We don't even celebrate Christmas. What will we talk about?"

Vic made short shrift of my anxiety. "We're human!" he said. "Humans find ways to communicate."

We got our first challenge at the entrance to the Lutheran home, where a lone elderly man sat in a wheelchair. We greeted him with the standard "Hi," but got no response.

He seemed so alone, and what touched us so much was that he was holding a small American flag in his hand. There he sat, on Christmas Day with his flag. But after several attempts at conversation, it struck us: He had lost the gift of speech. A stroke, perhaps, or some other infirmity.

I don't know what made me do it, but I stepped up close to his wheelchair, smiled and pointed to the flag. And I gave it a thumbs-up.

Suddenly, a smile as radiant as the sun spread across an old soldier's face.

Mind you, we don't know that he was one, but he seemed straight out of Central Casting as a World War II vet.

In that moment I knew we'd made a very good decision.

All around us were people in wheelchairs — some surrounded by families, some alone. There were staffers bustling around, leaning over to whisper something sweet or funny or just friendly. These are the amazing men and women who sacrifice their own Christmas Days to be there for the forgotten or the needy.

Suddenly, religion didn't matter a bit. Nor did shyness. All that mattered was the privilege of being a part of this day.

To pause to say "Merry Christmas!" To shake a hand. To offer a cookie.

But there was so much more to come.

We were ultimately assigned to the area where the Alzheimer's and dementia residents were finishing lunch, many of them slumped in their wheelchairs, a few with some small spark of awareness.

We'd been advised to meet these residents at eye level, to approach them from the front, never from behind, and to expect anything from total indifference to anger to a blank stare.

We got some of each.

But gradually, as we knelt down to try to connect — as we smiled, patted a shoulder, held a hand — there was a glimmer of something.

Eye contact. A hesitant smile. A word or two.

In some ways, that was a most difficult, even exhausting experience. But oh, the amazing rewards.

There was the tiny lady whose sweet face showed delight when we wished her a Merry Christmas. Her nails had been polished, her white sweater was clearly for special occasions, and her ability to connect and respond was in there somewhere.

So we talked without words. And yes, that's not just possible — it's amazing.

I handed her two soft little plush teddy bears that were available to these residents to have and to hold. She cuddled them close to her heart.

We repeated this again and again with men and women who didn't care what religion we were or why we were there, as long as we let them know that they were worthy of a smile or a touch.

And then we discovered the lady with a cap of silver hair who began to call us "Mommy" and "Poppy," and reminded us that we used to make Christmas pudding together. She was, she told us, seventeen years old.

Good for her! Maybe that's how she felt on this Christmas Day in her late senior years.

Our most astounding moments came with her.

The background music piped into the activity room was Christmas music, and almost instinctively my husband began singing along to the words of "I'm Dreaming of a White Christmas." Then I, the world's most self-conscious singer, joined in.

Then, suddenly, there was a third voice. Our silver-haired lady friend was singing every word of "Jingle Bells," and then of "Silent Night."

There we sat, two Jewish Christmas visitors and a sweet woman with a voice like an angel, singing together on Christmas Day.

Unlikely? Definitely.

Uplifting? Absolutely.

Meaningful? Certainly for us.

Hopefully also for the residents of this place, five blocks — and light years — removed from our lives.

When we tiptoed away, we noticed that our new friend had fallen into a peaceful sleep, with just a hint of a smile on her lips.

We left knowing that we'd just experienced our very own beautiful, wonderful Christmas miracle.

— Sally Friedman —

79

A Grandparent's Job

When you look into your mother's eyes, you know that
is the purest love you can find on this earth.
~Mitch Albom

While my daughter did not have any grandfathers, she was blessed with two wonderfully diverse grandmothers. "Nana" and "Momo" each played an important part in my daughter's life. One particular evening when I was busy with the usual chaos in our household, my mother, Nana, offered to give my daughter her bath. While I cleared the dinner dishes, I heard the usual laughter and exclamations that accompanied the bath time of a five-year-old, followed by a period of what seemed to be a serious whispered conversation.

After bath time, my mom came out to the kitchen and joined me in putting away the leftovers. She told me that she and Francesca had had a talk.

"I just want you to know that everything is alright," my mom said.

"What do you mean everything is alright? I didn't know anything was wrong."

"No, it's all good. She just needed to talk," my mom said with a confidence I certainly did not feel.

"Mom, I really need to know what she talked to you about."

"Oh, that's between a granddaughter and her nana."

We had been through a lot in my daughter's first five years of life — with my mother's cancer, my husband's cancer and him losing his job. We worried about how she processed all the stress that had transpired. We were always very open, answering any questions in a way a child her age could understand. So why could she not approach us? I felt a stab in my heart, followed by the immediate sense of fear that someone had hurt her. When I pressed my mom about it, she said not to worry. Not worry? Really?

I turned to my mom and said, "Why couldn't she ask me?"

My mother replied that she had asked Francesca the very same question, to which she had replied, "I know my mom and dad love me, but their job is to decide if I am doing right or wrong. You, Nana, just need to love me."

I never did find out what that whispered conversation was about—my mother has since passed, and Francesca can't remember—but I was grateful that my daughter had a confidante she could trust.

It has been thirty-two years since that conversation, but since I became a "Nana," I totally understand I hope that I can be the confidante to my grandsons that my mother was to my daughter.

A grandparent's job is not to judge, but to simply love. Oh, how I love my job.

— Loretta Schoen —

80

Wild Card

*Talent wins games, but teamwork
and intelligence win championships.*
~Michael Jordan

I hurled the pass into the end zone. Boom! Caught! Now I know how Tom Brady feels. Of course, I don't actually play any sport involving balls. But I am a grandma, always vying for number-one ranking among the grandparents. Last week, I nailed a big win against our chief rival. If you share your grandchildren with more than one set of grandparents, you get it. It's a competition.

My husband and I joined the league in 2010. We had the home-field advantage. Our first granddaughter was born in our town hospital and lived a mere three miles from our house. All the firsts — smile, rollover, sit-up, and steps — occurred in our stadium. The local fans supported our team — both sets of great-grandparents, cousins, great aunts and uncles. We understood the rules of possession. When the opposing grandparents visited from Ontario, we kept our distance. After their long weekend, we would resume our status as local resident grandparents.

In 2011, the advantage shifted, like the momentum after a hefty penalty. The parents moved our one-year-old granddaughter to Ontario. Suddenly, we became the underdog. More than simply moving the franchise from one city to another, it involved an international border. I felt the stakes magnify to playoff proportions. This relocation involved honoring a different national anthem, abandoning the Stars and Stripes for a maple leaf, and supplanting football with hockey. Her speech was just developing. The child would surely speak Canadian English, maybe even French, rather than Pittsburgh vernacular. In July 2012, the opposition took over first place The second granddaughter would be born in their country. It felt as if they sacked our quarterback.

We developed a defensive game plan. For weeks at a time in summers, we rented cottages near the Canadian venue, attempting to level the playing field. Over winter holidays, we traversed white-outs and ice storms to remain competitive. We stayed in rented houses, cottages and hotels over the next five years, investing in our franchise. We brought toys, gifts, our live Labrador mascot and, on several occasions, a set of great-grandparents, all in our effort to regain the number-one slot.

However, in the annual Christmas tournament, we always found ourselves coming from behind. With two small children, the parents were reluctant to travel treacherous roads to Pennsylvania for the holiday. The rival grandparents lived just three hours west, and they had the advantage of a two-holiday Canadian option — Christmas as well as Boxing Day. No matter how hard our son worked to make us feel viable, we recognized our status as second string.

The rivals pulled out their best play last summer when they took the children on a ten-day family trip to Europe. During any other year, that would have put us on the disabled list. However, we had a momentous game plan ready for this year. We moved permanently from northwestern Pennsylvania to northern New York, just twenty-five miles from the granddaughters. Thanks to our gutsy decision, like going for the two-point conversion, we tied the game.

Our new house features a bedroom for the children, and an art studio stocked with paper, markers, paints, modeling clay, and tubs of glitter. Any number of oak trees invites the construction of fairy houses, and we have checked out all the play structures within ten miles. Yet, all of that does not ease the drive, the bridge toll, or the long wait at the border when the parents bring the children to our place.

Coming into the 2016 holidays, we were in a dead heat.

The opponents took the offensive and hosted the grandchildren and their parents for Canadian Thanksgiving, which happens in October.

Of course, we Americans had yet to celebrate that holiday, so we took a bye that weekend. Little or no enthusiasm met us from team Canada for a second Thanksgiving. We lost that challenge and spent Thanksgiving at a hotel buffet.

I rebounded with a quarterback sneak. I had in my possession the American Girl catalog — a book of eighteen-inch dolls designed with exquisite care and detail. Each year, a Girl of the Year was marketed, complete with a personality profile and all the authentic trappings of a well-to-do young lady. I took the catalog with me to share with the granddaughters on my next visit. They loved Lea, that year's doll, and naturally I promised to order one for each of them for Christmas.

Then my doubts surfaced. When would we actually see the little girls? Would it be anticlimactic after the twenty-fifth? Would the dolls seem special amidst all of Santa's surprises? On impulse, I declared that the dolls would be here December first, and that would become American Girl Doll Day. I went online to place a rush delivery. The rivals could take Thanksgiving, and perhaps Christmas, but I would claim December first as my special holiday and win in overtime.

On December first, I drove my car to the border with the dolls gift-wrapped in the back seat. I endured a scolding for exceeding the sixty-dollar limit on importing gifts. Cheerfully, I promised to pay duty next time. At my son's house, I arranged the gift boxes on the coffee table and then drove to the bus stop to meet the granddaughters. Bursting with excitement, they asked if today was the day. Earlier, the older granddaughter had taken a corner of her bedroom and fitted it for the doll with a bed, play area, and work station, even wallpaper. I hoped the younger would love Lea just as much as she adored her baby dolls.

As we entered the house, they dropped their coats and book bags, and dashed for the boxes. The joy as they met their dolls and unpacked the realistic accessories lived up to my wildest hopes. The six-year-old raved about the small passport, complete with photo, so she could present it to the border guard on her next visit to our house. The younger gleefully examined the diminutive camera, compass, and duffle bag. They talked to Lea and tried on her extra outfits.

Of course, each doll was seated at the table for dinner and joined in our play the rest of the evening. We all had pictures taken. The older child used her photo with the doll as wallpaper on her iPad. The younger used my phone to take a portrait of her doll seated in the revered Minnie Mouse chair.

As I donned my coat for the return home, I savored the goodbye hugs and kisses — not just from my granddaughters, but also from the two dolls. "Now you have four granddaughters, Dede," Rayna announced. So this year, no matter what happens between now and January first, I've won the Super Bowl. Of course, a new year means a new championship. Game on.

— Cinda Findlan —

The New Normal

81

Going Places with Less

Don't settle down and sit in one place. Move around,
be nomadic, make each day a new horizon.
~Jon Krakauer

Walking along the trail with my husband, I took a deep breath and admired the view. Snowcapped mountains. Wildflowers blooming yellow, blue and red throughout the hillside meadows, their sweet scent carried in the breeze. A glimpse of a sapphire blue lake sparkling in the distance. We were in Glacier National Park, Montana.

One of the best, albeit scariest, decisions we made regarding our retirement was to sell our home of thirty years and travel across the country in an RV. Sounds great at first blush, but the reality of living in 350 square feet meant a drastic downsize. It would be quite a change for us. Oh, but our new back yard! We were downsizing with a purpose and we were excited to begin a new life chapter.

More than a year before our target departure date, we stopped buying anything except food. No more clothes. No more shoes. No more gadgets for the kitchen. It was actually quite freeing and easy to do.

As sad and difficult as it was, cleaning out my mother-in-law's home after her passing helped me. She was a borderline hoarder, purely as a result of her experience in East Germany during World War II, when she wasn't able to get simple things like sugar or coffee. While cleaning out her worldly possessions, I learned a very big lesson. Use it or give it to someone who can. All the excess things she had stored away — clothes, food, nylons, toys — were molded or moth-eaten and couldn't be used by anyone. It was so sad to realize the amount of her time, money and space that were wasted. She would have been sick had she known that everything would end up being thrown away. With that experience fresh in my mind, it was so much easier to make my own decisions on what to keep, give away or trash.

Slowly, we began downsizing. My husband and I each were responsible for our own "stuff," as were our grown kids. The downsizing was quite a challenge at first. It was easy to get rid of old Halloween decorations and the dated Christmas ornaments I had kept just in case we ever needed more for the Christmas tree. It got a bit harder when I was going through the boxes in the basement labeled "memories." There were my high school and college yearbooks, ribbons and a few trophies I had won as a child while on the town's swim team. When was the last time I even looked at those ribbons? And then there were the items I'd saved from our kids. The task at hand was to decide what to keep (in a storage unit), what to bring, what to give away, and what to trash.

Furniture was another story. We decided to just give it away. After family and friends took what they could use, we gave the rest to the young couple that bought our house. They were thrilled and we were happy to help this young family starting out.

As the downsizing momentum built, I tackled my photo collection — twenty-three shoeboxes to be exact. I could not bear to part with them so I scanned the photos into my computer and discarded the hard copies. What a feeling when that task was completed!

An avid and passionate knitter, I had accumulated lots of beautiful fiber for my creative pleasure. No. I could not give up even one skein. Or could I? This was one of the most difficult downsizing chores for me, and though I did well donating to various groups and fiber friends, I have a sizable stash to this day.

Fast forward to our current living conditions. We've been living in the RV for a year and a half and we want for nothing. We did a great job deciding what was necessary for our life on the road. There is not one item in our small kitchen that is not used. We have just enough clothes. Both of us have brought along our hobby supplies — yarn, computers and electronics paraphernalia. A few special pictures on the wall and a few select decorations make the motorhome into our "home sweet home." We even have a "garden" — several small pots of herbs we keep in our front window.

Because we are living so simply there is much less to clean and no reason to shop. If it doesn't have a purpose or enjoyment factor, it doesn't come in the RV. It really is that simple. Instead of collecting things, we are collecting such unbelievable experiences. It's a magical life we are living right now. Granted, much has to do with being retired, but I strongly believe that some of the freedom we feel is a result of downsizing.

My husband and I enjoy nature and being outdoors. We have the opportunity to explore national parks, hiking and marveling at the world around us. Early in our journey, we had very poor TV reception, so we rarely watched TV. Now, even when we do have access, it is more of a decision to watch... not just a habit. When we do watch TV or a movie, we really enjoy it. Not being tied to the TV habit, we spend more time on our hobbies. My husband has even branched out into quadcopters and other radio controlled vehicles. His eight-inch telescope came along with us for those fabulous night skies. My yarn collection is diminishing.

This journey of ours does not mean Nirvana. We did not win the lottery. We are living on a budget. We have endured illness (including cancer) and accidents (requiring stitches) while on the road thousands of miles away from family and friends. Things have broken down. The windshields have cracked on the car and the RV. We've had a few disagreements on the road.

Though it wasn't easy to downsize, the result has been such a feeling of freedom — not being tied down by material things allowed us to experience life differently. It is nice to know we can winter in the Arizona desert and not have to worry about a big snowstorm in New Jersey and our home there. Can you hear the sigh of relief? That is what simplifying and downsizing feels like to us. Living uncluttered and unencumbered by material things. A nice feeling. We have a very rich and fulfilling life, just with less stuff. Simple as that.

— Susan Leitzsch —

82

Confession of a Christmas Cruiser

I'd rather regret the things I've done
than the things I haven't done.
~Lucille Ball

Who skips out on Christmas? The Kranks tried it in both a novel and a movie but didn't succeed. So what made us think we could? And why would we?

All of the five Robbins kids had left the nest. They were scattered across the country, making it next to impossible to visit all of them at the holidays and a bit expensive for them to travel back home with their children. Bob and I truly didn't want to intrude on their family celebrations either. We remembered how much fun it was to celebrate on our own with them when they were little. Facing a Christmas with an empty house did not inspire a lot of Christmas decorating or cookie baking spirit. What to do?

The cruise brochure arrived just in time, filled with dreamy pictures of beautiful Tahiti and the French Polynesian islands. We sat at the kitchen table sipping coffee and watching the last of the autumn leaves swirl past the window. It wouldn't be long before the snowflakes fell. The brochure sat between us, already dog-eared and wrinkled from our perusal. A big grin spread across Bob's face.

"Let's give each other a cruise for Christmas!"

It didn't take long to sell me on the idea. But questions still arose.

Would we mind being away from home for Christmas? Would we miss not having a white Christmas? What would the kids say? We moved ahead with the idea anyway and made our reservations.

The ship was the Paul Gauguin, a beautiful elegant mid-sized cruise ship. We were welcomed aboard to a venue decorated with Christmas trees, gingerbread houses, and nooks and crannies filled with all the traditional decorations of the season. It was a ten-day cruise and Christmas fell in the middle of it. Bob decorated our mirrored vanity with a string of mini-lights and stuck a Santa hat on the small decorative bust that was in our room. I think our cabin steward giggled every time she saw it.

Christmas Eve we caroled and Christmas morning we awoke to another gorgeous view of luscious tropical greens draping the hills and mountains of Raiatea. In preparing for our trip, I had packed a couple of small Christmas stockings and some candy. Playing Santa's helper, I filled them and gave two to our cabin steward as she began her morning chores.

"One is for you," I said, "and one is for you to give to a friend."

Her eyes lit up and she clutched them to her chest as she ran down the hall hailing her friend in her own language to give her the second stocking. I didn't realize such a small gesture would be so welcomed.

After breakfast, we went on an excursion through the countryside. I was impressed that the driver of our open-sided truck had given up her Christmas morning to show us her beautiful island. Even more impressive was the young boy who quietly played with his Christmas present, a new truck, on the front seat next to his mother.

At noon we were tendered over to a private beach where there were picnic tables, a large barbecue pit, and plenty of beach chairs. Our Christmas dinner consisted of grilled lobster, steak, chicken, tropical fruits, and lots of delicious side dishes. I don't recall missing the usual pork roast with sauerkraut and dumplings that was a tradition at home for so many years.

After our dinner, we were treated to a visit from Santa. I'm sure he must have come to begin his vacation after his long night out delivering his presents. You see, he was dressed in a short-sleeved fur-trimmed red shirt, Santa cap, red shorts and flip-flops. He ho-ho-hoed his way down the beach and greeted all the passengers, gave a little extra treat to the children he met, and then disappeared to begin a long deserved rest.

Did we miss Christmas at home? Not in the least. As a matter of fact we enjoyed our time away so much that we have made it part of a new tradition. Every other year our kids know that we will be off cruising somewhere warm. They don't have to worry about Mom and Dad being alone at Christmas and we don't have all the work associated with the holiday season. I must confess, I love it.

— Karen Robbins —

83

Reconstructing Me

To practice any art, no matter how well or badly,
is a way to make your soul grow. So do it.
~Kurt Vonnegut

efore I met my late husband, I was very capable. I did a lot of things for myself, including building some of my own furniture. I never really doubted how capable I was. But then I married a guy who was so much better than I was at so many things that I just let him take charge. He was a general contractor and excellent carpenter. And even though I had always loved to garden and was even a garden writer, his green thumb was much greener than mine. He could just look at seeds and "will" them to grow. And then, when the tomatoes, eggplants and peppers he grew were ripe and ready, he could whip up a wonderful homemade meal without a recipe while my culinary skills were greatly lacking.

For the sixteen years we were together, we built many things, including our own home, owl boxes and garden structures for the yard, and two successful careers. But I always felt like he was the lead carpenter in our lives, and I was the apprentice in most things... and not just the construction projects. Of course, I didn't really mind. It made sense to let the person who could just envision a project and make it happen take the lead on most things. Projects would have been a lot slower if I was in charge, even though some things probably would have had a much more artistic flair.

Since he passed away, I have been trying to get my self-confidence back. After letting someone else take the lead for sixteen years, I got to the point where I was afraid to do anything or make decisions by myself.

During 2020, I was going a little stir-crazy being stuck at home during the pandemic. I decided to use all the scrap lumber and other materials I had around the house to build a new structure in my yard to hold orchids. I didn't have any plan to follow. I just looked up some things on Etsy and other places to get ideas. And then I started building. I hadn't built anything that large in a while, and I had to think about every corner, brace and angle — things my husband would have been able to visualize in his head with no problem. And, of course, I didn't really know what kind of lumber I had lying around. I didn't want to buy any because that defeated the purpose. I just made it up as I went along and worked to the point of exhaustion every night.

A million thoughts went through my head. First, I felt proud and accomplished. If my husband were still alive, he would have taken over the project and done it "right." Now, I kind of enjoyed doing it my way. I also know that if he were alive, it would have been done on the first day, and it would have been much more structurally sound but a little less "Bohemian" and arty.

He never would have added the old stained-glass window or the hand-carved wood trim to a project that was just going to be out in the yard. But they were leftover items that had been sitting around in the garage for years, and they fit right in with my creation. I thought a lot about how much I miss having someone in my life to do stuff like this with me. But when the whole project was done, it was completely, uniquely my own. And that feeling of pride and accomplishment made me realize how important it was for me to get back to being me.

It was a breakthrough project for me. I posted pictures of it online and got so much encouragement that it kept me going and made me want to build more things, exactly my way. So, this project was me time in more ways than one. It was not just me spending time doing what I love to do. It was also a project that helped to bring out the real me again.

My husband and I had designed and built the home I live in,

but I had somehow forgotten what a huge role I played in that and what an accomplishment it was for me. I had designed the cabinet layouts and the beautiful stone fireplace, and I'd made decisions like using wood trim throughout and putting in huge windows to capture the view outside. I even helped in the actual construction process by putting up cedar siding and helping my husband and his friend do the interior framing. I helped build this beautiful, wonderful home, and yet I felt like I couldn't accomplish things anymore!

I moved my new garden structure right outside a window where I can see it every day. It's a great reminder that I am a strong, capable, creative person in my own right. I'm not the same woman I was when I was part of that wonderful, powerful, successful team that my husband and I created. But I think I'm going to be okay if I just keep reminding myself that part of the reason that team was so strong and successful was because of me.

— Betsy S. Franz —

84

Gobble, Gobble

I believe that the ability to laugh at oneself is
fundamental to the resiliency of the human spirit.
~Jill Conner Browne

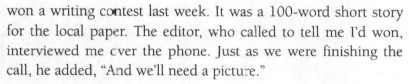

won a writing contest last week. It was a 100-word short story for the local paper. The editor, who called to tell me I'd won, interviewed me over the phone. Just as we were finishing the call, he added, "And we'll need a picture."

"Of me?" I asked.

"Yes."

"How about someone related to me?"

"Nope."

"Or a middle-aged actress who resembles me?"

The editor was probably wishing he had selected a sane person.

"Fine," I said.

Frantically, I began searching through my phone and computer for one decent picture. I e-mailed my daughter, asking her to send a good photo of me.

And she did.

But who was this less attractive, older version of myself? Oh, the horror!

Finally, I found a picture that was flattering. It was far away and blurry, and the person next to me partly obscured my face.

Jackpot!

The editor was less impressed. "We need a clear, solo, unfiltered photo."

A clear picture? Since when is clear better? For a glass of water, perhaps. But for pictures, let's not discount hazy.

And a solo picture? Who has a solo picture of themselves, besides real estate agents and convicts?

An unfiltered picture of myself? Filters were invented for a reason.

After not finding a single clear, solo, unfiltered picture of myself, I realized I would have to take a selfie. I examined my middle-aged face. Not bad. But really my face wasn't the problem.

It was my neck.

I didn't even know necks could be a problem until one of my friends (who will remain nameless, but we'll call her Carrie) recently told me about her neck woes. "I hate my neck," she said. "It's gotten so saggy, like a turkey."

That didn't sound like fun. I felt sorry for "Carrie" until I looked at my own neck in the mirror. Maybe it wasn't full-blown turkey, but it was turkey-esque.

Now I had to take a clear, solo, unfiltered photo that didn't involve my neck.

And then I remembered. Carrie once told me how she used tape to lift her eyebrows and soften the lines in between.

But tape on a neck? Wasn't that going too far?

I cut a piece of red duct tape, and while holding the tape in one hand, I pushed the left side of my neck back with the other hand. Carefully, I tucked the loose skin under the tape on the back of my neck. This stuff was amazing. My skin was firm, taught, years younger. Perfect.

Uh oh.

I could see red on one side, which could make one ponder, Is this a vampire story?

I started over, and it was going well until I ran out of tape. One side was smooth. The other, saggy. I was a before-and-after advertisement for duct-taped turkey necks.

I found more tape and finally got it on my third attempt. The skin was pulled back evenly on both sides without a hint of vampire or sag.

Just right.

After make-up and hair, I went in search of the best possible lighting in the house and snapped six selfies. Within minutes, I had made my selection, and one picture of a middle-aged neurotic writer, with a good neck, was en route to the editor.

His response? "Thanks."

The following week, my story, a short article on me, and the picture came out. My family, friends and colleagues had many kind words.

"What a great story."

"I love the ending."

"The imagery was powerful."

I thanked them politely, feeling a sense of pride. Still, it would have been nice if just one person had commented, "You know what was even smoother than your transitions? Your neck."

—January Gordon Ornellas—

A Year to Live

*Life is short, so live it. Love is rare, so grab it. Fear
controls you, so face it. Memories are precious,
so cherish them. We only get one life, so live it!*
~Author Unknown

We needed a new phone installation for a dictating device in the word processing center under my supervision as Central Services Coordinator in our combined school districts. But an old, heavy wooden desk was in the way and the serviceman refused to move it. With disgust, I muttered, "I am woman, hear me roar," as I shoved the massive obstacle out of the way. I covered up the wince in my fifty-six-year-old back until he left. It soon increased from pain to agony when I had to leave work and go home to bed. After a few days, when I could hobble to the car, I had it X-rayed.

The call from my doctor was unnerving. "Your back is not seriously injured, but there seems to be a dark spot on your kidney which requires further investigation." A CAT scan revealed a cancerous kidney, which had to be removed. Fortunately the cancer did not appear to have spread, but unfortunately it was a type of cancer that would not respond to chemo or radiation.

"Either we got it all… or we didn't," the nephrologist intoned. "I would recommend that you take that cruise you told me about, and do anything else this year that you have been putting off."

"My God," I pleaded. "The doctor expects this to spread and take my life within a year! I won't even get to claim any of the Social Security money I have contributed all these years. It isn't FAIR! Please help me!"

I hadn't intended to take an early retirement; my last child was still in college. But if I had only a year, I was going to make it count. A plea for volunteers at our local zoo appeared in the newspaper. I signed up for the twenty-three-week course to learn all about animals and how to handle them. The newsletter for my genealogy society arrived, hand printed, with genealogy misspelled and a plea for a volunteer editor. I had only a year, but I could surely do better than that! So I became an editor. I used the blessings of the new computers to resume writing and sold a few pieces.

I gave away many of my possessions, all my art supplies, and waited. As the year raced by and I was still around, I figured I still only had a few more years, maybe five. I marked off the years, filling them with everything I had procrastinated doing all my life. I took courses, Spanish and Russian; I taught night school courses in genealogy and family history. I savored every minute, soaking up visions of my new grandchildren I didn't expect to see grow up.

Now I've not only seen the first of the grandchildren grow up, but all ten of them and the first four great-grandchildren. I have been a zoo volunteer for over twenty-five years. After eighteen years as a genealogy society editor, I turned it over to another person and then walked into the editorship of a local historical society newsletter. I have had more articles and a couple of children's picture books published.

My "last year" of life continues to delight me, after a quarter century of making sure that every moment counts.

— Esther McNeil Griffin —

86

An "Aha Moment"

There's no place like home except Grandma's.
~Author Unknown

When my grandson was born, it was love at first sight. Tears of joy flooded my face as Randy's tiny fingers gripped mine. A proud grandma, I couldn't help but point out his sparkling dark brown eyes, handsome features and cute little grin. Whenever anyone suggested that he looked like me, I agreed wholeheartedly.

The older he got, the more I bragged. So handsome. And smart? It was obvious he was destined to be a rocket scientist. Or maybe an engineer. Did you see how he stacked those blocks? What a genius.

Time has a way of slipping by. An honor student and star athlete, Randy makes me proud. Now that he's almost a teenager he's become preoccupied with iPods, Xbox, cell phones and texting. Before I can hold a conversation with him, I have to remove the headphone from his ears. Our one-on-one time seems to be dwindling.

My recent foot surgery had me off my feet for several months. Randy lives next door and surprised me when he showed up every day after school to see if I needed help. We watched TV and played game after game of *Clue* just like old times.

Some afternoons he'd flop on the couch, and we'd talk about sports, summer and the future. He was so attentive, I worried he knew something I didn't. It was just foot surgery, right?

Every afternoon before he left, he asked to use my laptop. One day I peeked over his shoulder to see what he was working on. With a sheepish grin, he admitted he was chatting with friends on MySpace.

"That's my girlfriend," he said pointing to a cute little girl with long brown hair.

"You're way too young for that, but I love her dimples."

For two weeks, he visited non-stop. When he found out Grandpa was leaving for a trap shoot, he even offered to spend the weekend. What a wonderful grandson. Smiling, I caught myself remembering when he used to call and ask, "Are you thinking what I'm thinking? Come and get me."

One day, Randy's visits stopped as abruptly as they'd started. I assumed it was because I'd graduated to a walking boot and didn't need as much help. A week went by without us seeing each other. I knew he was busy with the new school year and sports, but I missed his company.

His mother checked on me daily. One day she called and said, "Well, I'm glad Randy's grades have improved."

"How can you do better than an A?" I asked.

She explained his study habits and marks had gone downhill since he'd started middle school. He'd put more effort into texting girls and making new friends than he had on homework. Thanks to online monitoring, she noticed his marks slipping well before progress reports came out.

Knowing he was capable of more, she'd taken away his electronic privileges, including his cell phone and computer. When she'd finished the litany of his punishment, there was silence on my end.

Finally, she said, "Mom, are you there?"

I chuckled, and then broke out in fits of laughter.

"Mom, what's going on?"

Choking back giggles, I said, "I've just had an aha moment. That explains our bonding the past few weeks. It wasn't my charming company after all. It was my wireless connection."

Randy must've heard his mother's end of the conversation because he stopped by later that afternoon and said, "Grandma, are you doing okay?"

Trying to hide my smile I said, "Yes honey. And so are you."

— Alice Muschany —

87

The Comeback

*To give anything less than your best
is to sacrifice the gift.*
~Steve Prefontaine

t was New Year's Eve 2011. I sat on my couch with my two dogs and was reflecting on the year. I had turned fifty in February and was taking some time to learn about myself. I was learning to embrace solitude and I was discovering peace.

As I sat on my couch, I recalled the joy I had experienced back in my glory days, running ultra marathons, winning National Championships, representing the United States at the World Championships. I thought of all of the friends I had made in the sport.

It had been a decade since I had entered a competition. Strangely, tears began to roll down my cheeks. Then, for the first time in many years, I wept openly. I tried to compose myself and walked to the bathroom to wash my face. It was there that I took a good, long, hard look at myself in the mirror.

I was no longer that ultra marathon runner. I had to confront reality. I was a middle-aged man in decent enough shape to sit behind the desk in my office for the day. Sure, I could still go out and run easily for an hour or go down to the gym and lift weights. I still worked out every day, but I was not the same person, the same athlete that I was in the late 1990s.

In the time away from competing, I'd raised my daughters and developed my law practice in Vermont. I attributed it all to growing up. It was easy to tell myself that. I had grown content in my life and appeared comfortable with the increase in the size of my waistline.

When I took a serious look at myself, I knew it was time to change. I lacked discipline and had no readily identifiable goals.

I shut off the TV. I began to contemplate what it was that I wanted in my life. Did I want to remain in my present state? Had I grown so old that I could no longer imagine a better me? Could I see myself transforming back into a competitive athlete? Did I have it in me? What was I made of? Was there something in me that desired more? Did I dare to dream?

A strange quiet came over me. I was going to transform my life. It was time to reinvent myself, to become all that I could imagine. I had to see it. I had to believe it. I began to think of myself as that thin, super fit athlete that could accomplish anything he set his mind to. This was not just about diet, exercise, and my routine. This was much deeper. It was going to be a complete transformation — mind, body and spirit.

I saw the end result as I sat there that night. The only things in the way of my desired result were effort and time. I asked myself one more question: "What are you willing to do to make this dream a reality?" The answer was a very simple one: "Whatever it takes!"

I slept well that night and was prepared for Day 1 of my metamorphosis. I gulped down a couple of cups of coffee and visualized my results. I was going to do this, but I was going to accept and forgive myself. It was time to be kind and loving to myself. It was going to be one day at a time. Day after day, doing whatever was required to reach my goal. I had not deteriorated into this condition overnight, and I expected it was going to take some time to achieve my ultimate goal. I understood the level of commitment that was needed and prepared myself for the battle that was ahead.

The first few days, I was filled with enthusiasm and it was easy to stay on track. I expected some plateaus and prepared myself mentally for the difficult days. As the days went by, my newly discovered discipline developed into more discipline. I vowed to abstain from alcohol and to remain true to my restricted diet of 1,200 calories per day. I was running for an hour every morning and lifting weights for another hour three or four days per week. Weight began to disappear. I lost approximately three pounds every week. This was feeling good. I was gaining momentum and strength as each day passed. There was no doubt in my mind that I would get down to my desired weight. I was planning a return to ultra marathons by the end of 2012. It was all going to happen.

By the beginning of June, I was down to my desired weight. My health was good and I was running well. I was running faster and my efforts were getting easier. It was time to up my mileage and forge ahead. I would start increasing my mileage by adding time and distance to my Sunday runs until I could run for four or five hours.

In my down time, I would read and study anything that I could on a wide range of topics. I was reading two to three books each week and increasing my knowledge base. My life was transforming. As my waist shrunk, my mind expanded. I was transforming myself in mind, body and spirit. It was as if a spark inside me had burst into flames. I became passionate about inspiring others, sharing what I was learning and helping others to grow in areas that they sought.

I would often remember Ralph Waldo Emerson's words: "Make the most of yourself, for that is all there is of you."

I decided to run a six-hour race in October and diligently trained for it. As race day approached in late October, I could feel those old feelings of excitement and anticipation. It was now time to come back and experience the joy that I always felt while competing in the sport that I loved so much. The results would not be nearly as important as the journey. The journey is, after all, the most important part. That is where we find success.

The six-hour race was a wonderful event. It was there that I shared my passion with fellow runners and experienced bliss for the entire event. Since that race, I have competed at numerous ultra marathons at distances ranging all the way up to 100 miles and timed races of up to twenty-four hours.

What has become abundantly clear to me is that it is not the achievement of our goals that define us, but rather what we become in the pursuit of those goals. As Ernest Hemingway stated, "It is good to have an end to journey toward; but it is the journey that matters, in the end."

— Brian Teason —

Gray

*It is not by the gray of the hair that
one knows the age of the heart.*
~Edward G. Bulwer-Lytton

I was walking my dog when a friend pulled up and rolled down her car window. "Oh, my God!" she said. "I've wanted to do that for ages! You are so brave!"

It was the first time Elyse had seen me since I let my hair go gray.

I'd been thinking about taking the plunge for a couple of years. I was sick of coloring my hair. Sick of the outlay of time and money. Sick of the seaweed hue the chlorine in the pool turned it only weeks after coloring.

I was also weary of colluding with a culture that saw a sixty-year-old man's silver-gray crown as "distinguished" but expected women of the same age to have hair that was impossibly golden or brilliantly brunette. I was fed up with the cultural expectation that I look younger than my age.

About twelve weeks elapsed between the day I stopped coloring my short, afro-styled hair and the day I left the last vestiges of my chemically prolonged youth on the salon floor. During those awkward months when the top of my head looked like a vanilla cupcake with chocolate frosting, I felt like a walking Rorschach test. What did my friends see in this morphing design?

Many women, some good friends and some barely acquaintances, decided that my decision was sufficiently universal that they had to share their thoughts and feelings with me. They voiced many concerns: What would my kids think? Would my spouse like it? When I look in the mirror, would I see my mother? Or worse, my grandmother?

What happens when one defies cultural norms and brazenly courts ageism? I was struck by how many women ended their conversations about my hair with "It's so great that you're doing this. Good luck!" They vicariously wished to live the dream but also recognized that, for the granny who suits up to cross skydiving off her bucket list, a little luck couldn't hurt. Like the canary in the coalmine, they collectively waited to see if I would survive.

Most of them, like Elyse, applauded my courage for having traveled somewhere they were still too timid to go. Still, I was struck by the number of women who ended the conversation by reminding me, "You can always color it again if you don't like it." It was a sisterly gesture of unconditional acceptance should my silly experiment turn out to be a bust.

Brave is laudable but not safe. For so many of us, there is something dangerous about not looking young. The pressure to look young drives us to purchase youth-enhancing concoctions so implausible we would never consider buying into such hokum in any other realm of our lives. It drives some into misery, others to the dermatologist for injections, and others under the knife.

Even my older friends who color their hair admit that they've been thinking about going gray for years, but feel they just aren't ready. Ready for what?

As un-PC as it may sound, I think the most honest answer to this question is: not ready to look old. This is particularly true of my women friends who work in corporate settings. They have earned their high-level positions through years of study, sacrifice, and hard work. Still, they are afraid that to look their age would somehow jeopardize their... what? Their credibility? Their value? Their power? Or is it something deeper? Their sense of self-worth?

Although I was (mostly) comfortable with my decision from the start, there were some false starts.

"How old were your parents when they died?" This awkward question was posed to me by a young intake nurse when I changed physicians recently. Before I went gray, the question had always been: "Are your parents still alive?"

I had only been fully gray for a few days and wore my new identity like an aging Peter Pan, full of bravado and uneasy with the range of feelings that could pop up in new circumstances. Reactive and relentless, I shot back, "Did you ask that question like that because I have gray hair?" The poor woman was flustered and mortified, but I would take no prisoners. "Do you assume I'm too old to have living parents just because I have gray hair?" She apologized profusely. I thought she might cry. With my defensiveness on full display, it was my turn to feel mortified.

Empowerment is an inside job. Giving oneself permission and authority to challenge norms is not for the faint of heart, and this gray business is a complicated endeavor. From hour to hour, I am resolved but insecure, freed but self-conscious.

As time passes, I am increasingly comfortable with my decision. Being gray suits the way I live the rest of my life. Simple. Quiet. Counter-culture. With this decision not to take action against my body's natural course, I have given myself permission to look my age, trusting that my esprit de corps will compensate for whatever assumptions onlookers may associate with a silver crown.

Early in my pilgrimage, I was jolted when I passed a mirror and was confronted with my gray-haired reflection. I was caught off guard but was not unhappy. I felt eager to embrace this familiar stranger, knowing that by accepting her, I was one step closer to more fully accepting me.

— Audrey Ades —

89

Itching for a Change

Becoming acquainted with yourself is a price well
worth paying for the love that will really
address your needs.
~Daphne Rose Kingma

I wanted to be a receptionist in a doctor's office when I grew up. As a kid, I played with a blue plastic phone and a calendar, answering the phone with a smile and filling in time slots for patient appointments. Fifty years later I am still filling in my calendar, but my plastic phone has been replaced by an iPhone and as a clinical psychologist I serve as my own receptionist. A vanilla candle on the corner of my desk perfumes the air with a subtle scent as I listen to life stories in forty-five minute intervals — sound bites of love, loss, dreams, and tragedy. Worn green leather chairs cushion our time together. I have a photographic memory for only two things: my patients' lives from one week to the next, and baking recipes.

One Christmas holiday a few years ago, my work stress was intensifying due to the difficulty of cases and the number of clients I chose to see in a day. It was a cold Thursday evening that I sat listening to a young woman recount a horrific car accident she had witnessed the previous night: "She flew through the air as the car careened around the curve and slid off the embankment. I knew it was my neighbor when I saw her red and green socks through my headlights as she hit the pavement. She always wore funny socks with her snow boots."

I drove home holding tight to the steering wheel, snow beginning to fall. As I opened our front door to the smell of baked potatoes, my neck suddenly became hot and itchy.

My daughter asked, "What are all those red spots, Mom?" A warm bath seemed to help but the next week it happened two more times after a long day of work. I realized I was itching for a change. I had to figure out how to simplify and live my next fifty years more peacefully.

Shortening my workweek and seeing fewer patients was only the beginning. More importantly my mid-day is now reserved for someone special whose self-care trumps all others. My blue yoga mat sits regally in the corner of my office, always a reminder of the importance of my own physical, emotional, and spiritual alignment. I steal away to a small yoga studio around the corner. It is my sanctuary where I connect to myself. I need to do that — it's at the core of my ability to help heal and connect with others.

Yoga is like putting on my reading glasses, allowing me to see what is closest to me, which can get blurred when caring for others. When I am centered and balanced, I can better read my patients' stories. A therapist's work is all about change and transition — both our personal growth and that of our clients. The inevitable pain and challenge of our journey is softened in yoga class as we experience a sweet calm in the transition between our in breath and our out breath and from one pose to the next. Standing poses challenge my balance, reminding me of the importance of finding that equanimity in our busy lives. I try to wear clothes that easily travel from one practice to the other, from mat to office, my seams holding the healing energy.

Like the soothing bath on a cold night just a few years ago, I now bathe in the light of daily yoga and meditation to sooth the inevitable rough spots in life. As I meet my true self on the mat I am better able to meet the truth in others. What an honor to hold on to the simplicity of that receptionist job I dreamed of as a child.

— Priscilla Dann-Courtney —

90

Long-Distance Love

Distance means so little when
someone means so much.
~Author Unknown

grew up with my grandma right in our house. She was my best friend until she passed away when I was thirteen. Now, even though my own grandchildren live far away, I want to be just as special to them as my grandmother was to me.

All four of my granddaughters were born in South Africa, so I made ten trips there over seven years just to make sure I built a strong and lasting bond with them. It was expensive, exhausting, and exciting — but worth every minute I spent in cramped airplanes and crowded airports. Thankfully, the family moved to the States a year ago, and although they don't live near me, they are just a few hours away by plane. I make every effort to get together with them regularly.

Recently, I returned from taking care of all four children — ages one, four, six, and seven — for nearly a week while their parents were away. I can't remember ever being so tired. Still, my time with them was full of love and laughter. We made daily outings to special places around their city, and I homeschooled the two oldest in the afternoons while the little ones slept.

We made so many sweet memories that week — like helping the seven-year-old master double-digit subtraction; seeing the six-year-old swim like a dolphin; and watching the four-year-old fearlessly climb to the top of the jungle gym. In turn, the girls taught me how to use Alexa and showed me how to travel on the light rail. And the seventeen-month-old? Her smiles and hugs melted my heart.

Even when I'm not there, I still see our beautiful grandchildren, hear their sweet voices, and watch them grow — through Skype or FaceTime. We learn about their day-to-day activities on Facebook or Instagram, and we get photos through e-mail or Dropbox and see videos over WhatsApp. We can even order them gifts via the Internet, and don't have to worry about how they'll get there.

As a family, we make connecting a priority even though we're all so very busy. We've established weekly Skype traditions that we count on and love. Grandpa often has a milk-and-sweetie party with the girls since he's known to love sweets. And since I am a former teacher, I love to read to them.

The best tradition of all, so far, is our blowing-kisses tradition. We started saying goodbye with the girls blowing a few "girly kisses" my way and me blowing some "Grandma kisses" back. But now simple goodbye kisses have become "hurricane kisses" that blow me off my chair and "baseball kisses" that Grandpa catches in his invisible baseball mitt. What will be next? Maybe it's time to think of some new kind of kisses to blow through cyberspace and right into their hearts.

It still hurts to be so far away from them. I have to admit that I search the Internet for special deals to fly out and see them.

But I'm thankful that we have all this wonderful technology at our fingertips. We have so many ways to connect via our smart phones and the Internet. Yesterday, I watched the toddler sing "Itsy Bitsy Spider" to me on a FaceTime chat. Today, I saw a video of the six-year-old riding a pony. I'm sure my granddaughters are building their own memories of good times with their grandparents, too, and some day they may not even remember which of those good times happened in person and which happened over the Internet.

— Susan G. Mathis —

Chapter
10

Who Are You Calling Old?

91

Over Superman's Dead Body

I have a warm feeling after playing with my
grandchildren. It's the liniment working.
~Author Unknown

My daughter purchased season tickets to Six Flags St. Louis that included guest passes. All summer long, my grandsons begged me to join them. Since school would be starting in a week, I finally agreed to go, but my husband could tell I wasn't enthused.

"Honey, what's wrong?" he asked.

"It's been almost thirty years since I've been to an amusement park. Don't forget, I just turned sixty."

He chuckled. "Is your life insurance paid up?"

When they pulled in the drive to pick me up, I trudged to the car like a prisoner on death row.

Wiggling with excitement, six-year-old Clayton squealed from the back seat, "Grandma, we're gonna have so much fun!"

Despite my fears, I smiled and said, "I can't wait"—to get back home.

As soon as we arrived at the park the car doors flew open and the boys hit the ground running.

Eleven-year-old Randy said, "Let's ride Mr. Freeze first. It goes the fastest and turns upside-down."

I froze.

When Clayton saw the look on my face, he added, "Unless you're chicken."

Was that a triple-dog-dare? Who couldn't survive twenty-three seconds? Twenty-four seconds later, I had my answer — my stomach. After Mr. Freeze, everything else was uphill. Next we approached the wooden Screamin' Eagle, and I bragged about riding it with their mom when she was a little girl. Oh, my aching back! I didn't remember it being so rickety and rough. But that was nothing compared to the Ninja. My head snapped from side to side as the sharp curves turned into sheer drops. I wobbled off the ride trying to regain my balance.

Randy shouted, "Wasn't that awesome, Grandma?"

"What?" My ears felt like Mike Tyson had used them for a punching bag.

My favorite part of the day was when the boys finally agreed to stop for the picnic lunch we'd packed that morning. They spread a blanket under a large oak tree, and I plopped down kicking my shoes off my aching feet. What I wouldn't have given for a short nap. Before I could swallow the last bite of my sandwich, my ambitious grandsons jumped up, raring to go. When my daughter said we'd leave after we rode the roller coasters on the other side of the park, my aching body screamed in protest.

We soared through one terrifying ride after another, but the real challenge of the day was our last ride — the Superman Tower of Power. *Great,* I thought, *a new way to be terrorized.* An eternity passed as we waited to be hurled toward the ground. What was I thinking when I'd agreed to spend the entire day at an amusement park? Luckily, we survived the extreme free fall, and the look of admiration in my grandsons' eyes was worth every frightening second.

On the way home, I swallowed an ibuprofen and wondered what time the chiropractor's office opened the next morning.

Clayton beamed. "Grandma, you were super."

Randy chimed in, "Yeah, I can't believe you rode every roller coaster in the park. You're going with us next time."

If I could've moved my head, I would have hung it. Under my breath, I mumbled, "Over Superman's dead body."

— Alice Muschany —

92

Technology 101

Technology is anything that wasn't
around when you were born.
~Alan Kay

Grandparenting these days is all about technology. I'm not talking about e-mail, Facebook, iPads and tweeting. We're pretty good at that. It's those strollers and car seats. When our kids were little, life was simple. We had carriages that got pushed around the block, but never entered an automobile. They were as big as a car themselves. And we used lightweight fold-up umbrella strollers when we travelled by car or bus, and then switched to a child carrier when we got where we were going. Sure, babies slumped over like a sack of potatoes from little support in those strollers, and fingers got pinched when they folded up, but they were cheap and replaceable.

Now the SUV strollers come with airline pilot-type instructions, and we need the coordination of a NASA astronaut to open them, install a child and prepare for takeoff.

When I was telling a friend and fellow grandmother that I was babysitting my grandchildren for a week, she confided that she has been afraid she'd never get her grandchild out of his car seat. I've felt the same about high chairs, double strollers, single strollers, automatic indoor baby swings, and outdoor baby swings. The grandchild had to show me how to stick my finger inside to release the shoulder clasp on the swing's seatbelt mechanism. This newest generation will never conceive of doing anything at all without a seat belt and shoulder harness. My two-year-old granddaughter is able to climb in and out of her stroller herself, and when she climbs in she immediately secures the safety belt herself.

When my daughter gave me my child-minding instructions, she told me the four-month-old drinks when he's thirsty and sleeps when he's tired; no need to follow a schedule. She was right; he smiled his way through the day while sucking his two middle fingers. The challenge was the single stroller in which I had to place his car seat with him buckled in, while remembering the diaper bag, rain cover, sun cover and assorted paraphernalia. And that was only when his sister was at Montessori, and I was just taking him on an outing to No Frills, cramming the groceries into the bottom of the stroller.

Early morning and late afternoon, the transportation of the day was the double stroller, with options for which way each could face. Of course, each child had to be buckled in and adjusted so that kicking each other was not an option. It wasn't easy to maneuver the stroller on city streets and get through traffic lights. I felt like a long-haul truck driver, with the arm muscles to match.

After a week of it, I was getting pretty good, and had a new appreciation for those Strollercize mothers who pack the coffee shops. I salivated outside the Starbucks, but the thought of negotiating the stairs and the lineup with my two-person spaceship had me drinking from a sippy cup outside.

— Louise Rachlis —

93

Who's That Girl?

A ship in harbor is safe, but that is
not what ships are built for.
~John A. Shedd

I stopped short when I caught my reflection in the bathroom mirror. The silver hair that shone back at me still threw me a bit off balance. Only a year or so ago, my hair had still borne the deep rich mahogany color of my youth, thanks to that all-too-frequent appointment with the dye bottle. And, truth be told, had I been able to stop the hands of time, I would have remained that striking brunette of my youth. But last year, I had decided that if the change was to come — and clearly it was already here — then I would take control of it and not just survive it... but thrive in it. So, much to my friends' chagrin, I went silver — on purpose. And what a glorious silver it is: thick, long, soft, and shiny. Who knew all that sparkle was waiting there underneath all that pretense?

So here I was just past my fifty-fifth birthday. The world referred to me as a "senior" now. I could get a discount at the grocery store. I was a wife, mother and, yes, grandmother. And still, I was startled by how fast the years had flown by. Why hadn't someone warned me that when we cross a certain birthday barrier, the world begins to think of us differently? Ads for certain medicines began to show up in my newsfeeds. Was this how my mother had felt when she crossed this line? I blinked back tears as once again I felt the pang of missing my mother, who had passed away five years before. As I thought of her, I began to mentally count. When my mother was fifty-five, I had been a mere nineteen years old, newly married and sure I knew everything. My, how time changes things. What was it that Bob Dylan said in his "My Back Pages" song? "I was so much older then. I'm younger than that now."

Lately, my reflection in the mirror seemed to be taunting me, as if it were asking, "Is this it? Is this all you got? Your comfortable life. Your comfortable job. Your comfortable drive to work and back every day. Is this the way you're spending the rest of your life? Nice. Comfortable. And bored out of your mind?"

And I was comfortable. I had a good, if somewhat predictable life. A few precious, if predictable, friends. Every day, my husband and I ate dinner at the same time. We watched the same television shows. We shopped at the same grocery store. Life was pleasant, and I felt grateful and blessed.

But somewhere deep inside that fifty-five-year-old exterior, an ember of my younger self still remained. And it was that part that kept telling me that this was not all there was to life. It kept reminding me that I did not have to go quietly into that good night. Maybe there were still things to be learned and new experiences to be had if I dared step out of my comfortable rut. I thought again of my mother. At about this same age, my mother, who had been a housewife all her life, had gotten her driver's license, and gone back to work and school. At the age I was now, my mother had not given up. In fact, it was at this age that my mother had truly started to live.

Did I dare take a back page from her book? Could I finish that second degree I had started? Could I quit that comfortable job and comfortable life and go out there to see what else was waiting? My husband was retired. Our kids were grown. In fact, our sons were constantly asking the two of us to come to the city and live near them. But could I give up everything I knew and remake myself? How would employers react to a silver-tressed woman competing with Millennials for a job?

I wondered what my mother would have said about this crazy plan. Then I laughed. I knew exactly what my mother would say.

Six weeks later, the boxes were almost packed. The deposit had been paid on the exciting new apartment in the city. I had a new job. My silver hair had not been a deterrent after all. In fact, my new employer had rather liked my self-assured, authentic, experienced self. And, truth be told, I was liking myself more these days, too.

I felt a small pang of sadness as I hugged the girls at work one last time. But then I jumped into my new car with the stick shift that I had just bought a month before. That car was now packed to overflowing with things the movers couldn't fit into the van. As I slipped on my sunglasses and adjusted my rearview mirror, I again caught a glimpse of myself. Only this time, I thought, *Who is that beautiful, confident, excited woman staring back at me? And where is she going?*

As I downshifted and accelerated, leaving behind my old office and old life, I wondered what the next chapter of my life would bring. I didn't know, but I was sure going to find out. And I wasn't afraid.

— Geneva France Coleman —

94

My Everest

What you get by achieving your goals
is not as important as what you
become by achieving your goals.
~Henry David Thoreau

t was October and I was at a bookstore to hear the author and mountain climber Heidi Howkins. She looked intense. "Mountaineering is a life-or-death situation," she explained. "And I have to be ready for whatever challenge I may face. I take it seriously." Heidi proceeded to read and comment from her newly released book entitled *K2, One Woman's Quest for the Summit*.

Her obvious excitement built as she continued: "K2 is a deadly mountain. Only five women had made the summit and all died either on the way down or in subsequent climbing accidents. I wanted to summit that mountain!"

In her two prior attempts on K2, Howkins had seen climbers swept away by avalanches and had seen frozen bodies along the trail. And yet K2 kept calling her.

I had never been a particularly daring person. I had attempted many things in my life, but never felt I had mastered any of them: knitting, sewing, skiing, scrapbooking, rafting, running, foreign languages, sailing, water skiing and the litany goes on, without ever reaching perfection in any of them. I was about to turn sixty and become a grandmother, too.

I needed to prove something to myself. I raised my hand and

asked, "How does one actually get started?" The author turned her full attention to my question and replied, "Love of mountains and the sense of accomplishment in achieving goals." I thought to myself: Hey, I'm there, I have always loved mountains, read every book I could get my hands on about mountain adventures, flew over Mount Everest in Nepal, went to see the IMAX films on Everest and Eiger, not once but three times! I am there; I can do this… maybe.

After the book signing session was over, I was able to speak personally with Heidi. "Do you think a woman my age could ever achieve a personal goal of actually climbing a mountain?" I timidly asked, thinking she might laugh at such a preposterous question. She looked directly at me and said, "Follow your heart and achieve your goal. Climb your personal Everest, but do it with the most knowledge, planning, training and professional guidance that you can find!" She wrote inspirational words in my copy of her book, smiled and said, "You go for it, girl!" I left that evening filled with inspiration and determination.

I thought to myself, "I have my goal. Now I have to achieve it!" I even knew which mountain I wanted to climb. It was in my back yard and a source, for many years, of great family memories. I had skied, summer camped, snowshoed and photographed that mountain many times: It would have to be Mount Hood. Heading home from downtown Portland that evening my mind was reeling. I walked in the door to my house and abruptly announced, "I am going to climb Mount Hood!" My husband raised his eyebrows as he often did when I made one of my pronouncements, and said, "Really, now wash up, dinner is ready!"

I began my research right after dinner. A community college featured an adventure course in the spring. Starting in early May, a mountaineering course designed for first time climbers was being offered. It was perfect. All I had to do was get in the best physical condition I could achieve in the next six months. I was not a novice in physical conditioning as I had always had a gym membership and used it at least once a week. I felt reasonably certain I could intensify that routine and achieve greater cardio and endurance conditioning.

Months passed. When I wasn't on a treadmill or pumping weights at the gym, I was running the hills around our neighborhood. By early May, I felt I was ready to learn the climbing techniques. I enrolled in the one-day "snow school," which taught the intricacies of climbing as part of a rope team and using an ice axe for self-arrest. There were six of us in this class, and I was filled with anxiety as I realized I was old enough to be the mother of my classmates, who would become my climbing partners. What in the world had I been thinking?

Dave, the instructor, a middle-aged, rugged and gruff individual, began to speak. "In essence, I will be asking you to carry a fifteen-pound backpack with gear, wear a heavy pair of boots and walk on varied slope angles for six to eight hours, much of which will be during the night. In addition, we're going to diminish the amount of available oxygen along the way." Dave proceeded to say, "Not all of you will be physically able to summit. You need to be honest at all times so that you do not jeopardize the safety of the group. We will be roped together." My heart sank, as I was certain that speech was directed at me.

Dave continued, "Mount Hood, Oregon's highest summit at 11,240 feet, is a volcano. It is considered a technical climb with crevasses, ice and falling rocks. It is a mountain where weather can change without warning signs. 157 climbers have lost their lives on Mount Hood!" Why did he have to say that?

It was May 25th and it was time. We would start to climb at midnight. There was no visibility beyond the direct arc of our headlamps. By starting at midnight, we would be off the mountain before the sun melted the high walls of ice on the upper slopes. We roped into two teams of three and started to climb. We climbed and climbed, at first with no more effort than climbing stairs, but gradually getting more breathless as the altitude increased.

Dave kept repeating his mantra: "One foot in front of the other in a very slow pace." He also kept asking me "Are you with us? Are you pacing yourself?" He must have been concerned about my abilities but it was starting to irritate me. All the faces around me displayed a mask of extreme fatigue and I knew mine was no exception, probably more obvious because of my age. It was almost dawn; we climbed at a pitch that seemed wildly steep, perhaps forty-five degrees. We negotiated around rocks, crevasses and large chunks of ice.

Resting briefly, we noticed a hot, sulfur odor escaping from a nearby fumarole; a reminder that Mount Hood is an active volcano! I no longer paid attention to the complaints of fellow climbers who were verbalizing their every discomfort. I was cold too, but my hunger had been replaced with raw nerves. I had to pull deep within myself to focus! The air was definitely thinner and it was harder and harder to take deep breaths. No longer did our team chat endlessly. There was an eerie silence. Only our crampons could be heard crunching on the frozen ground. Would this ever end? I told myself to keep moving and squelched my doubts.

I pictured the mountain, where we might be on its flanks and how close we were to the summit. Someone yelled, "We're at the Pearly Gates"—a narrow icy and extremely dangerous gully. A small slit of sun was breaking though the darkness of the night. We continued to climb, and then we suddenly stopped climbing. There were no more places to climb! We were there!

I stepped onto the peak's windblown summit, more than two miles above sea level! Lights from faraway places twinkled magically. Incredible! Exhilarating! I had done it! The view was magnificent!

A sudden strong gust of cold wind served as an abrupt reality check. And then, I thought to my very weary self, "I have to get down from here!"

— Shirley Deck —

95

The Happy Golfer

Of all the hazards, fear is the worst.
~Sam Snead

When I was sixteen years old my father bought me a set of used golf clubs. "Here," he said, "I think you'll be good at this sport; golf is something you'll enjoy." I'll never forget those clubs. They were Bobby Jones Signatures, made by Spaulding. I loved them, as I loved my father.

His first prediction proved to be somewhat accurate. I did get pretty good at the sport — at my best, I had lowered my handicap to four, a merit few golfers are able to achieve. But it was his second pronouncement where I truly shined. I didn't just enjoy golf, as my father had predicted, I became obsessed with it, fanatical. As my long drive developed, golf became the driving force in my life.

Golf has been an enduring passion since that day. In the six decades since my father first handed me those clubs, the sport has served as both my teacher and my savior. Golf has helped me learn the virtues of patience and steadiness. Golf has helped me cope with the tragic loss of our daughter on her eighteenth birthday. Golf has given me a reason to get out of bed in the morning. On days when the mood is somber and dark, golf has compelled me to get out the door and keep on keeping on. In short, golf has given me a reason for living.

Still, after six decades it was time to stamp a crowning achievement on this sport I so loved. But what could that be? I'd played literally thousands of rounds of golf. What more was there? What challenge was left? I thought about it. There was one other activity that appealed to me as much as golf, and that was travel. Why not combine the two? I pulled out a map of the United States. What about taking that RV of ours and heading out on a golfing extravaganza, a quest to play a round of golf in each of the contiguous U.S. states? Wait, would that even be possible?

I put the map away. That would be impossible.

But the idea possessed me. I kept wondering whether it could be done. The question continued haunting me so I decided to talk to my doctor about it. He cautioned me that attempting such a feat would put a lot of stress on my heart.

"Doc, I'm seventy-two years old. Going to the bathroom puts a lot of stress on my heart. I'd rather go out in a blaze of glory doing what I love, than slumped over a toilet seat."

He advised against it.

I decided to go for it.

But how? Where to begin? I thought about writing a golf company to see if they might be interested in sponsoring my trip. But I was certain that golf companies were besieged with such inquiries about sponsorship. My proposal really needed to stand out. So I decided to propose playing not one, but two, rounds of golf in each of the lower forty-eight states, a total of ninety-six rounds of golf in ninety-six days.

Callaway bought into the idea. They either liked what they heard or were so confused by the math they gave up.

Soon, boxes of Callaway gear started arriving on my doorstep. It was all top-of-the-line and beautiful. They also assisted with some of the coordination, which was quite helpful. And they even agreed to set up a blog for me on the Callaway website, which was amazing, except I was seventy-two years old and had no idea what a blog was. So they found a bright young Millennial to handle that.

There was lots of planning and logistics that went into the trip, and soon maps and guidebooks started piling up in our kitchen. Eventually the mound grew to take over the entire house. Thankfully, I have a very understanding wife.

Anticipation mounted as the day of departure drew near. Finally, the morning came. My family gathered at the house to bid me farewell. As I pulled out of the driveway they all waved and hooted; I felt both confident and comforted by their support. After months of planning and preparation, this would be my Forrest Gump of golf moment.

I didn't get very far. My wife was screaming and yelling and holding something over her head. I'd forgotten my CPAP machine and blood pressure medication. Ah, the delights of growing old.

But from that point forward I never looked back. Thankfully, hemorrhoids aren't one of my problems because the drive from California to Cerbat Cliffs Golf Course in Kingman, Arizona took seven hours. There were many long drives during the odyssey, some on the golf course but mostly on the roadways. Eventually I got into a rhythm, I found my groove. It went something like this: EAT. SLEEP. DRIVE. PLAY GOLF. REPEAT.

As my trip progressed, people started learning about my pursuit and they started showing up at golf courses. They were reading the daily blog updates and my undertaking was serving to inspire them. People started calling me "The Happy Golfer" and golf courses started comp'ing my greens fees and inviting me to pose for pictures in the pro shop afterward. Reporters began calling. Soon I had interviews and media obligations. This whole endeavor was proving to be quite a sensation. I started growing a beard, just like Forrest Gump. I was on a roll.

Then I had heart palpitations and my left shoulder went numb. Next, my right. I checked myself into a hospital. The cardiologist confirmed that my arteries were clogged and I would need surgery. It wasn't a matter of *if*, he explained, but when.

When? It became the defining question of my life. When would I need to have this procedure done? Was it possible to continue onward and realize my dream? Or must I stop? The doctor had his opinion, and I had mine. The two didn't necessarily reconcile, but I decided to play on.

I mostly stayed at campgrounds along the way, or sometimes with friends and relatives, and in a pinch, Walmart parking lots. After the hospital scare, my diet became very regimented. I only ate healthy and wholesome foods, like salads and fresh vegetables. I started feeling better. Maybe it was just psychological, but my scores began improving and I felt less sore in the mornings.

You would think that such a whirlwind tour would be a great blur, but I remember each and every day quite vividly. It was as though someone had granted me a new lease on life so I could fully immerse myself in these grand ninety-six days and experience them to their utmost.

The final day, as you can imagine, was quite emotional. Putting in the last shot on Hole 18 of the Gold Hills Golf Course in Redding, California brought a torrent of feelings and reflections. I'd completed two rounds of golf in each of the contiguous forty-eight states for a total of ninety-six rounds of golf in ninety-six days. Mission accomplished.

It had been an amazing journey, one that required me to overcome many fears and doubts. After seventy-two years of living I finally proved to myself that I was more courageous than I'd ever given myself credit for being. I still don't know what a blog is, but if anyone needs a resource for locating a nice golf course in any state, or finding a Walmart parking lot to camp in, I'm your guy. Beyond that, if anyone harbors a dream of trying something really bold and outrageous in his or her life, think of The Happy Golfer… and go for it.

— Nick Karnazes —

96

The Geri-hatricks

It's not the men in my life that count —
it's the life in my men.
~Mae West

fter forty years of marriage, my husband and I have shared many fun adventures together, such as living on a houseboat when we were first married, rafting down the Colorado River at the bottom of the Grand Canyon, buying and moving a huge barn to our property so we could reassemble it and renovate it ourselves... you get the picture. Oh — and because we couldn't afford to have our home built for us, my husband surprised me by enrolling me in a plumbing, wiring and carpentry class when I was pregnant with our second of three children so I could be a certified helper. We obviously don't fit into any box that's remotely considered "normal."

And so it is that my husband, who just turned seventy-five, still has a passion for ice hockey. Not watching it... playing it! Throughout our marriage, he has belonged to many different hockey leagues and played in a variety of pickup games; largely dependent on what age group he was in. Now that he is a senior-senior, he still plays twice a week. My favorite team of all the ones he has played on is his current over-seventy group: the Geri-hatricks. Is that a genius name or what? The men who play with him come from all walks of life, from one who is a mortician to others who are journalists or doctors. In fact, the mortician suffered a mild heart attack one night during a practice, and it was largely thanks to a doctor on his team that this man is still alive and skating.

The men who share ice time with my husband come from the Washington, D.C. metropolitan area, which includes parts of Maryland and northern Virginia, where we live. That is why two years ago the Geri-hatricks were invited by the Washington Capitals professional hockey team to skate during one of their intermissions on a game night. The "boys" were all thrilled.

I nominated myself to be the head cheerleader, as I'm admittedly loud and enthusiastic. I had a great time gathering items for our large fan section, since the logo for the Geri-hatricks is a set of false teeth, biting down on a hockey stick. I found in a catalog some of those long-handled grabbers, with the top of them being plastic false teeth! You squeezed the handle and the teeth at the top of the pole opened and closed! They were hysterical! I also bought colorful pom-poms for us to shake, as well as inexpensive medals we could place around our husbands' necks after they had skated, changed, and returned to their seats.

One of our married daughters happened to be in town and joined our cheering section. Right before the Geri-hatricks took to the ice, my daughter saw her father and the other men all lined up in their uniforms and she said to me, "Now I think I know what you and Dad felt like whenever you came to watch any of us in our activities. I'm a nervous wreck!"

The crowd went wild when the Geri-hatriks were introduced and began warming up for their brief exhibition. The announcer seemed as excited doing the play-by-play for their mini-game as he was when the Capitals were playing! There was a little concern at one point when an eighty-two-year-old player fell and didn't get right up. Others noticed and helped him get vertical again. He wasn't injured, fortunately.

Through the years, I've heard wonderfully funny stories from my husband about his fellow hockey players. My favorite was about a goalie with tri-focals who wasn't able to see the puck very well as it quickly passed through the different lenses of his glasses. Many of the players have had various parts of their bodies replaced or repaired.

My husband is going to have knee replacement surgery this spring. He's put it off for several years, because he's concerned it might end his hockey career. But several other Geri-hatricks who have already had this surgery have assured him he will only play better afterwards.

On a hook in my husband's office hang several medals he's won with his teammates in the Senior Men's Olympics. One of them is even a gold medal! On his wall are photos of the different teams he's played on in these national competitions. I smile whenever I pass them.

So here's to the Geri-hatricks who enjoy fun, fellowship and falling down together as they show younger hockey players just how enduring this sport can be.

— Bobbie Wilkinson —

Melba Faces Assisted Living

A good laugh is sunshine in the house.
~William Thackeray

I was very proud of myself for having persuaded my eighty-two-year-old mother to tour an assisted living facility. I had even found one that was near the home in which she had lived on her own following my father's death ten years earlier.

My mother was tough. She was the descendant of hearty pioneer stock that had braved the elements before settling in Salt Lake City. And she was the ninth and last child of a polygamous dad and, as such, had been forced to fend for herself in order to get her fair share of the family's limited resources.

Yes, my mother Melba was a toughie for sure — a terror on the road, and aggressively independent. She didn't cook anymore, but subsisted largely on McDonald's Filet-O-Fish sandwiches. She didn't need to clean the kitchen that way, and, in fact, she found the racks in her automatic dishwasher were ideal for filing and sorting her mail.

Nevertheless, it was time for her to move out of her house and into a facility where she could have some assistance as she continued to age. I thought that she was accepting my decision, too, because she handled the tour of the facility so well. She was the essence of grace, nodding politely to those I hoped would be her new "neighbors" and complimenting the tour guide on the cleanliness of the public areas and private rooms. She didn't even grill the guide on how frequently fish sandwiches were served in the dining room.

Everything was going beautifully and according to my plan. But then, as we stood outside the business office, Melba gently took my hand and asked, "So, Gordon, do you think you're going to be happy here?"

— Gordon Osmond —

98

It's Never Too Late

It's never too late to be what you might have been.
~George Eliot

M y mom sprinkles joy wherever she goes. Right now she is probably writing an encouraging note to a friend, complimenting someone she has encountered in the hallway, or reading the newspaper to an ailing resident in her retirement community. Or maybe she's planning the next show by the Prime Life Follies, an entertainment group she started ten years ago for assisted living complexes and nursing homes.

Growing up, my mom thought about becoming a dancer, but she didn't have the opportunity until after retirement. Then she joined her first group, The Hot Flashes. Once she donned the tap shoes, "Dancin' Grammy" was born.

There seems to be no end to her energy as she tap-dances her way into people's hearts, bringing smiles to sad places. But this is nothing new for my mom.

A lifetime educator, she was recognized in the 1980's as her school district's Teacher of the Year. I remember the evening phone calls to students' homes when she took a break from grading papers. They were not the typical bad-news calls many parents would expect. Usually she was calling about something positive. She recognized students who made small steps forward and helped even the unruly ones reach their full potential, revealing gifts they often did not see.

I was the youngest of seven children and life wasn't easy for my mother. I remember sitting on the back of her bike as she took me to a daycare center for low-income families on her way to Rosary College, where she was pursuing an education degree. At home she was tough because she had to be. It was not an easy childhood, but we learned from watching her. Her work ethic and determination trickled down to all of us.

I could write a book about my mom, and maybe I will someday. Better yet, we may write one together, as her dream to be a writer has not yet been fulfilled. But she got one step closer by attending the Erma Bombeck Writers' Workshop in Dayton, Ohio. We were a mother-daughter pair of newbies. Actually, we were known as virgins, officially "Erma Virgins." My mom was a lifelong Erma fan and for years she had talked about writing a book, so I knew attending this workshop would be a perfect Christmas gift. The three-day conference was jam-packed with information and helped launch our writing careers.

Day one started with our decision to "divide and conquer," a strategy designed to soak up more knowledge from concurrent sessions. But by the end of the day we had conquered not a thing except finding bathrooms and snack tables.

By day two we focused on companionship and together attended a workshop on the use of social media tools to build a digital brand. I peered over at Mom's notes, knowing she had no idea what Facebook Live was on "The Facebook," as she called it. Next, we found our way to lunch as the program began with the announcement of the conference king and queen. As the master of ceremonies spoke of a mother-daughter team she had met the previous day, I realized she was talking about us. I was overcome with emotion when we heard, "Will our new queen, Lori Mansell, please come forward with her daughter Julie?"

On the stage, the keynote speaker placed a bejeweled plastic crown on Mom's head, and the new queen was offered a moment at the microphone. "I've always wanted to be a writer, and you've all inspired me," she began. "This is a new beginning. I'm going to write a book. It's never too late!"

With that, the Erma Virgin had become the Erma Queen, inspiring more than 350 attendees from all over the country. Throughout the afternoon, fellow writers greeted her with bows and hand kisses. Selfies with the royal family became commonplace. The queen perfected her regal wave.

And just before we departed for our Indianapolis castle—home—we had a divine hallway encounter with the Bombeck family. After a photo shoot with Erma's children, we made our way to the car, and the Queen was on a cloud the entire drive home. The next day she sat down at her computer to draft her first story, "Queen for a Day," typing away with the crown still proudly secured on her head.

From mother of seven to grandmother of eighteen, Dancin' Grammy, now better known as the Erma Queen, continues to inspire everyone she meets. She has many titles, but my favorite is Mom. She has been a symbol of sacrifice, encouragement, perseverance, selflessness, and joy—all wrapped in bountiful, unconditional love.

May my mom's zest for living create a ripple effect, serving as an empowering example of kindness and encouragement to all who cross her path as she continues to tap-dance her way through life. No doubt her book will one day become a bestseller. There's nothing she can't do—even now at the ripe young age of eighty-eight.

Indeed, it's never too late!

—Julie Osborne—

99

The New Refrigerator

The best babysitters, of course, are the baby's
grandparents. You feel completely comfortable
entrusting your baby to them for long periods,
which is why most grandparents flee to Florida.
~Dave Barry

Since I am the grandmother of seven, blessed with vast experience and lots of free time, I'm used to being called to help out in a variety of different situations, ranging from picking up a sick child at school, taking one to a doctor's appointment, or providing a place to hang out when there is a school holiday. So when my daughter called to ask if I would stay with her twenty-year-old son, Geoff, who had just had four wisdom teeth pulled, I quickly agreed.

Since my daughter had taken the day off to be with Geoff, she also arranged for delivery of a new refrigerator in the afternoon. However, she had just been called into work for an emergency meeting. All I had to do was keep an eye on Geoff, change his dressings and get a glass of water down him every two hours. Nothing sounded easier.

Arriving at my post, I showed the proper sympathy to my six-foot, five-inch grandson, who was curled up on the couch, his mouth stuffed with cotton and drool running from his slack lips.

The counter that separated the kitchen from the living room was covered with food items that are normally housed in the refrigerator and I assumed that the old appliance was ready to be replaced.

I settled myself down with a good book. At the appointed time, I woke up the patient, who insisted that he didn't want to have the packing replaced nor did he want a drink of water. I won, the cotton was changed and the soggy slimy packing discarded.

When the phone rang, I was surprised to hear my oldest grand-daughter's voice. She had just been called in to interview for her dream job and she needed a sitter for her thirteen-month-old daughter.

"It will just be for an hour or maybe a little more. You're my only hope," she pleaded. I quickly weighed my options and realized I had none — I was needed.

Before long I had a grandson drooling and sleeping on the couch, a baby balanced on my hip and a dog scratching at the door to get in.

Thirty minutes after the baby's mother left with a wave and a smile, the refrigerator deliveryman made his appearance, early. He refused to make the delivery through the back door because there was a dog in the yard.

So I plopped the baby in the large overstuffed chair with a bottle and opened the sliding door to get the dog. The dog, thrilled to be included in the fun, bounded into the house and jumped on the baby, who started screaming. Geoff flopped over on the couch, mumbling. I grabbed the dog and dragged him into the master bedroom just as two men appeared with the dolly. They asked me if the old refrigerator was empty, and to my dismay I found the freezer crammed full. The men waited patiently while I unloaded the food. The baby was leaning over the back of the chair watching with fascination and the patient appeared to have returned to his peaceful slumber.

As the old kitchen appliance was being hauled off, things began to fall apart. I was faced with an empty space behind the old fridge that was littered with stray dog and cat food, dried peas, pet hair, milk bottle lids, bread wrapper clips, a broken pencil and dust.

Trying to keep one eye on the baby, I got busy with the broom, finishing up just as the shiny new refrigerator was wheeled in and positioned at the end of the counter — blocking my exit. The delivery-men returned to their truck to get some tools.

So, here's the situation: Geoff was on the couch, the dog was in the bedroom, the baby was in the chair, I was stuck behind the new fridge in the kitchen and the sliding door was open.

The baby spotted the open door and off the chair she went. My calls of, "No, no, Makayla. Don't go out!" were unheeded as she headed for the wide world beyond. I couldn't squeeze between the refrigerator and the cabinet so I had to force my ancient knees and legs up and over the counter, being careful not to kick any food onto the floor. I reached the baby just as she got the first handful of dog food into her mouth.

The deliverymen finished their job, I put the dripping items back in their new home and the dog was put back outside. All was well in the world.

Geoff stirred, peeked his tousled head over the back of the couch, and through soggy cotton and drooling lips, he muttered an indistinguishable sentence ending in "dog."

Dog! I forgot the dog. With the baby clinging to my neck, I threw open the sliding door and tore around the corner of the house to confirm my worst fear — an open gate and no dog. I closed the gate, as my mind sorted through excuses, hoping to find one my daughter's family would accept for the loss of the family pet.

Back in the house, I changed a now fragrant diaper, replaced Geoff's packing and forced water down his throat. I dug around in the closet until I found the dog leash and headed out for what was expected to be a fruitless search. To my delight, when I opened the front door, there sat a silly brown dog with her tongue hanging out, panting after a good run.

The baby's mother returned to find a sleeping baby. My daughter came home to a new fully stocked refrigerator, a tired dog in the backyard and a son sleeping peacefully on the couch.

Smiling, I said, "A good time was had by all."

I stopped by the store on the way home to get a good bottle of wine.

— Ruth Smith —

100

Swipe, Don't Tap

*I realized something on the ride. I realized
if I wait until I'm not scared to try new things,
then I'll never get to try them at all.*
~Marie Sexton

My phone buzzes. "I have something to tell you," she texts, "but it's a secret."

She knows I am powerless against clickbait.

"What kind of secret?" I ask.

Moments later, I hear clunking on the stairs.

She shuffles to my door and pokes in her head. Her face glows with mischief, and she is unable to mask her glee. Mom makes a show of checking for eavesdroppers, though we both know it's only us.

"I'm going to drive for youber!" she exclaims.

Her smile is practically wrapped around her head.

"Oh... you mean Uber?"

I am bemused. My mother is great at making sales, packing snacks and cussing out retail managers. But driving competently and using technology? Not so much.

I am half-expecting her to abandon this idea before it fully percolates, like her foray into jewelry sales or the time she tried to make a scrapbook. But then she asks me to help her download the app.

Mom has sworn me to secrecy because she thinks my dad and sister will judge her. She is probably right. Under the cover of midday, while the rest of the family works, we download the app, watch the training videos, and talk about how to pronounce the "U" in Uber.

We practice driving on Tuesday morning. I order the ride to our house while we sit in the car one block away. We go through the motions of picking up a rider and dropping her off in our neighbourhood. It does not go smoothly.

The navigation system is too quiet. The screen is distracting. The GPS doesn't know the best route. The destination requires a U-turn. The button is a slide instead of a tap. It is confusing. It is stressful. The ride ends in tears.

"Don't worry," I say. "We can try again tomorrow." Mom decides one hour later that she is ready for the road.

On her way home from grocery shopping, she turns on the app, which matches her quickly with a rider named Matthew. As she makes her way toward him, the panic from the morning creeps in. The silent navigation. The screen confusion. The swipe/tap debacle. It is just too much.

Naturally, she turns off her phone. She does not cancel the ride. She does not contact him to explain. She does, however, feel an imminent need for acupuncture. Mom spins her Lexus 180 degrees and races toward her practitioner.

A few minutes later, Mom turns on her phone to check her text messages. She has several missed calls from Matthew, who has been watching her on his screen and has seen her drive in the opposite direction for the past five minutes.

A word to the wise: Turning off your cellphone does not cancel an Uber ride.

Matthew calls again. She hesitates, and then picks up the phone.

"Why are you driving in the opposite direction?" he asks.

"Listen," she pleads. "This is my first time with youber, and I don't know how to use it. Please cancel the ride."

Matthew is late for work and doesn't want to foot the cancellation fee. Somehow, he coaxes her into picking him up. Mom finds the destination, trolls the parking lot for a while, and eventually he waves her down and hops in.

Matthew is a handsome man in his early thirties with a kind face and a crisp suit. A GoodLife duffel is slung across one shoulder, and a messenger bag hangs off the other. He is overseeing a grand opening event at the mall. Mom realizes how unprofessional it would be to show up late.

She mutters an expletive and gets ready to gun it, telling Matthew he'll need to manage the technology if he wants to arrive on time.

"So, start the trip," she barks and tosses her iPhone to the back seat in what is surely a breach of protocol. He obliges.

As Matthew co-pilots the ride, Mom gathers intel. They chat about his career, education, home life, and aspirations. She jokes about how incompetent she feels and about how embarrassed her daughter will be once she finds out about this. They laugh, talk and eventually arrive at Yorkdale — albeit at the wrong entrance.

"Crap, I'm sorry," she says.

"It's okay, Paddy," laughs Matthew. "Everyone is a beginner at some point."

He ends the trip, returns her phone, and starts to climb out of the car.

"Hold on," she says. "Will you show me how to do that?"

So Matthew explains, with the time that he doesn't have, how to use features on the Uber driver app.

"Matthew," she calls from her window, "you better not rate me one star."

"I'm rating you five right now!" he says, and he really does.

Matthew disappears into the mall, smiling. She smiles, too, proud that her first ride was such a success.

— Bronwyn McIntyre —

Racewalking

Your body is built for walking.
~Gary Yanker

fter years of pounding my knees and ankles in dashes and the long jump, pain ended my decades of track and field competition. But how do you live without the adrenaline of racing? That's simple. You just become rational at age sixty and turn to competitive swimming! Suddenly, the pounding was gone, and so was the pain. And I was gone, too, in less than a month, bored by pool laps and no scenery. Now what?

A friend in the Annapolis Striders had the answer. This marathoner said he had stayed fit by vigorous walking while healing from a running injury. "Try it," he said, "it's even a competitive sport." Sure enough, a certain kind of energetic walking is a 100-year-old Olympic event called Racewalking. It's the most efficient way that a biped can move, and that shows in Olympic competition where winners of the men's 50K race will finish at an average of 7 minutes to the mile for those 31 miles.

I took to this sport immediately because there was no pounding involved, and thus no pain. Its special way of moving is so smooth that no cushioning is needed in the shoes. Many people use this method of striding just for health benefits. You don't have to enter races to be a racewalker.

However, those who compete must follow two rules and must please numerous hard-eyed judges or be disqualified (DQ). The first rule says one foot must be on the ground at all times. Horse racing offers a comparison: if a trotter breaks the required style in harness racing, and goes into a gallop, it gets DQ'd.

The second rule is designed to guarantee no running. How? Well, it's impossible to leap or jump or run unless the knee is bent to spring you up or ahead. Thus, on the advancing leg, a racewalker's knee must be straight at a given point in its movement.

Violation can cause a DQ. It took me many months to become fluid in the style.

But I was "off and running," so to speak. I took group-coached lessons from Dave McGovern, a world class racewalker. (To see his style in walking the mile in 6:00:72, visit www.racewalking.org and click any photo at the top of the page.) In time, I earned age-group gold medals in Senior Olympics' and USA Track & Field Masters' competitions. Hallelujah! I had lost a sport but had found another.

Then came a disaster. All the words in my saga start with "S." They surge, surely and swiftly, on a slippery slope. This sequence shows the segues: stride, stroll, saunter, shuffle, stagger, stop. The cause? Another "s": suffering. Lower back pain had arrived.

"Surgery is a last resort," I was told. But months of therapy didn't help.

The culprit was a slowly closing foramen, pinching a nerve passing through.

The cure was to enlarge that bone hole and relieve pressure. I saw it as akin to expanding the Holland Tunnel from the inside while traffic flowed. Some loss of leg control was predicted from nerve damage during removal of surrounding bone in tight quarters. I took the chance because the pain would only worsen.

Dr. Clifford Solomon, super-surgeon of Annapolis, Maryland, worked the cure. It left me with full leg control, but a flopping foot. I would be able to jog care free, but not meet racewalk rules. Months of therapy didn't help. My spirits sank to the level of that foot until by chance I tuned the TV to an old movie showing Fred Astaire dancing up a storm. From the ankle down, his feet swiveled like pivots, in the very motion I needed. I turned off the TV and went to the Senior Center.

As the only man among twenty-nine students in the tap dancing class I learned that grandmothers are programmed to care for any wounded creature. Some fussed over this seventy-five-year-old invalid, staying after class to guide and inspire. Many had been childhood dancers; some were from chorus lines. They were there to recapture lost skills. They knew the value of repetition on performance and muscle memory. And they knew how the magic of music can make therapy endurable and even playful. With example, humor, encouragement, advice and team drill-drill-drill, they taught me to tap dance. The guy whose wife always claimed he had two left feet had learned to dance. Those grande dames cured my flopping foot. I will be forever grateful.

Within a year, I was competing well enough to enter the USATF Nationals at Boston and break the American record for the 3000 meter racewalk. The article about my race is on the wall of Dr. Solomon's office, with a "thank you" inscription. And now, at eighty-six, I'm still competing and often thinking of dancing ladies.

— Charles Boyle —

Meet Our Contributors

We are pleased to introduce you to the writers whose stories were compiled from our library to create this new collection. These bios were the ones that ran when the stories were originally published. They were current as of the publication dates of those books.

Linda Williams Aber is a writer, editor and packager of more than one hundred and fifty novels, activity books, and humor books from clients including Scholastic Inc., Random House, Reader's Digest Children's Publishing and many others. Her latest book, *500 Things to Do with Your Kids Before They Grow Up* was co-authored with her son Corey Mackenzie Aber.

Lynne S. Albers earned an Elementary Education degree from Fort Hays State University in Hays, KS, and taught for several years before raising their now-grown children, Jennifer and Wade. Lynne and her husband Bob enjoy exploring the picturesque New Mexico landscape with their dog, Phoebe. You may e-mail her at lynnealbers@yahoo.com.

Born and raised in northern British Columbia, **Marty Anderson** has raised four daughters and now currently resides with his wife in a remote community where the Wi-Fi is slow so no one is tempted to move back home. His hobbies include hiking, dog walking, shoveling snow and listening to his wife.

Violetta Armour is a former bookstore owner. She has published four books, including the award-winning *I'll Always Be with You* and sequel *Still with You* in addition to *A Mahjongg Mystery* and *S'mores Can Be Deadly*. She lives in Sun Lakes, AZ where she enjoys an active retirement lifestyle, including pickleball.

Sandra Bakun is a retired newspaper reporter and medical secretary.

She held the dual positions while bringing up her four children in Stow, MA. She retired to Cape Cod in 1995 and now splits her residency between the Cape and Myrtle Beach, SC. She loves to read, golf, and walk the beaches with Art.

Linda Barbosa is the author of *How Can I Smile at a Time Like This?* She also writes under a pen name for a popular advice website. When not jumping out of perfectly good airplanes, Linda enjoys the retired life with her husband Joe in their quiet, two-horse town.

Rosemary Barkes won the Erma Bombeck Writing Competition in 2000, which began a writing career. She subsequently published *The Dementia Dance: Maneuvering Through Dementia While Maintaining Your Sanity*. She holds B.A. and B.S. degrees from The Ohio State University and an M.S. degree from University of Dayton.

Ann Barnett grew up in a factory town in Pennsylvania. Moving to New York she raised two daughters, taught school, and lived on the Hudson River in an old wooden boat. Now retired, she surrounds herself with good books, sharp pencils, and an up-to-date passport.

Garrett Bauman has published fifteen stories in various *Chicken Soup for the Soul* books. His work has also been in *Yankee*, *The New York Times*, *The Chronicle of Higher Education*, and many other publications. He and his wife live nearly a mile off the nearest road in rural New York.

Arlene S. Bice is an author, speaker, and teacher of poetry and memoir. She is a member of IWWG, and founding member of Warren Artists' Market. She lives in South Hill, VA.

Janet Newlan Bower is a retired professor of history teaching for over thirty years. Her publications include contributing a chapter to *Women in the Biological Sciences: A Bibliographic Sourcebook*, *Tigerpaper*, *National Parks and Conservation*, *The Explorer*, *Environment Southwest* and *Child Life*, among others. Read her historical blog at historyallaround.com.

Charles Boyle worked thirty-five years at NASA. He is the author of *Shuttle Rising: Rendezvous with a Rumor*, and two kids' picture books titled *Tailey Whaley* and *The Sandpiper's Game*. He is a scuba diver and sailor.

Barbara Brady lives in Topeka, KS with Merris, her husband of sixty-two years. She is an active member of the Kansas Authors Club and believes everyone has a story to share.

D.E. Brigham has taught English as a Second Language for several years in Turkey, Saudi Arabia, and the United Arab Emirates. He has retired from teaching and lives and works as a writer in Eastern Tennessee, where he enjoys pickleball, kayaking, and hiking. E-mail him at davidebrigham@gmail.com.

Kristine Byron worked as a trainer for Tupperware and in later years as an interior designer. She loves to cook and entertain. Kristine also loves to travel with her husband and spend quality time with her five grandchildren.

Monica Cardiff homeschooled her three beautiful daughters. Married to the love of her life, she now has an empty nest and is working on writing her second novel. She appreciates all the support she gets from her family, friends, church family, and the ladies in her empty nest group.

Elynne Chaplik-Aleskow, a Pushcart Prize-nominated writer, is founding general manager of WYCC-TV/PBS and distinguished professor emeritus of Wright College. Her stories have been performed throughout the U.S. and Canada and are published in anthologies and her book, *My Gift of Now*, which *Conversations Magazine* named an inspired book.

Geneva France Coleman is a freelance writer from Eastern Kentucky. Having grown up in Louisa, she moved to Pikeville when she married her husband, Mike. Although always Appalachian at heart, she and Mike recently moved to the beautiful Bluegrass region of Lexington, KY to be closer to their children and grandchildren.

D'ette Corona received her Bachelor of Science degree in business management and is the Associate Publisher of Chicken Soup for the Soul. D'ette and her husband of nearly thirty years recently downsized and look forward to their new adventure. Their son is currently attending medical school in the Caribbean.

Priscilla Dann-Courtney is a writer and clinical psychologist living in Boulder, CO. Her columns have appeared in a number of national magazines and newspapers. Her book, *Room to Grow: Stories of Life and Family*, is a collection of her essays. Yoga, meditation, running, writing, family, and friends light her world.

Barbara A. Davey is the Director of Community Relations at Crane's Mill, a retirement community in West Caldwell, NJ. She received her bachelor's degree in English and master's degree in education from Seton Hall University, and teaches business writing at Caldwell University. She and her husband live in Verona, NJ.

Shirley Deck is a retired Clinical Microbiologist living in the Pacific Northwest, where the rainy days inspire creativity. Shirley has a passion for reading, writing, drawing and engaging in outdoor activities. Her stories are most often centered around her priceless family, personal recollections and life's lessons.

Mary Grant Dempsey, a former teacher and bookstore owner, resides in Bluffton, SC. Her writing has appeared in newspapers, magazines and three *Chicken Soup for the Soul* anthologies. She is a freelance writer for a local newspaper and recently published a book of her short stories. E-mail her at Marydemp27@yahoo.com.

Melissa Face lives in Prince George County with her husband and two young children. She is an English instructor at the Appomattox Regional Governor's School. Her essays have been published in local and national magazines, as well as in twenty *Chicken Soup for the Soul* books. Learn more at www.melissaface.com.

Jean Ferratier writes to inspire and honor others who face life challenges. She is a retired teacher who promotes self-development through her Clarity of Now Coaching Practice. Jean is the author of *Reading Symbolic Signs: How to Connect the Dots of Your Spiritual Life*. Visit her website at synchronousmoments.wordpress.com.

Cinda Findlan, a retired professor of Education, lives with her husband on Wellesley Island, NY. She dedicates her time to writing, painting, and enjoying her two granddaughters. Cinda looks for humor and meaning in life as a senior, recounting weekly experiences in her blog at PowerAgers.com.

Writing about exceptional events and wonderful people, **John Forrest** has had seventeen stories appear in the Chicken Soup for the Soul series. He has published the Christmas anthologies *Angels, Stars, and Trees* and *Home for Christmas*. He lives in Orillia, ON, with his wife Carol. E-mail him at johnforrest@rogers.com.

Betsy S. Franz is a freelance writer and photographer specializing in nature, wildlife, the environment and both humorous and inspirational human-interest topics. You can visit her online at www.betsyfranz.com, on Facebook at www.facebook.com/thenaturelady, or e-mail her at backyarder1@earthlink.net.

Victoria Otto Franzese has degrees from Smith College and New York University. She owned, operated, and wrote for an online travel guide for fifteen years before selling it to a major media outlet. Now she writes about a variety of topics and all of her travel is for fun. She lives in New York City with her husband, two sons, and a Goldendoodle named Jenkins.

Peggy Purser Freeman is the author of *The Coldest Day in Texas*, *Swept Back to a Texas Future*, *Cruisin' Thru Life: Dip Street and Other Miracles*, and *Spy Cam One*. Her experience as a magazine editor, student writing workshop teacher and her many published works in magazines across Texas inspire readers. Learn more at PeggyPurserFreeman.com.

Peggy Frezon is the contributing editor of *All Creatures* magazine, and a regular contributor to *Guideposts*. She is the author of *The Dog in the Dentist Chair: And other true stories of animals who help, comfort, and love kids* (Paraclete Press, 2018) and dog mom to Pete and Ernest. Look for her new book about miniature therapy horses (Revell, 2021).

Sally Friedman is a graduate of the University of Pennsylvania. Her personal essays have appeared in *The New York Times*, *Family Circle*, *Ladies' Home Journal* and *The Huffington Post*. Her family provides ample material for musings about how we live our lives. E-mail her at pinegander@aol.com.

Sandy McPherson Carrubba Geary lives with her husband and old dog in the house built for her maternal grandparents. She enjoys gardening, theater events, and encouraging other writers.

Sam Georges practiced law for seventeen years in Ohio and subsequently was the CEO/President and General Counsel of the Anthony Robbins Organization in San Diego, CA for twenty-two years. He served in the United States Air Force with the Strategic Air Command in the U.S. and Asia. He is now retired and lives in Las Vegas, NV.

T'Mara Goodsell is an award-winning multi-genre writer and teacher who lives near St. Louis, MO. She has written for various anthologies, newspapers and publications and is currently working on a book for young adults.

Esther McNeil Griffin, a graduate of SUNY Geneseo, volunteers at the Ross Park Zoo in Binghamton NY. She has written *Alex, the Lonely Black-Footed Penguin*, and written and illustrated *Which Witch is Which, Today?* and *My Mom Hates Violence*. E-mail her at Eltiemblo@aol.com.

Carol Harrison earned her Bachelor of Education from the University of Saskatchewan and is a Distinguished Toastmaster. She is a motivational speaker and author of *Amee's Story* and has two stories in *Chicken Soup for the Soul* books. She enjoys time with family, reading, scrapbooking and speaking. E-mail her at carol@carolscorner.ca or visit her website www.carolscorner.ca.

Eileen Melia Hession is a former teacher and publisher's representative whose writing has appeared in various publications. She has one daughter and enjoys running, yoga and ceramics. She believes there is a need for more levity in life and her writing reflects that belief.

Miriam Hill is a frequent contributor to the *Chicken Soup for the Soul* series and has been published in *Writer's Digest*, *The Christian Science Monitor*, *Grit*, *St. Petersburg Times*, *Sacramento Bee* and Poynter Online. Miriam's manuscript received Honorable Mention for Inspirational Writing in a Writer's Digest Writing Competition.

Linda Hoff Irvin is a psychotherapist in private practice who has been practicing for more years than she cares to admit. She is happily re-married and her son is doing well. E-mail her at lhofflcsw@gmail.com.

Jennie Ivey lives in Tennessee. She is the author of numerous works of fiction and nonfiction, including several stories in the *Chicken Soup for the Soul* series. Learn more at www.jennieivey.com.

Nick Karnazes (AKA: The Happy Golfer) is an avid golfer and active community member living in San Clemente, CA. When he's not golfing he enjoys Greek food and Greek dancing. This is his first submission to the *Chicken Soup for the Soul* series. E-mail him at nickthgp@gmail.com.

Lynn Kinnaman is a writer, web designer, marketing coach and tech-savvy woman. She's published books and magazine articles for decades. Owner of Works by Design, she builds websites and also coaches/ advises small businesses and individuals. She continues to write and publish fiction and nonfiction in her spare time.

April Knight is a freelance writer and artist. She began writing stories when she was twelve years old and had her first story published when she was thirteen. She is happiest when she is horseback riding or beachcombing.

Kathleen Kohler writes stories about the ups and downs of family life for numerous magazines and anthologies. She and her husband live in the Pacific Northwest, and have three children and seven grandchildren. Visit www.kathleenkohler.com to read more of her articles or enter her latest drawing.

Susan Leitzsch, a retired microbiologist, lives and travels full-time across the United States with her husband Tom. She has two grown children (twins), and one grandson. Her many interests include traveling, nature, hiking, knitting and several other creative outlets.

Beth Levine is an award-winning writer whose work has been published in *O*, *Woman's Day* and many other national magazines. She was last seen on stage as Villager #6 in *Fiddler on the Roof*. Critics are still referencing her breakout performance (cough). Learn more at www.bethlevine.net or through twitter at @BethLevine75.

California State Employees Association (CSEA) employed **Linda Lohman** for several years after her retirement from the State of California. Since retiring she has been published in several *Chicken Soup for the Soul* anthologies. Enjoying retirement, she writes extensively on grief issues. E-mail her at lindaalohman@yahoo.com.

Christine Long received her Bachelor of Arts in English in 2009. She teaches sophomore English in North Texas. She enjoys camping, sewing, writing, and spending time with her family. She plans to write a how-to guide for second-generation parents.

Patricia Lorenz is an art-of-living writer and speaker, the author of thirteen books and contributing writer to nearly sixty *Chicken Soup for the Soul* books. She and her husband "hunka-burnin-love" Jack live in Largo, FL, but she enjoys traveling to other parts of the country speaking to various groups. Contact her at www.PatriciaLorenz.com.

Melinda Richarz Lyons earned a Bachelor of Arts in Journalism from the University of North Texas. Her freelance work has appeared in numerous publications, and she is the co-author of *WOOF: Women*

Only Over Fifty (Echelon Press). She enjoys genealogy and currently resides in Tyler, TX.

JoAnne Macco worked for thirty years as a mental health therapist in a nonprofit agency. Since retiring, she paints angels, volunteers with first graders, and has published her first book, *Trust the Timing: A Memoir of Finding Love Again*. JoAnne lives in North Carolina with her husband, David, and their two dogs.

Carol L. MacKay's funny stories and poems for kids have been published in *Highlights*, *Cricket*, and *Babybug* magazines. Carol lives on Vancouver Island with her husband, James, and their cat, Victoria, who have both provided many laughs over the years. This is her third story published in the *Chicken Soup for the Soul* series.

Doug Malewicki of Irvine, CA has a Masters of Science degree from Stanford University and is the author of *Fit at 75!* Doug turned 80 this year. He is doing a year-long series of trail running, hiking and cycling challenges meant to inspire others that they too can retain their physical powers into their elder years. See his 80th year challenge list at www.InventorDoug.com.

Elaine Maly teaches the art of creative engagement for meaningful connections with elders through her work with TimeSlips. She writes about her life as a native Milwaukeean and is an active participant in her local storytelling community. She's the grandmother of three spunky grandsons who give her plenty of material.

Irene Maran, retired and living at the shore with her four cats and six turtles, enjoys writing about life, family and everyday topics humorously expressed in her two bi-weekly newspaper columns, *The News-Record of Maplewood/South Orange* and *The Coaster of Asbury Park*. She is also a storyteller and artist.

Susan G. Mathis is a grandma of four and multi-published author of historical fiction: *The Fabric of Hope: An Irish Family Legacy, Christmas Charity*, and *Katelyn's Choice*. She has five books coming out soon and is also a published author of two premarital books and two children's picture books. Learn more at www.SusanGMathis.com.

Jeremy Mays currently resides in Mt. Vernon, IL where he is an English teacher at the local high school. In his free time, Jeremy enjoys writing (typically horror stories), ghost hunting, collecting horror movie memorabilia, and spending time with his wife, Courtney, and his nine children.

Jane McBride considers writing her dream job. The mother of five children and grandmother of ten, she spends her time being with family, going to garage sales, and, of course, writing.

Bronwyn McIntyre is a writer on a mission to make every story more fun and more human. In her spare time, she walks dogs and drinks coffee in alarming quantities. You can check out her other works at jollywriter.com.

Tamara Moran-Smith is a freelance writer and contributor to the *Chicken Soup for the Soul* series. She is the proud mother of an adult son and a furry daughter, a Border Collie named Rosy. Her favorite subjects are God, family, and friends. E-mail her at hotflashofgenius@cox.net.

Ann Morrow is a writer, humorist and frequent contributor to the *Chicken Soup for the Soul* series. She and her husband live in the Black Hills of South Dakota. Recently, she committed to living "gluten free" and no longer accepts gifts disguised as baked goods.

Alice Muschany lives in Flint Hill, MO. She loves being retired and spending time with her grandchildren. Her hobbies include hiking, photography and writing. E-mail her at aliceandroland@gmail.com.

Cindy O'Leary has been in education for thirty years. She is married to her college sweetheart, has three daughters and three grandchildren. Cindy enjoys spending time with her family, traveling, scrapbooking, and painting. She has also written a children's chapter book, *Leprechauns on the Loose*.

January Gordon Ornellas is a comedy writer, teacher, wife, and mom. She enjoys traveling, working out, and spending time with her family. She writes humorous stories on her blog at midlifebloomer.com and recently published one of her short stories, "Rookie's Triathlon Lessons" in the *Los Angeles Times*, June 2019.

Julie Osborne is a former editor, feature writer, and columnist for Current Publishing in Carmel, IN. She recently launched into the freelance world with her blog *Tales of Oz* at julieosborne.com. Her best friend is a rescue dog whose name happened to be Toto when they met.

E-mail her at info@julieosborne.com.

Gordon Osmond is a graduate of Columbia College and Columbia Law School. He is the author of eight produced stage plays, three published novels, and three published nonfiction books about English, his life, and sports. He loves dogs, cats, and select humans. E-mail him at fertile1@aol.com.

Laura L. Padgett is an award-winning author who received her M.A. degree in Storytelling, with honors, from Regis University in Denver in 2009. She loves writing, dancing and traveling with her husband, Keith. Her first book *Dolores, Like the River*, about beauty and purpose in aging, was published in 2013 by WestBow Press.

Kristi Paxton lives life in Iowa woods and eastern rivers. Her happiest moments include family, friends, coffee, and the great outdoors. Kristi writes, teaches, walks, reads, and loves to kayak. The Paxtons and pup embark on their Great Loop adventure September 2014. E-mail her at kristi.a.paxton@gmail.com.

Laurie Penner works full-time in computer assisted design (CAD). When she's not helping her husband David build their house, she enjoys gardening, quilting, rock hunting, and spending time with their four grandchildren. Laurie plans to expand her writing career in her retirement years. Please e-mail her at writer7laurie@gmail.com.

Ava Pennington is a writer, speaker, and Bible teacher. She writes for nationally circulated magazines and is published in thirty-two anthologies, including twenty-five *Chicken Soup for the Soul* books. She also authored *Daily Reflections on the Names of God: A Devotional*, endorsed by Kay Arthur. Learn more at AvaWrites.com.

Connie K. Pombo is a freelance writer and author of three books. She is a regular contributor to the *Chicken Soup for the Soul* series and *Coping with Cancer* magazine. As a professional speaker, she loves to encourage cancer survivors, their families, and healthcare professionals. Learn more at conniepombo.com.

A resident of Ottawa, Ontario, **Louise Rachlis** is a perpetual writer, acrylic artist and runner with her fellow "Antiques of Steel." To her grandchildren, she is "BabaLou."

Connie Rosser Riddle is a middle school nurse and writer who lives in Durham, NC with her husband, David. She continues to take yearly solo journeys and has recently completed a memoir that describes these adventures. E-mail her at ConnieRosserRiddle@gmail.com.

Known as the Wandering Writer, **Karen Robbins** and her husband have visited all seven continents and circumnavigated the globe. Karen is the author of five novels. The most recent, a historical romance, *Ruby*, is set in the Cleveland area where she grew up and still resides.

Loretta Schoen grew up in Brazil and Italy and now resides in Florida. She loves traveling and spending time with her grandsons. She conducts workshops on how to survive medical adversity and has just published her debut book, *Surviving Medical Mayhem: Laughing When It Hurts.*

Beverly LaHote Schwind writes a column, "Patches of Life," for her local paper. She teaches at the jail and rehab center. At eighty-three she won a gold medal playing basketball in the National Senior Olympics. She and Jim celebrated sixty-five years of marriage. They have four children and eighteen grandchildren. She was Patches on a children's TV show.

Dana Sexton is a freelance author who has recently moved from Houston, TX to Nebraska. In 2012, she received the Susanne M. Glasscock award from Rice University in both poetry and fiction. Long ago and far away she earned a BA degree in English Literature from San Diego State University.

Since retiring from a career in adult education, **Marilyn Cohen Shapiro** is now writing down her family stories as well as the accounts of ordinary people with extraordinary lives. Read her blog at theregoesmyheart.me.

Lori Shepard retired from the Orlando Police Department in 2008. Since then she has traveled extensively, stopping long enough to adopt the brilliant cat Libby. Lori enjoys performing and teaching at a local improv theater. Currently she works part-time as a librarian, enjoying all things books.

Allen R. Smith is an award-winning freelance writer living in Vail, CO. He writes about health, fitness and outdoor sports. Smith has a master's degree in exercise physiology and exercise specialist certification with the American College of Sports Medicine at San Diego State University.

Ruth Smith was raised in Golden, CO. Ruth has been married to her husband, Ralph, for fifty-seven years. She is mother to three children, grandmother to seven and great-grandmother to six. She enjoys reading, traveling, family gatherings and recording her memories in stories. E-mail her at msgslbc@bak.rr.com.

Jan Kendall St.Cyr is a wife, mother of four and grandmother of six. Always an avid reader, journal writer, and writer of a monthly column in her hometown paper, Jan uses the experiences of her family as fodder for her many stories.

Brian Teason is an attorney. He was the 1997 and 1998 U.S. 50 Mile Road Champion, 1997 50 Mile Trail Champion and has represented the U.S. at two World Championships. Since his comeback, he has set the national age group road record for 100 miles.

Heather Truckenmiller is a farm wife in central Pennsylvania. Recent empty nesters after raising and homeschooling four children, including twins, she and her husband enjoy geocaching and exploring local small towns and their unique restaurants. Heather runs a blog for crafters, and is currently writing a book about the empty nest years.

Miriam Van Scott is an author and photographer whose credits include children's books, magazine articles, television productions, website content and reference books. Her latest titles include *Song of Old: An Advent Calendar for the Spirit* and the *Shakespeare Goes Pop* series. Learn more at miriamvanscott.com.

David Warren and his wife of twenty-eight years reside in Kettering, OH. They have one daughter Marissa. David's stories have been in multiple titles in the *Chicken Soup for the Soul* series. He is Vice President of Lutz Americas and continues to inspire with positive views on life!

Roz Warren writes for everyone from the *Funny Times* to *The New York Times* and is the author of *Our Bodies, Our Shelves: A Collection of Library Humor* and *Just Another Day at Your Local Public Library: An Insider's Tales of Library Life*, both of which you should buy immediately. E-mail her at roswarren@gmail.com.

Dorann Weber has been a fan of *Chicken Soup for the Soul* books since they were first published in 1993. She loved them so much she tried her hand at writing stories. She is a freelance photographer for a local newspaper and a Getty Images contributor. She lives in New Jersey with her family. E-mail her at dorann_weber@yahoo.com.

Kate White was an only child who made up imaginary friends to play with. At a young age she began writing stories about her imaginary friends and when she was thirteen she sold her first story. Her lonely childhood made her a writer, and through writing she has made many real friends and has had some great adventures.

Bobbie Wilkinson is a writer, artist, and musician who works from her home in northern Virginia. She and her husband Tom have three married daughters and two grandchildren. They also run a home business that sells Bobbie's inspirational jewelry, cards and artwork. Visit her at theflipflopheart.com.

Ferida Wolff is author of seventeen books for children and three essay books for adults. Her essays appear in anthologies, newspapers and magazines. She also writes online at www.grandparents.com and is a columnist for www.seniorwomen.com. A former elementary school teacher and Yoga instructor, she now teaches stretching and meditation. Her website is www.feridawolff.com.

Marjorie Woodall works as a freelance copy editor and lives in the Sierra Nevada foothills with her husband. E-mail her at marjoriewoodall@hotmail.com.

Phyllis W. Zeno has stories in eight *Chicken Soup for the Soul* books. She was the founding editor of *AAA Going Places* for twenty years and editor/publisher of *Beach Talk Magazine* until she met Harvey Meltzer on Match.com. They were married in 2009. Now eighty-six years old, they are on a perpetual honeymoon.

Jerry Zezima writes a nationally syndicated humor column for his hometown paper, the *Stamford Advocate,* in Connecticut. He is the author of three books. He lives on Long Island, NY, with his wife, Sue. They have two daughters, three grandchildren and many creditors. Mr. Zezima has no interesting hobbies.

Meet Amy Newmark

Amy Newmark is the bestselling author, editor-in-chief, and publisher of the *Chicken Soup for the Soul* book series. Since 2008, she has published 198 new books, most of them national bestsellers in the U.S. and Canada, more than doubling the number of Chicken Soup for the Soul titles in print today. She is also the author of *Simply Happy*, a crash course in Chicken Soup for the Soul advice and wisdom that is filled with easy-to-implement, practical tips for enjoying a better life.

Amy is credited with revitalizing the Chicken Soup for the Soul brand, which has been a publishing industry phenomenon since the first book came out in 1993. By compiling inspirational and aspirational true stories curated from ordinary people who have had extraordinary experiences, Amy has kept the thirty-one-year-old Chicken Soup for the Soul brand fresh and relevant.

Amy graduated *magna cum laude* from Harvard University where she majored in Portuguese and minored in French. She then embarked on a three-decade career as a Wall Street analyst, a hedge fund manager, and a corporate executive in the technology field. She is a Chartered Financial Analyst.

Her return to literary pursuits was inevitable, as her honors thesis in college involved traveling throughout Brazil's impoverished northeast region, collecting stories from regular people. She is delighted to have come full circle in her writing career — from collecting stories "from the people" in Brazil as a twenty-year-old to, three decades later, collecting stories "from the people" for Chicken Soup for the Soul.

When Amy and her husband Bill, the CEO of Chicken Soup for the Soul, are not working, they are visiting their four grown children and their spouses, and their five grandchildren.

Follow Amy on Twitter @amynewmark. Listen to her free podcast — Chicken Soup for the Soul with Amy Newmark — on Apple, Google, or by using your favorite podcast app on your phone.

Thank You

e owe huge thanks to all our contributors, who share their most important life events, milestones, and advice with our readers. We are both entertained and improved by reading their work.

Here at Chicken Soup for the Soul we want to thank our Associate Publisher D'ette Corona for reviewing our story library and presenting us with hundreds of stories to choose from for this new collection. Publisher and Editor-in-Chief Amy Newmark made the final selection of the 101 that are included here, all personal favorites, and D'ette created the manuscript. None of these stories appeared in previous Chicken Soup for the Soul books about aging. They first appeared in books on other topics.

The whole publishing team deserves a hand, including Senior Editor Barbara LoMonaco, Vice President of Marketing Maureen Peltier, Vice President of Production Victor Cataldo, and our graphic designer Daniel Zaccari, who turned our manuscript into this beautiful, entertaining book.

Changing your life one story at a time®
www.chickensoup.com